PRACTICAL MASONRY
A GUIDE TO THE ART OF STONE CUTTING
COMPRISING THE CONSTRUCTION

PRACTICAL MASONRY

A GUIDE TO THE ART OF STONE CUTTING

COMPRISING

THE CONSTRUCTION, SETTING-OUT, AND WORKING OF STAIRS, CIRCULAR WORK, ARCHES, NICHES, DOMES, PENDENTIVES, VAULTS, TRACERY WINDOWS, ETC.

TO WHICH ARE ADDED

SUPPLEMENTS RELATING TO MASONRY ESTIMATING AND QUANTITY SURVEYING, AND TO BUILDING STONES AND MARBLES, AND A GLOSSARY OF TERMS

FOR THE USE OF STUDENTS, MASONS, AND CRAFTSMEN

BY

WILLIAM R. PURCHASE

BUILDING INSPECTOR TO THE BOROUGH OF HOVE

With 52 Lithographic Plates, Comprising over 400 Diagrams

FIFTH EDITION, ENLARGED

KALPAZ

ISBN: 978-93-5128-848-0(PB)

First Published in 1904
Indian Reprint in 2017

Published by

Kalpaz Publications
C-30, Satyawati Nagar,
Delhi – 110052
E-mail: kalpaz@hotmail.com
Website: kalpazpublications.com
Ph.: +91-9212142040

Cataloging in Publication Data—DK
Courtesy: D.K. Agencies (P) Ltd. <docinfo@dkagencies.com>

Purchase, William R., author.
Practical masonry : a guide to the art of stone cutting, comprising the construction, setting-out, and working of stairs, circular work, arches, niches, domes, pendentives, vaults, tracery windows, etc., to which are added supplements relating to masonry estimating and quantity surveying, and to building stones and marbles, and a glossary of terms for the use of students, masons and craftsmen / by William R. Purchase.
pages cm
Reprint of fifth edition, enlarged: London : C. Lockwood and Son, 1904.
"With 52 lithographic plates, comprising over 400 diagrams."
ISBN 9789351288480

1. Masonry. 2. Stone-cutting. I. Title.

TH5401.P87 2017 DDC 693.1 23

PREFACE.

THIS work has been compiled, not with the view of superseding any of the works already published dealing with the architectural or geometrical side of the stone-cutter's art, but as a means of introducing the student of Masonry to the practical work of everyday life in the workshop and on the building. It has no pretensions to instruct skilled workmen, but is intended to initiate young beginners in the craft into the rules and principles of good masonry. It is the result of many years' attentive observation and practical experience, acquired by the Author first as an operative stone-mason, and afterwards as a foreman mason, on some of our largest public buildings.

All the cases commonly met with are worked out, and, when the general principles applying to these are understood, their extension to any unusual question which may occur should not be difficult. The student is assumed, however, to have some knowledge of geometrical drawing and projection, which indeed is indispensable. Most of the examples given are from actual work.

In further explanation of his aim in compiling the volume, the Author may be allowed to cite the subjoined extract from an address delivered a couple of years ago by Mr. J. H. Morton, F.R.I.B.A., President of the Northern Architectural Association.* Mr. Morton said that "it must be allowed that "no trade could be properly learned out of the workshop; "although the men would certainly understand better the "instruction given in the workshop, if they had had the benefit "of a theoretical foundation before proceeding to practice. It

* Address at opening of winter session of the Association at Newcastle-on-Tyne, reported in the "Builder" of December 9, 1893.

"was useless to expect the technical school to entirely replace "the apprenticeship system; but having laid the foundation "before entering the workshop, the technical education of the "artisan might go on contemporaneously with the workshop "employment. Many workmen, of excellent practical skill, "worked entirely by rule of thumb, and their efforts would "assuredly prove more successful if guided by the enlightenment "and precision of scientific knowledge. Thus technical educa- "tion might be the means of exalting labour, and of enabling "capable workmen to raise themselves to a higher standard by "the acquisition of a more perfect knowledge of the art of "building."

Any suggestion with which the Author may be favoured, with a view to the improvement of the work in future editions, will be duly acknowledged, and carefully considered as opportunity occurs.

W. R. P.

HOVE. *October*, 1895.

NOTE TO THE FIFTH EDITION.

The reception accorded to the previous editions of this work has been very gratifying, no adverse criticism having come to the Author's knowledge. On the contrary, besides very favourable notices in the Press, he has received numerous letters conveying the assurance that the work has been found of the greatest value. At the request of correspondents, two additional Plates, illustrative of Grecian and Roman mouldings respectively, and also a GLOSSARY OF TERMS, were added when the second edition was issued; and the usefulness of the work has now been further extended by the addition of new sections relating to MASONRY ESTIMATING AND QUANTITY SURVEYING, and to BUILDING STONES, MARBLES AND GRANITES, including carefully compiled Lists of Stones actually in the market. TABLES OF DIAMETERS, CIRCUMFERENCES, AND AREAS OF CIRCLES are also appended.

W. R. P.

HOVE. *June*, 1901.

TABLE OF CONTENTS.

TOOLS AND APPLIANCES.—PLATES I. to III.

ARCHES AND JOINTS.—PLATES IV. to VIII.

MASONRY DETAILS.—PLATES IX. to XI.

STAIRCASES.—PLATES XII. to XV.

CIRCULAR WORK (RAMP AND TWIST).—PLATES XVI. to XIX.

ARCHES, CIRCULAR ON PLAN.—PLATES XX. to XXIII.

SKEW ARCH AND NICHES.—PLATES XXIV. to XXVI.

CYLINDRICAL VAULTING.—Plates XXVII. to XXIX.

DOMES & PENDENTIVES.—Plates XXX. to XXXIII.

GROINED VAULTING.—Plates XXXIV. to XXXVII.

GROINED VAULTING (*continued*).—Plates XXXVIII. to XLI.

TRACERY WINDOWS.—Plates XLII. to XLVI.

GOTHIC MOULDINGS.—Plates XLVII. to L.

GRECIAN MOULDINGS.—Plate LI.

ROMAN MOULDINGS.—Plate LII.

SUPPLEMENTARY MATTER.

PRACTICAL MASONRY.

Plates I., II., III.—TOOLS AND APPLIANCES.

Fig. 1.—The square is of various sizes, and generally made of iron plate about one-eighth of an inch thick; the edges are parallel and at right angles to each other.

It is important that the square should be true, as the accuracy of the work depends entirely upon it, and for this reason it should be frequently tested for correctness.

Fig. 2.—The set square is of several sizes, and made of iron, brass, or zinc plate; it contains a right angle and two angles of forty-five degrees, and is used chiefly for mitres, and setting out on bed of work.

Fig. 3.—The bevel, or shift stock, made of iron or brass, and used for sinkings, bevels, &c.

Fig. 4.—A small tee square of unequal sides, and with right angles, used for sinkings, &c.

Fig. 5.—Mallet of beech, or other hard wood, of various sizes, for striking the cutting tools.

Fig. 6.—Hand hammer of steel, about five pounds in weight, used principally with punch for removing waste, and, in very hard grit stones, it is used also with hammer-headed chisels.

Fig. 7.—The punch: the cutting edge of this tool is about a quarter of an inch wide, and chisel-pointed. It is used with the hammer for removing all superfluous waste.

Fig. 8.—The point, with edge similar to punch, is used with mallet, generally for hard grit or lime stones, and for reducing the irregularities left from punch, leaving the stone in narrow ridges and furrows close down to face.

Fig. 9.—Chisels, of various widths, from a quarter of an inch to one and a half inch wide, used for mouldings, fillets, sinkings, &c.

Figs. 10 & 11.—Boasters, from one and a half inch to three inches wide, used for dressing stone down to smooth faces, and cleaning or finishing mouldings, &c.

Fig. 12.—Broad-tool, about four inches wide, used for tooling.

Fig. 13.—Claw-tool. These are of various sizes, the teeth being cut coarse or fine to suit the texture of the stone. For hard lime stones the teeth at point are about an eighth of an inch wide, and for softer stones from a quarter to three-eighths of an inch wide.

The claw-tool is used after the punch or point, dressing down the ridges still closer to finished face.

Figs. 14 & 15.—Small chisels, of various sizes, for carving, letter-cutting, &c.

Note.—Numbers 8 to 15 are mallet-headed tools, and must never be struck with the hammer, the heads being made to receive the blow of the mallet only.

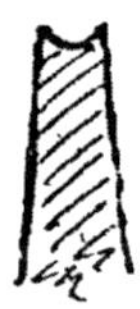

Fig. 16.—Small chisels, called "splitters," of various sizes; the heads are concave, or cup-headed, as in sketch. When used with an iron hammer (Fig. 21), they cut very smooth and sweet.

They are used mostly for marble work, carving, lettering, &c.

Fig. 17.—Pitching tool: this has a bevelled instead of a cutting edge, and is used with the hammer, for pitching or knocking off the irregularities or waste lumps on stone.

Fig. 18.—Jumper, chisel-pointed and slightly round-nosed; it is wider at cutting edge than the diameter of tool, so that it clears itself in cutting circular holes, for which it is used, chiefly in granite.

PLATE . I.

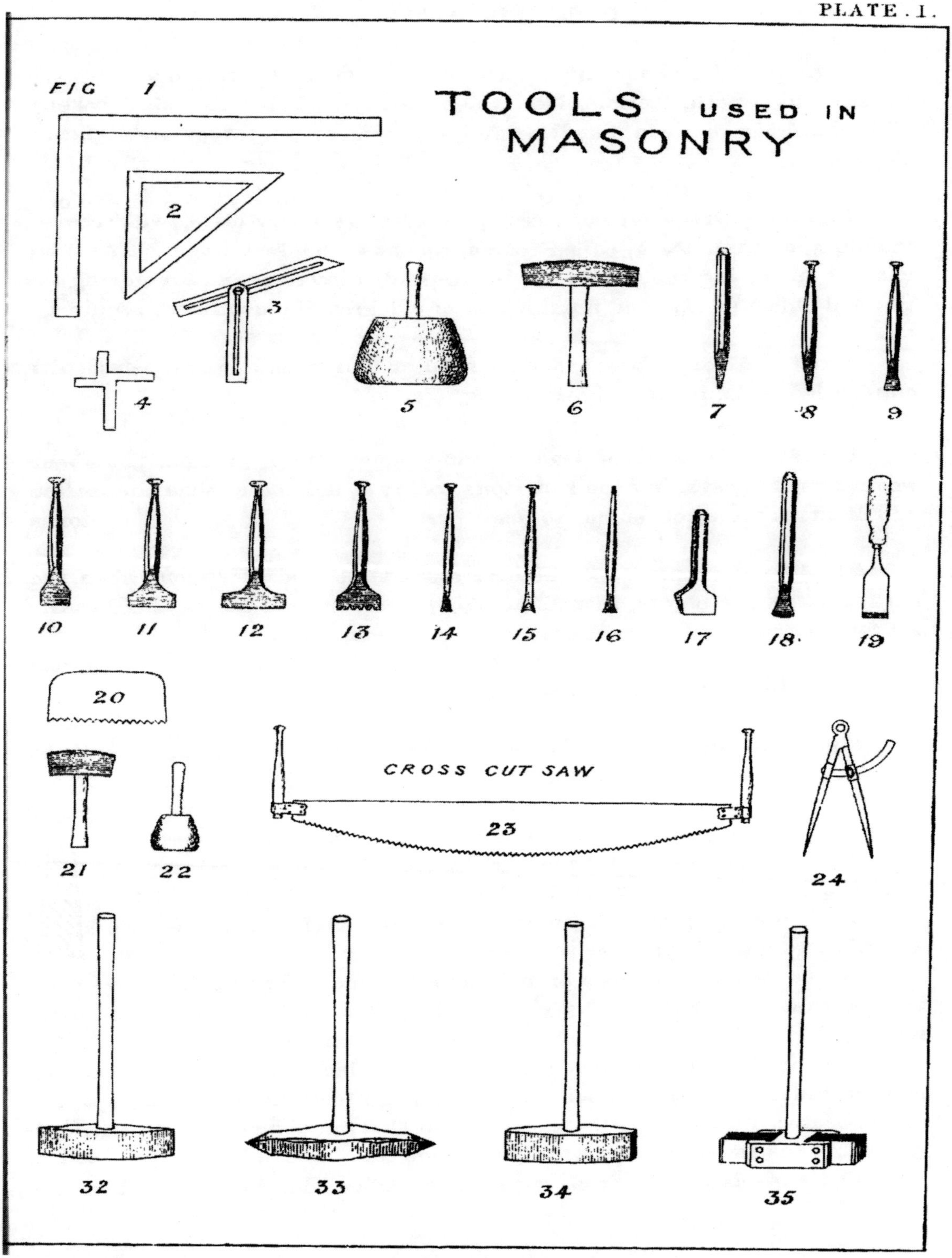
TOOLS USED IN MASONRY
FIG 1
2
3
4
5
6
7
8
9
10
11
12
13
14
15
16
17
18
19
20
21
22
CROSS CUT SAW
23
24
32
33
34
35

Fig. 19.—Chisel for soft stone (this is a general term, and comprises varieties like Bath, Ketton Beer, Caen stone, &c., as well as Alabaster). The chisels have wood handles, and are similar to carpenters' "firmer chisels."

Fig. 20.—Drags for soft stone, of best steel saw-plate, with coarse, middling, and fine teeth, called coarse, seconds, and fine drags. These are used by traversing the face of the stone in all directions, and removing the saw and chisel marks, and finishing to any degree of smoothness required.

Fig. 21.—Iron hammer, about three or four pounds weight, used with cup-headed tools, for carving, lettering, &c.

Fig. 22.—Dummy, of lead or zinc, about three or four pounds in weight, used for striking the soft stone tools; it is handier than the mallet, and at times more convenient to use.

Fig. 23.—Cross-cut saw, of best steel plate, and of various sizes, for cutting soft stone blocks, scantlings, &c.; the teeth are coarse, and broadly set for clearance. Two men are required in using it.

Fig. 24.—Compasses, for setting-out work, &c.

Fig. 25.—Shews sketch of a saw-frame, for hand-sawing, which in practice requires some little skill in framing up to the various sizes.

The frame generally, for good working, should be about two feet longer inside than the length of stone to be sawn, so as to allow for draft.

The heads or ends of frame are made of 4″ × 3″ deal, tapered from near the top to $3\frac{1}{2}''$ × 2″ at the bottom, with a groove or slot for the saw four inches deep by half an inch wide, the angles being rounded off or smoothed to make it easy for the hands.

The stretcher is a piece of pole about three inches in diameter, with iron ferrule at each end, varying in length. Packing pieces are used against the head at each end of stretcher, as shewn.

The couplings are in wrought iron, half an inch in diameter, of various lengths and shapes, as in sketch. These are tightened up with a union screw in the centre, which keeps the saw taut, so that no difficulty is experienced in getting the saw-frame to the required length.

The saw-plate is of iron, about four inches wide by one-tenth of an

PLATE. II.

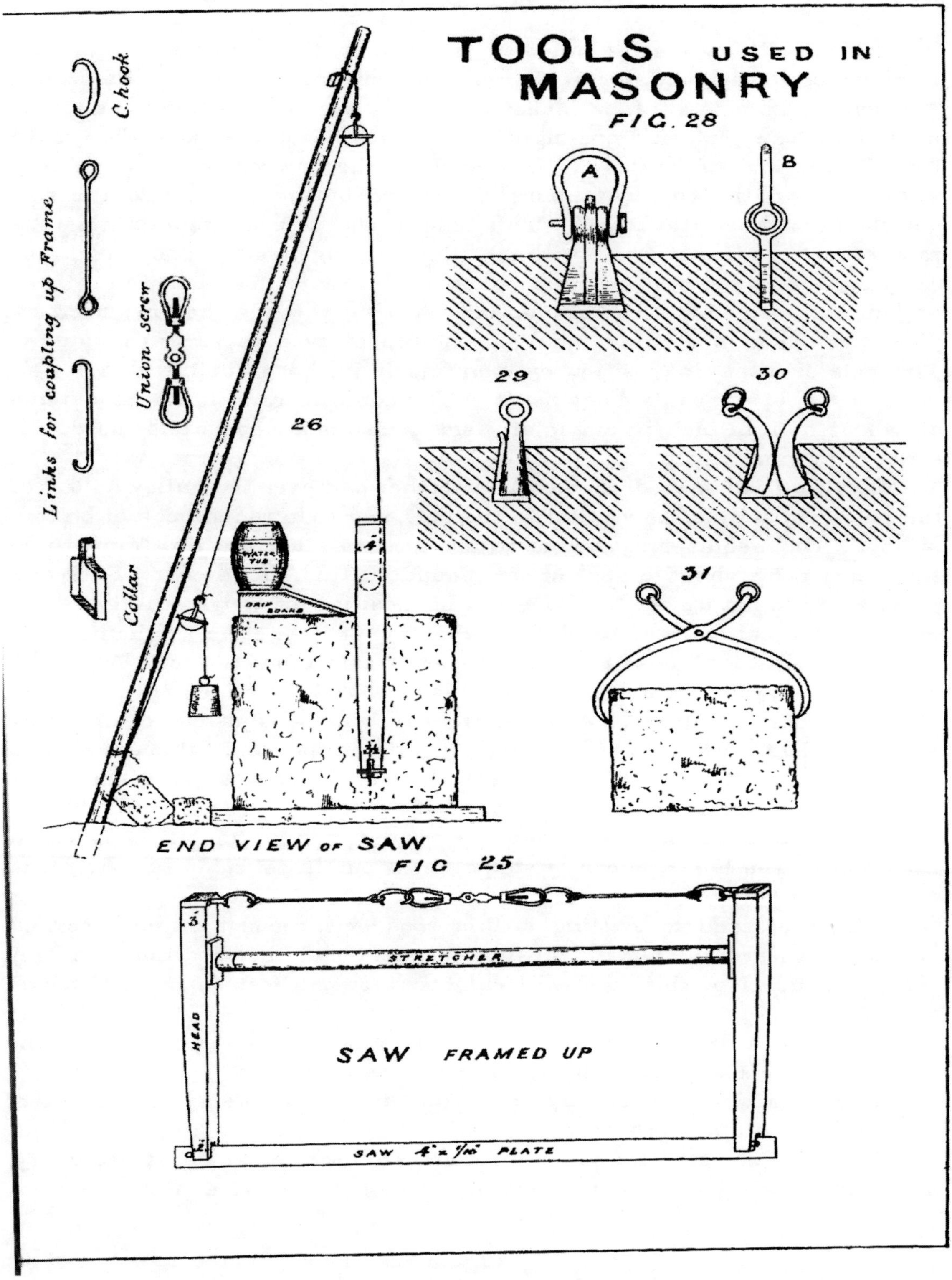
TOOLS USED IN MASONRY
FIG. 28
A
B
29
30
31
C. hook
Links for coupling up Frame
Union screw
Collar
26
WATER TUB
DRIP BOARD
4
END VIEW OF SAW
FIG 25
3
STRETCHER
HEAD
SAW FRAMED UP
SAW 4" x 1/10" PLATE

inch thick, with two holes punched through it, three-quarters of an inch in diameter, at each end, for iron pins, which are inserted to keep the saw in position. The pins are four inches long, and have a small slot the thickness of the saw-plate and one-eighth of an inch deep, fixed with the groove towards the end of the saw; this enables the sawyer to keep the saw straight down the cut, by tapping either end of the pin, should the saw deviate from the vertical line. This slot in the pins is important, as the saw cannot be kept true without this arrangement. The pole, for carrying the saw-frame, is from sixteen to twenty feet long and three or four inches diameter at bottom, and tapering towards the top; a cross-piece and chain is secured nearly at the top of pole to carry the pulley. The pole is kept in position by planting it in the ground, and a rough piece or two of stone is laid against it. The cords for carrying the saw-frame are about half an inch in diameter; small chains are sometimes used, but cords work more easily.

The cord is fastened round the stretcher and over the pulley on top of the pole (which must be vertical to the cut), and then round hook of bottom pulley. The weight must be so adjusted as to allow the saw-frame to be the heavier by about eight or ten pounds; this, however, will depend greatly on the nature of the stone. The position of weight can be raised or lowered to suit the cut by shifting the cord at the bottom of the pole.

The drip-board is of deal, as in sketch, and about two feet long, with sloping side against the cut, and on this is placed the water tub; a small spigot is inserted in the bottom of the tub, and is adjusted to allow the water to trickle down the board, carrying with it the sand, which is also on the board, into the cut. To regulate the supply of water and sand, the sawyer uses a small rake with long handle.

The line of cut for saw should be set out with a plumb rule or bob at each end of the block, and a V shape chase cut in to guide the sawyer in keeping to a true line.

The best sand for cutting is flint road grit, washed through several sieves, all the coarse and fine being rejected, and the medium size only used. A bushel of this sand will cut about twelve feet super of Portland stone.

The saw is drawn backwards and forwards, and the stone cut by the attrition of the saw-plate with the sand and water.

A good sawyer can cut by hand from fifteen to twenty feet super of Portland stone in one day of ten hours.

On large jobs steam stone saw-frames are used, in which, if necessary, from one to twenty cuts may be put in one block at the same time.

Fig. 27.—Shews a method of coping or splitting a block of stone to a required size.

Begin by cutting a V chase on top and two sides of the block, as at *g f e*; directly under this place a wood skid, and on the top of the skid a long iron bar, which should bone with the line *g f*, or a punch driven in on each side, as at *e*, will do nearly as well. At extreme end place a short skid, as at *h*, and packed up to within an inch of the underside of the block. This is done to prevent the coped piece from breaking under by its own weight, as the fracture would not take the line of direction proposed, but would probably break away from *j* to *k*, and spoil the block.

Sink wedge holes with the punch (at distances apart varying with the nature of the stone) to as fine a point as possible at the bottom of the hole, as in sketch at *b*, so that the wedge will bite or hold when struck with the hammer. The apex of the wedge, which is of iron, is blunt-pointed and about a quarter of an inch wide, so that it does not touch the bottom of the hole, or when struck it would jump out. The holes being cut, the wedges are inserted in each one: care must, however, be taken to keep them upright, so that the cleavage takes the line of direction required. The wedges are now gently tapped with a heavy hammer, till all have got a hold; then harder blows are given in quick succession, and the fracture takes place.

a shews sketch of wedge, made of iron, and from four to five inches long and one and a half inch wide.

In coping or splitting granite, wedge holes are not cut as in stone, but circular holes are "jumped," one inch or one and a quarter inch in diameter and about five inches deep, at distances apart varying with the obstinacy of the material, and plugs and feathers are inserted and driven in as for stone. The plug is of soft steel, and made tapering as at *c*.

The feathers are thin pieces of iron, concave in section, as shewn at *c* 1. These are first put in the holes, the plugs are then driven in until they become tight, and a few sharp hard blows are all that is necessary to complete the process of splitting. *c* 1 is a plan of *c* to a larger size.

Fig. 28.—Shews a pair of iron lewises used in lifting worked stone for fixing. The lewis consists of a dovetail of three pieces, the two outer pieces being first inserted in the hole, and then the centre piece, which acts as a key, and tightens up the dovetail; the shackle is next put on, and the bolt is passed through the whole.

Care must be taken to cut the hole to a dovetailed shape, and of the size of the lewis.

A is the front view, and *B* the side view, of the lewises.

Fig. 29.—Shews an iron conical-shaped lewis plug, which is placed in a slightly larger dovetailed hole, a small curved iron plug being inserted by its side, which keys it up. This is used chiefly for worked granite.

Fig. 30.—A pair of chain lewises, consisting of two curved iron plugs with rings for chain; these are inserted in a dovetailed hole, and when tightened up act similarly to the ordinary lewises.

Fig. 31.—A pair of iron dogs, or nippers, with steel-pointed claws, used for lifting rough blocks, and also for fixing.

Fig. 32.—Axe, about twelve or fourteen pounds in weight, chisel-pointed, used on granite for removing the inequalities left by the pick and dressing it similarly to tooled work in stone, shewing the marks or indents in parallel lines.

Fig. 33.—Pick, about sixteen pounds weight, used chiefly on granite, for dressing the inequalities of the rough or rock face down to within half an inch of the finished face; and also used for scabbling blocks of stone roughly to the required shape.

Fig. 34.—Spalling hammer, about twelve to fourteen pounds weight. This has a square edge of about an inch and a quarter, and is a very effectual tool for knocking off rough lumps.

Fig. 35.—Patent axe. The body of this is of iron, with a slot at each end, into which a number of parallel thin plates of steel, chisel-sharpened and of equal length, are inserted and tightly bolted together. This is used for granite, and produces the finest description of face, next to polishing.

Fig. 36.—A pair of trammel heads, or beam compasses, used chiefly for setting out arcs of circles full size; those made of gun-metal, with steel points, are the best, and a set should be large enough to take a rod thirty feet long.

Fig. 37.—A spirit level for fixing.

The following appliances are also required for setting out work:—

A large platform or drawing-board, about ten or twelve feet square; or

TOOLS USED IN MASONRY

Trammel heads & Rod

36

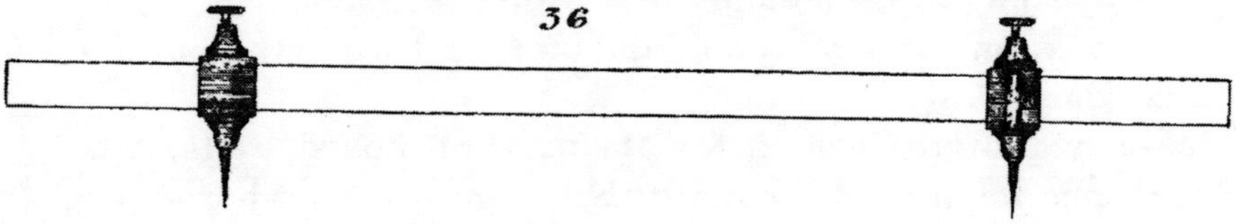

FIG. 37

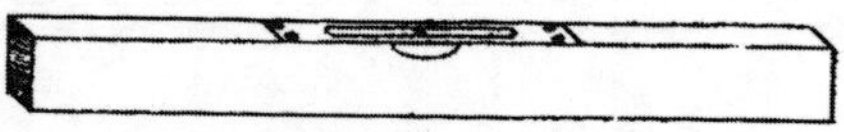

LEVEL

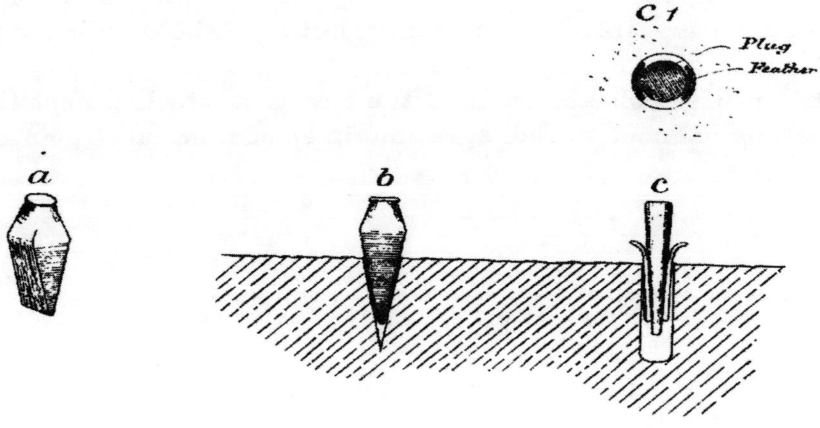

FIG 27

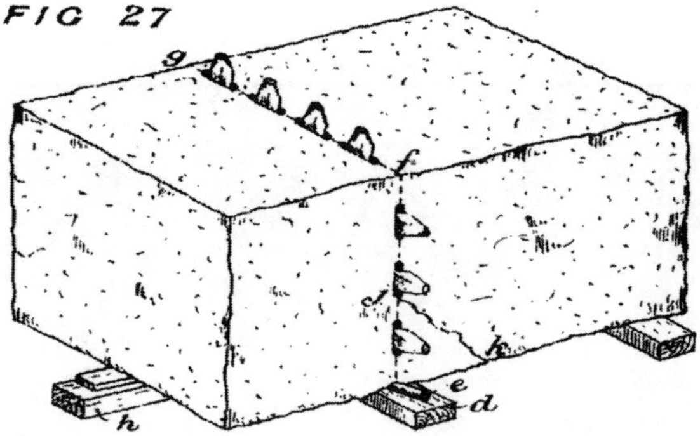

COPING OR SPLITTING BLOCK
BY WEDGES

if larger than this, the better. It may be fixed either vertically or horizontally.

A standard five-foot rod.

Two or three straight-edges of various lengths.

Deal rods for storey rods, and for setting out lengths of cornices, modillions, dentils, &c.

Pipe-clay and stiff brush, for cleaning off board, rods, &c.

Sheet zinc for moulds, usually No. 9 gauge, this being a good workable thickness. The lines for face, bed, and section moulds have to be carefully transferred to the sheet zinc, and cut to their proper contour or shapes with shears and files.

The foregoing lists do not comprise all the tools and appliances required for every branch of masonry, but only those which are in common use.

All cutting tools are made of the best cast steel, except the pick, axe, and spalling hammer, which are sometimes of iron, steel pointed and faced.

Plates IV., V., VI., VII., VIII.—ARCHES AND JOINTS.

The terms used in connection with the arches here shown may be thus defined :—

The face of the arch is the *front*, or that portion shown in elevation.

The *under-surface* or *soffit* is called the *intrados*, and the outer surface the *extrados*.

The *voussoirs* are the separate arch blocks composing the arch, the central one being the *keystone*.

The *springers* are the first or bottom stones in the arch on either side, and commence with the curve of the arch.

The *skewbacks* generally apply to segmental arches, and are the stones from which an arch springs, and upon which the first arch stones are laid.

The *span* of the arch is the extreme width between the piers or opening ; and the *springing line* is that which connects the two points where the intrados meets the imposts on either side.

The *radius* is the distance between the centre and the curve of the arch.

The highest point in the intrados is called the *crown*, and the height of this point above the springing is termed the *rise* of the arch.

The *centre* is a point or points from which the arch is struck ; and lines drawn from this centre or centres to the arch are radiating joints, and are also called *normals*.

All joints in arches should be radii of the circle, circles, or ellipses forming the curve of the arch, and will therefore converge to the centre or centres from which these are struck.

Fig. 1.—Shews a segmental arch, in which the above-mentioned terms are illustrated.

Fig. 2.—Is a semi-circular arch, *A B* being the span and *C D* the rise ; the left-hand half has the ordinary joints radiating from the centre

C, and the right-hand half, with rebated or step joints, also radiating from the centre *C*. This last is a sound and effective joint where great strength is required, and there is also no tendency to sliding of the voussoirs.

Fig. 3.—Shews a semi-oval arch, approaching in form that of the ellipse, and struck with three centres. This form of arch has a somewhat crippled appearance at the junction of the small and large curves, and is on that account not pleasing to the eye.

It may be here observed that the true ellipse is obtained from an oblique section of the cone, and no portion of its curve is any part of a circle, and cannot, therefore, be drawn by the compasses or from centres.

The method of setting out and drawing the joints requires but little explanation, *A B* being the span, *C E* the rise, and *D D* and *F* the centres, from which the curve is struck, the joints converging to their respective centres.

The left-hand half is shown with square bonding on face, and the right-hand half shows line of extrados.

Fig. 4.—Is a semi-elliptic arch.

On comparing this with the arch shewn in Fig. 3, which is of the same span and rise, the gracefulness of the elliptic arch will be apparent.

To draw the arch joints :—

Divide the soffit into any convenient number of parts, and find the foci by taking *C* as centre and *A E* equal to half the major axis as radius, and describe an arc cutting line *A B*, giving the foci *F* and *F*. From *F* and *F* draw lines to *H* (one of the divisions for the arch joints) and bisect the angle *F H F*; the bisecting line *H O* produced will be perpendicular to the tangent of the curve, and will give a true radiating joint.

The other joints are found in the same manner.

Fig. 5.—Shews an equilateral arch, described about an equilateral triangle *A B C*, the centres *A* and *B* being at the extremities of the span.

The joints are drawn to the radii or centres *A* and *B*.

Fig. 6.—Is the lancet-shaped arch, described about an acute-angled triangle *A B C*, the radius *D E* being longer than the span of the arch.

The joints are drawn from the centres *D* and *D*.

ARCHES AND JOINTS

FIG. 1

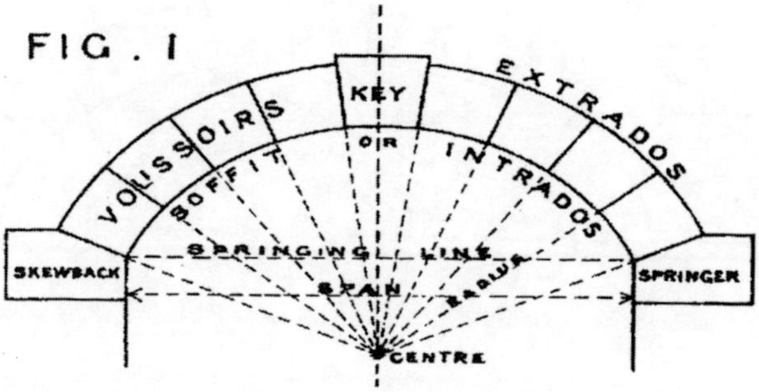

FIG. 2

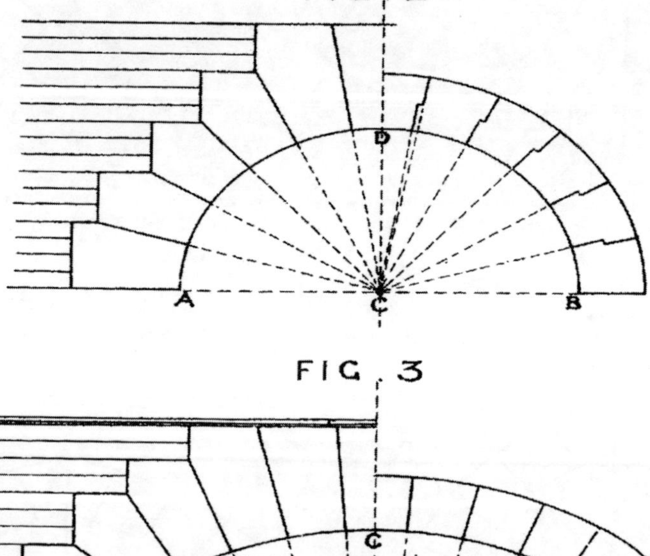

FIG. 3

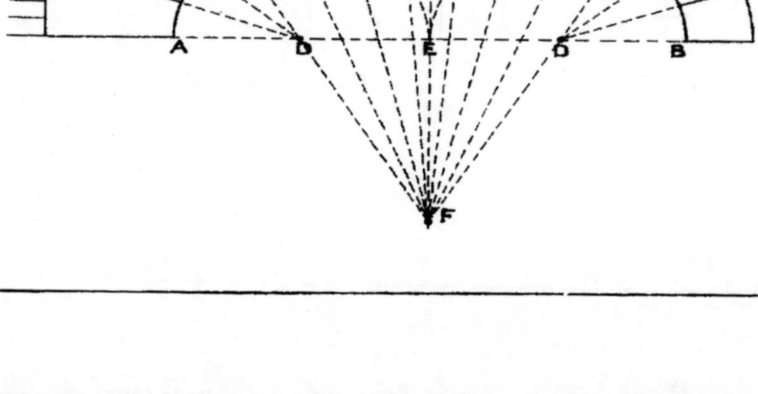

ARCHES AND JOINTS

FIG. 4

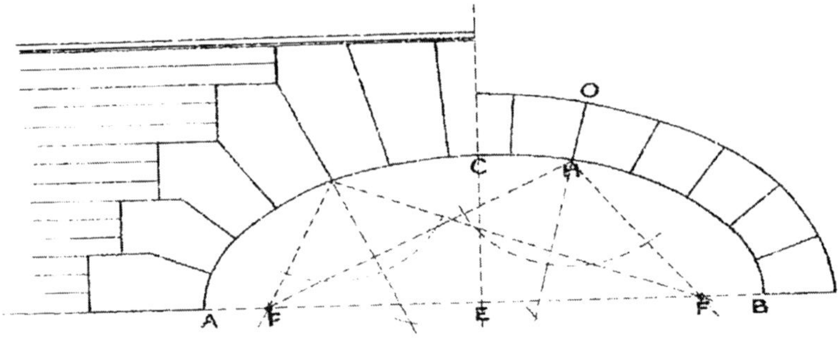

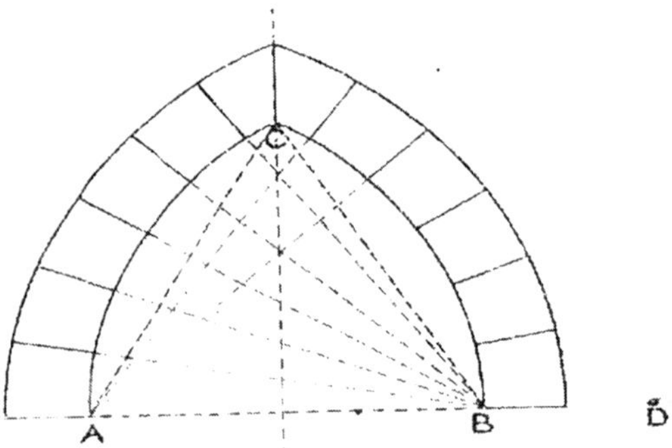

FIG. 5

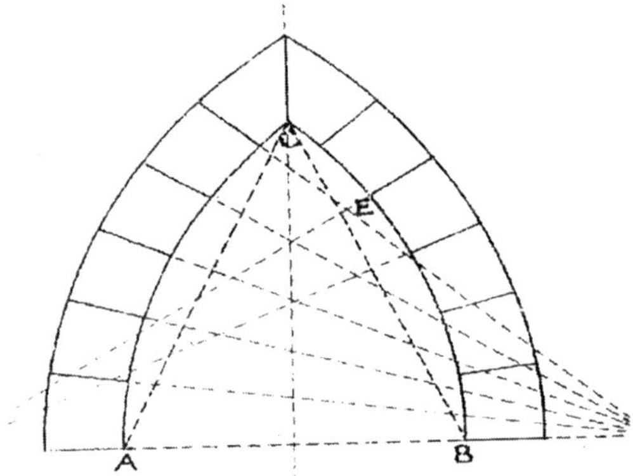

FIG. 6

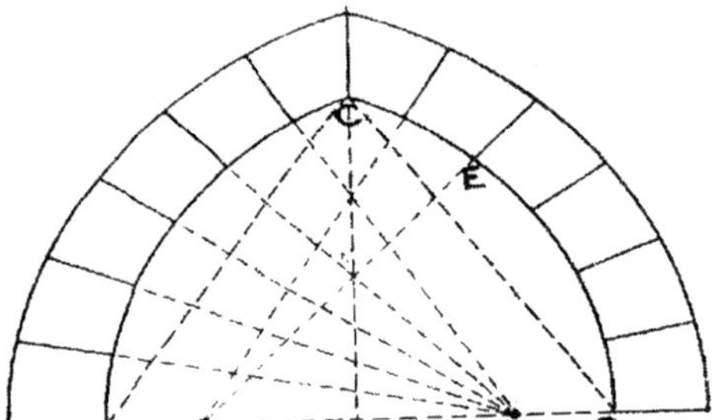

FIG. 7

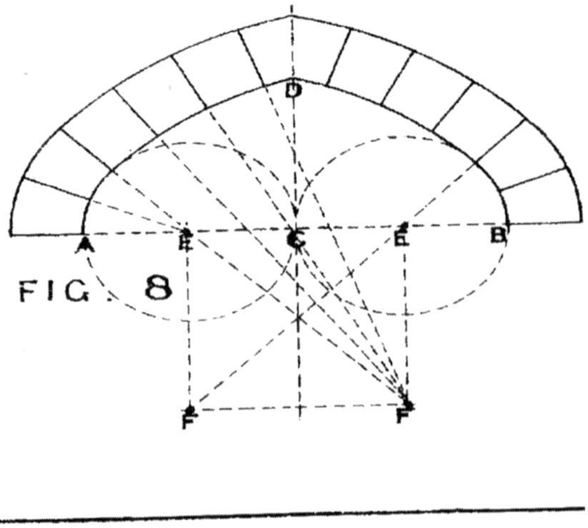

FIG. 8

Fig. 7.—Is the drop arch, described about an obtuse-angled triangle *A B C*, the radius *D E* being shorter than the span of the arch.

The joints are drawn from the centres *D* and *D*.

Fig. 8.—Shews the four-centred or Tudor arch, *A B* being the span and *C D* the rise; two of its centres, *E E*, are on the springing line, and the two others, *F F*, below it.

The joints are drawn from the centres *E E* and *F F* as shewn, and require no further description.

Fig. 9.—Is a Tudor arch, based on the curve of the hyperbola.

Let *A B* be the span and *C D* the rise of arch: erect perpendicular at *A*, and make it equal in height to two-fifths of the rise as at *A C*, and draw the line *C D*. Now divide the lines *A C* and *C D* each into six equal parts, and draw lines from 1 to 1, 2 to 2, 3 to 3, &c., and the line drawn through the intersection of these points gives the curve of one side of the arch. The other side is obtained similarly.

A thin flexible lath is generally used for guidance in drawing an easy curve through the points of intersection.

To draw the arch joints:—

At any point in the curve, say at *E*, drop a perpendicular on to the springing line, as *F*, make *B G* equal *B F*, and from *G* draw line to *E*, which is a tangent to the curve, and erect the perpendicular *E H*, giving the arch joint required.

The other joints are described in the same manner.

Fig. 10.—Is another example of the Tudor arch, and is a parabolic curve.

Let *A B* be the span and *C D* the rise, erect a perpendicular at *A* and make it equal in height to half the rise, and proceed as in previous figure.

To draw the arch joints:—

At any point in the curve, say at *E*, draw the chord line *B D* and bisect it in *F*; join *F G* cutting the curve in *H*, and from the point *E* draw line *E J* parallel to *E F*, cutting *F G* in *J*; on the line *F G* make *H K* equal to *H J*, join *E K* and draw *E L* perpendicular to *K E*, thus giving the joint line required.

The other joints are described in a similar manner.

Fig. 11.—Shews a straight or flat arch, the joints radiating to a common centre.

On the right-hand half the joints are not continued through to soffit or top, but have a small portion squared on, thus relieving the acute angles of arch blocks, which are otherwise liable to fracture.

The springer on left hand has additional strength in having a square seating on skewback.

In flat arches a camber of an eighth of an inch in a foot to soffit is usually given to allow for any depression or settlement.

Fig. 12.—Is another example of the flat arch; the left-hand half has rebated or step joints, and the right-hand half has joggle joints. All these joints converge to a common centre.

Fig. 13.—In this figure a lintel with double joggle vertical joints is given.

Fig. 14.—Shews a lintel with curved joggle joints, and is an example not often met with.

The form of joint in figs. 12, 13 and 14 is a little wasteful of material; but where stone is plentiful and in small blocks, good lintels may be obtained. Many examples of these may be seen in our modern Gothic buildings.

Fig. 15.—Illustrates a window or door head with quadrant corners; the stretching-piece or key is in one stone, with arch-joints resting on the skewbacks.

Fig. 16.—Is another form of head, the square seating on each stone giving additional strength, and the joints converge to a common centre.

Fig. 17.—Shews three joints used in landings.

A is a joggle joint, commonly called He and She joggle. A tongue is cut slightly tapering on one edge, fitting into a corresponding groove worked in the other edge. Run in with cement it forms a strong and secure joint.

B is a rebated joint; this is sometimes undercut.

C is a bird's mouth joint. Grooves are roughly cut in on the edges of these joints opposite each other, and the cavities run with cement grout. Slate dowels are also laid longitudinally in the joint and run with cement.

ARCHES AND JOINTS

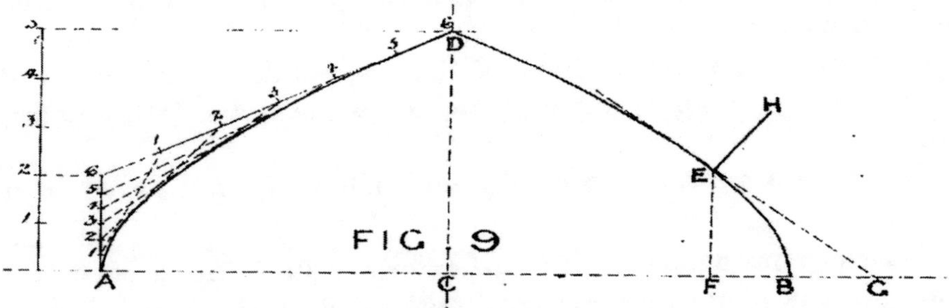

FIG 9

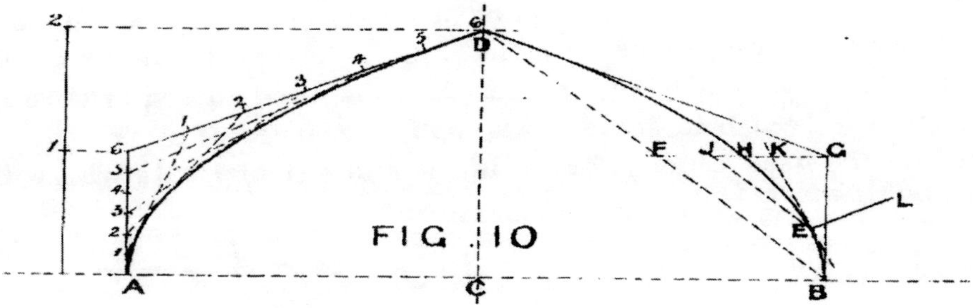

FIG . 10

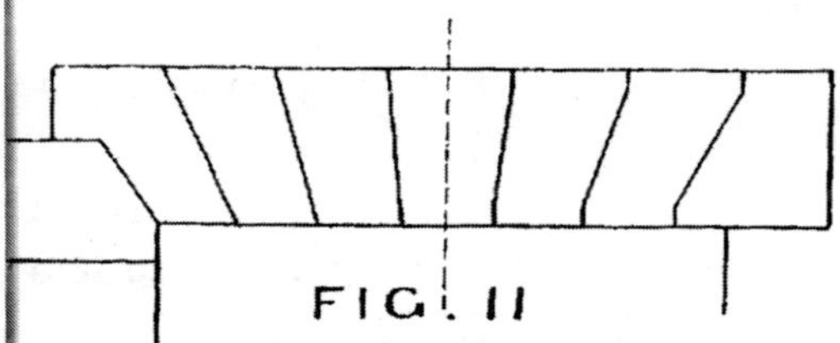

FIG . 11

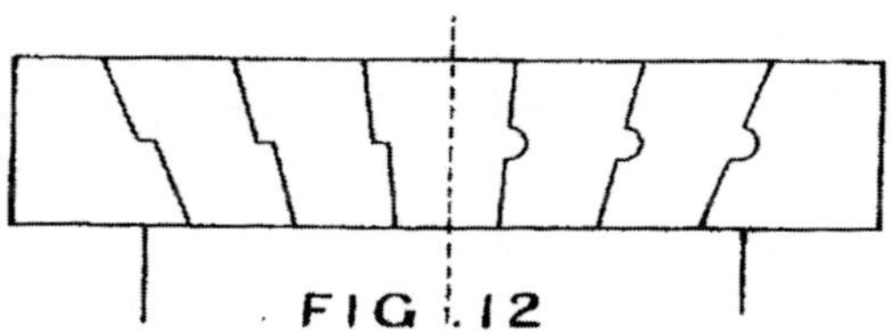

FIG . 12

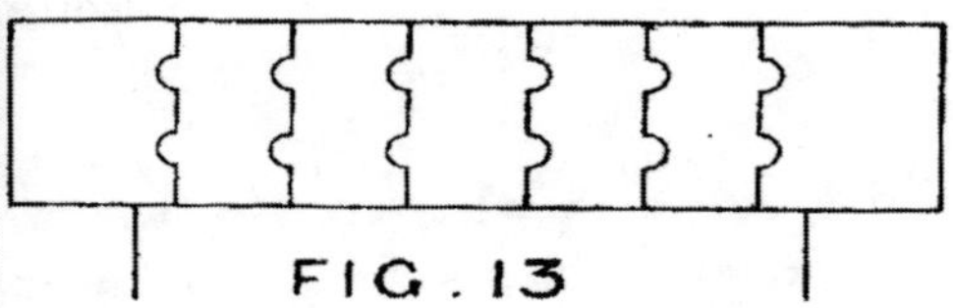

FIG . 13

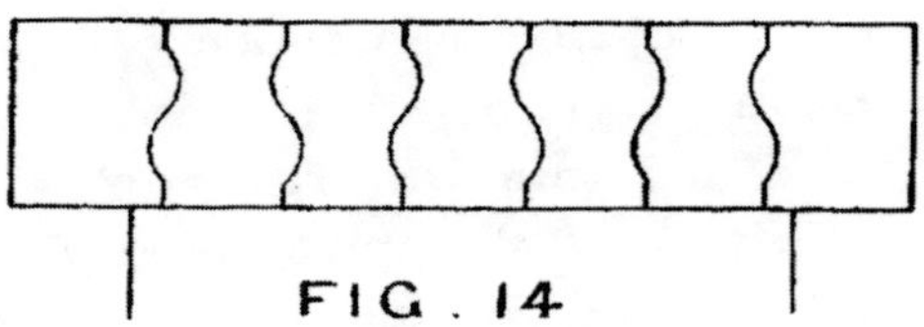

FIG . 14

FIG . 15

Fig. 18.—A horizontal lintel or architrave spanning an opening, with an apparent vertical joint, but concealing a secret arch joint.

This is used chiefly in colonnades, porticoes, &c., where stones of a sufficient length are not attainable, and sometimes also for convenience of hoisting and fixing.

An indent is formed the shape of the reverse of a wedge in joint of abutment, and a wedge-shape projection is cut in keystone fitting neatly into the indent.

This makes a good and secure joint without dowelling or cramping.

Fig. 19.—Shews sketch of weather or saddle joint in cornice.

This joint is made by leaving at each end of the stone a ridge or roll, the formation of which is generally left till after fixing. This roll effectually prevents the water running through the joint. The roll is not usually seen from the front, as the nose of cornice is continued straight through the joint, although it is also in some cases made a feature of.

This joint is used chiefly for cornices and window sills where there is a large projection.

A cross-section of the joint shows thus : 

Fig. 20.—Exhibits a rebated joint in gable coping.

This joint is serviceable, inasmuch as it keeps the water out of the joint and the wall dry, although it is somewhat expensive.

Fig. 21.—An example of various bed joints in stone spires, being respectively—

A. A horizontal bed joint.

B. A bed joint at right angles to batter.

C. A rebated or stepped bed joint.

D. A joggle or tabled joint.

The bed joints of the stones are usually cut at right angles to the batter or face of the spire, as at *B*; but horizontal beds, as at *A*, are supposed not to involve so much thrust at the base. But for obviating any outward tendency, a chain or rod-bond united at the angles, and inserted in a cavity at the base of the spire, is sometimes used.

The two bed joints *C* and *D* are both a little wasteful of material, but for stability and strength these are by far the best form of joints.

A word may be said as to the thickness of the work; this will depend

ARCHES AND JOINTS

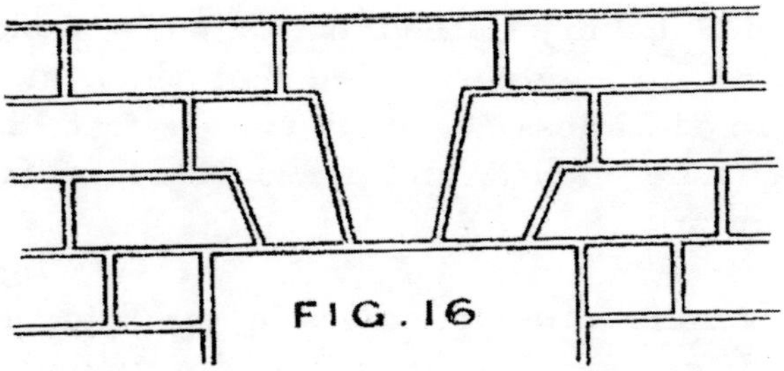

FIG. 16

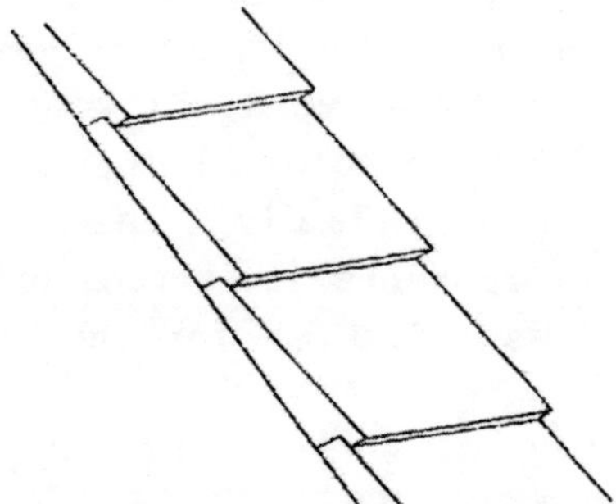

FIG. 20

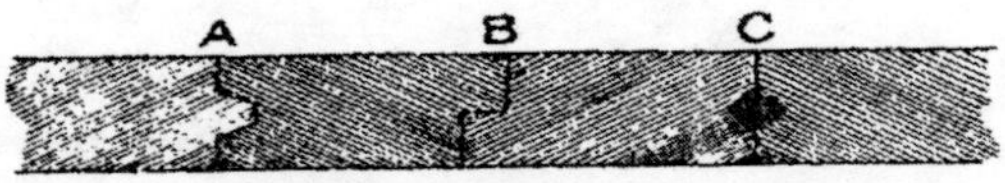

FIG. 17

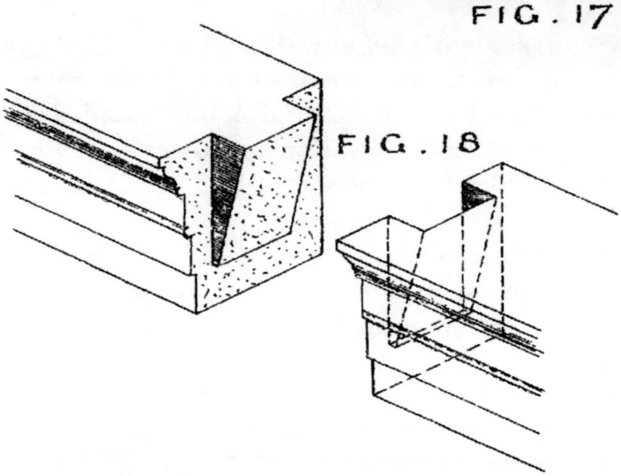

FIG. 18

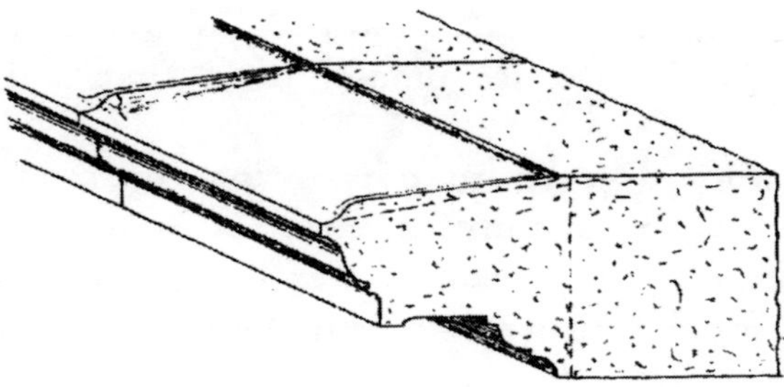

FIG. 19

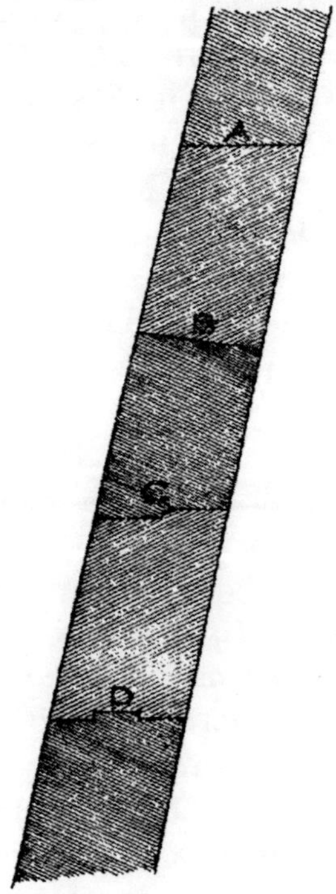

FIG. 21

chiefly on the height of the spire and the quality of the stone. From ten or twelve inches at the base, diminishing to six inches or even less at the top, may be generally considered sufficient.

The stone-work of the spire of Salisbury Cathedral (the spire, reckoning from the tower, being 204 feet in height), is two feet thick at the base, and gradually diminishes in thickness to about twenty feet above the tower, where it is reduced to nine inches, and is continued at that thickness to the capstone at the summit.

Fig. 22.—Gives plan of part of one course of stones in the Eddystone lighthouse. The stones are held in position by being dovetailed one into the other.

This form of joint is seldom used, except in works requiring great strength, such as sea-walls, breakwaters, &c. It is also an expensive joint, on account of the large amount of labour, and the waste of material.

Fig. 23.—Shews ashlar in courses with joggle joints.

This is a very unusual form of joint, and is used no doubt more for effect than utility. There is a waste of material and labour, and a better result may be obtained by the use of slate cramps. However, there are several examples of it in modern buildings in London.

Fig. 24.—A seating to sill, with a slate or copper dowel to prevent lateral motion. Mortices are cut opposite to each other in the two beds, and the dowel made secure by being run in with cement.

The dowel is a most useful adjunct in good and secure fixing.

Fig. 25.—*A* is a metal cramp for securing joints together. A chase or groove is cut in the stone of a sufficient width and depth, and at each end a mortice hole is cut to the exact size of inside of cramp, so that it fits tightly, and requires to be tapped into its place; it is then run with melted brimstone or cement.

The use of iron cramps and dowels in connection with stone is generally attended with some danger, on account of the iron rusting, which causes an increase in size, and subsequent fractures and discolouration of the stone. But if the iron is properly protected by galvanizing or japanning, the risk is reduced to a minimum.

The best metals for cramps, dowels, &c., are copper, gun metal, or brass, but these are expensive and are therefore not much used.

B is an example of a slate cramp also used for connecting joints

ARCHES AND JOINTS

FIG . 22

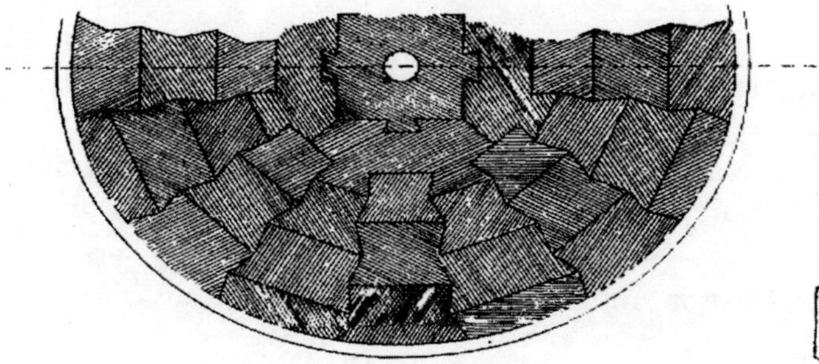

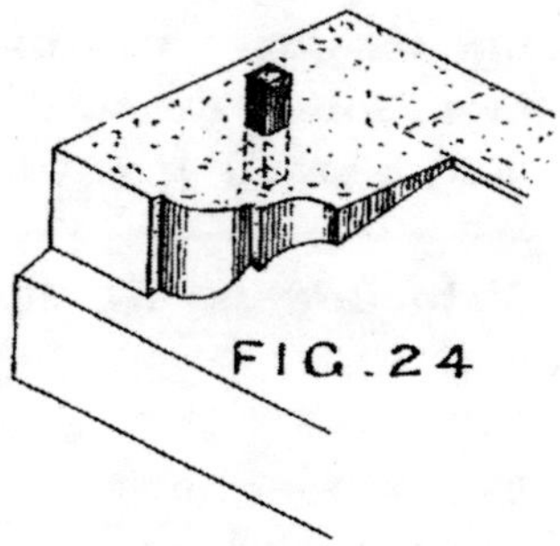

FIG.24

FIG . 23

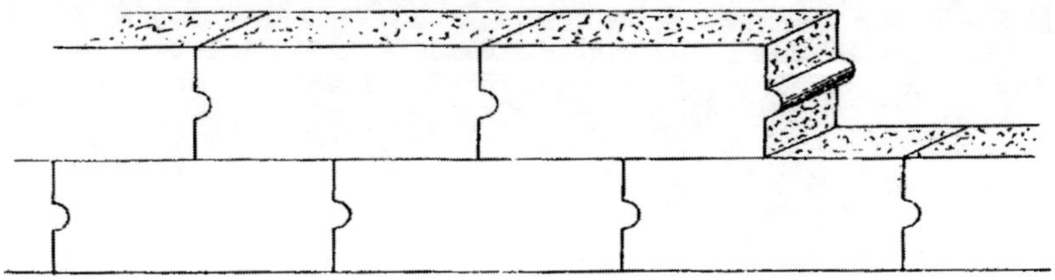

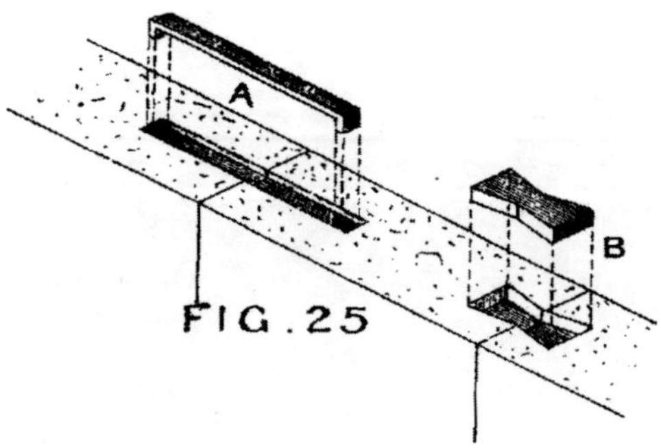

FIG.25

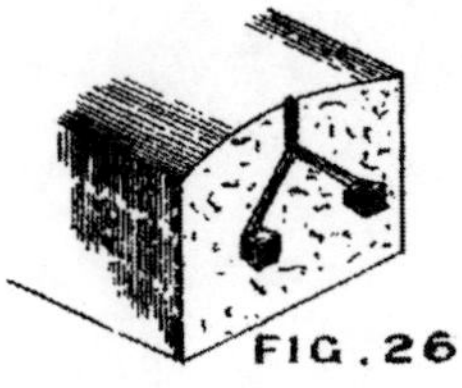

FIG.26

FIG.27

together, and is an excellent and economical substitute for metal. It is made dovetail in shape, let in flush to the bed of the stone, and then run in with cement.

Fig. 26.—Shews a plugged or lead dowelled joint. This is chiefly used in copings, curbs, strings, arches, &c., and prevents the joint working loose or "drawing."

Two holes, dovetail in shape, are sunk in the joints opposite each other and a small groove is cut from the top to each hole and run in with lead.

Slate dowels are sometimes used for this purpose, and run in with cement.

Fig. 27.—Shews a lewis, or holding down bolt, let in a dovetail hole and run in with lead.

Plates IX., X., XI.—MASONRY DETAILS.

Fig. 1.—To form a Plane Surface from a rough block, when the surface is of considerable size.

Four small cubes of beech, or any hard wood, about two inches square, wrought perfectly true, are used for this purpose, and are termed *boning pegs.*

Commence at the end of block by chiselling at each corner a sinking sufficiently low to take out any irregularities which from observation can be seen, and repeat the operation at the opposite end; place the pegs at each corner, and apply straight-edge on them as at *a b* and *c d*, sight through (or "bone," as it is usually termed), and adjust sinkings until the bottom of straight-edges are out of winding and in one plane. This being done, work straight drafts from sinkings *a* to *b*, *c* to *d*, *b* to *c*, and from *d* to *a*, point off superfluous stone and dress to a finished face.

To prove that the face is a true plane, apply the straight-edge on the diagonals *a* to *c* and *b* to *d*; these should be perfectly straight, and the surface also in every part should coincide with the straight-edge.

The use of the "boning pegs" on large surfaces is obvious, as all that is necessary is to sink the small corners where the adjustment is required, instead of reworking a long draft each time.

When the surface to be formed is not too large, a draft may be sunk across at each end of the stone, and boned through with straight-edge, and the above operation repeated without the pegs.

With regard to beds and joints, these are worked to perfectly true and straight surfaces, and the chisel drafts round the margin should form sharp and straight arrises.

The point may be freely used in the centre of bed, but care must be taken not to work the bed hollow, because when the stone is bedded, there would be undue pressure on the outer edges, which would be liable to cause fracture of the stone.

Fig. 2.—To form a WINDING SURFACE.

For this purpose two rules or straight-edges are used, one having parallel edges, the other with divergent edges giving the amount of twist that is required. The distance apart at which the two rules are to be placed is generally defined by two light iron rods connecting them together.

Commence by working drafts across each end of block, and apply the rules as at *c d* and *e f*, and bone the upper edges of rules until they coincide. Work straight drafts on sides at *c e* and *d f*, dividing each end into an equal number of parts as *g h i*, and cut straight drafts through from *g* to *g*, *h* to *h*, and *i* to *i*. The remaining portion is now to be subdivided, and straight drafts worked through from corresponding point to point until the whole surface is finished. The drafts must not be worked parallel to sides, or a correct winding surface will not be formed.

Winding surfaces are used chiefly in skew arches, with spiral beds and joints, and in the beds of coping to curved wing walls, and also to the soffit of winders in stairs, an example of which will be given in the next section.

Fig. 3.—To form a CYLINDRICAL SURFACE.

Square the ends of block off to a plane bed or joint, and scribe in section mould of cylinder ; mark the centre and diagonal lines on as *a b*, *c d*, *e f*, *g h*, at each end, care being taken to keep these lines each in the same plane, as the accuracy of the cylinder depends on their coinciding.

Point off superfluous stone roughly to near the surface, and chisel straight drafts from *a* to *a′*, *b* to *b′*, *c* to *c′*, &c. ; divide the spaces from *a* to *e*, *a* to *g*, &c., into as many parts as are convenient, and work drafts through to corresponding divisions, until the whole surface is finished to a true cylindrical face.

Fig. 4.—To work a LENGTH OF CORNICE out of a rectangular block of stone.

The beds, joints, and nosing being first worked, scribe in section mould on each joint, draw a line at pleasure close to the profile of moulding as at *a b*, forming a wedge-shape piece to be removed, which rough off with the punch right through the block, taking out smaller checks roughly as shewn at *c d e*, *e f g*.

Fig. 5.—The next process is shewn here, from *A* to *B*. This is to roughly chisel out the shape of mouldings to within about an eighth of an inch of the finished surface. This being done, clean through the mouldings, as shewn at *B* to *C*, by aid of round-nose and narrow chisels, and some-

MASONRY — DETAILS

FIG. 1

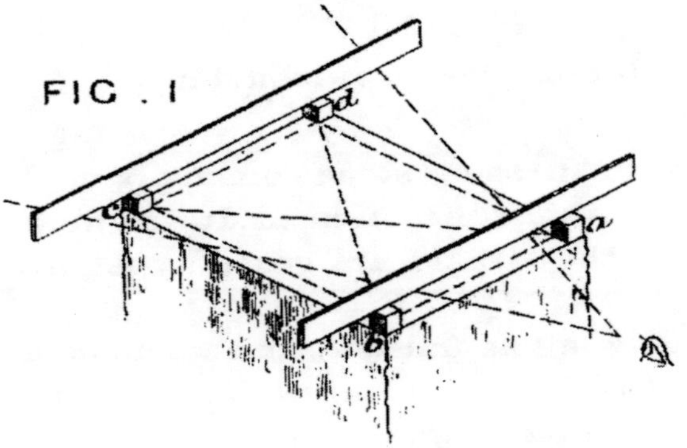

FIG. 2

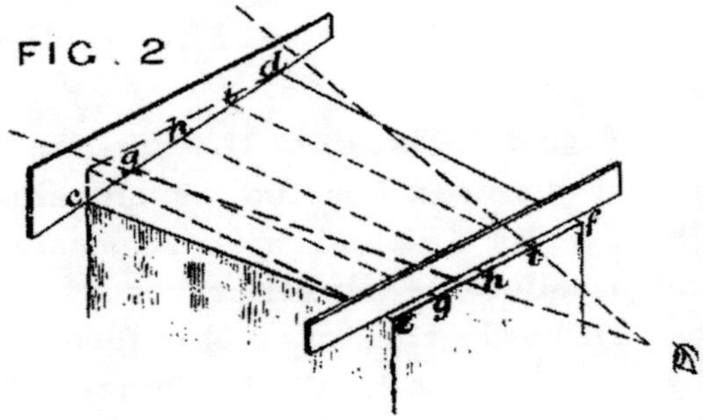

FIG: 3

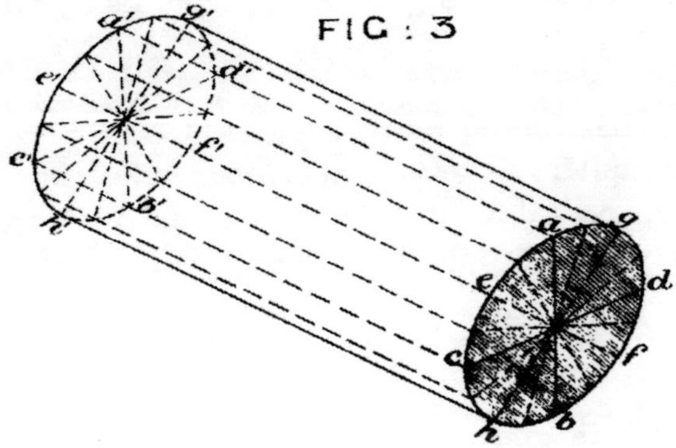

FIG. 4

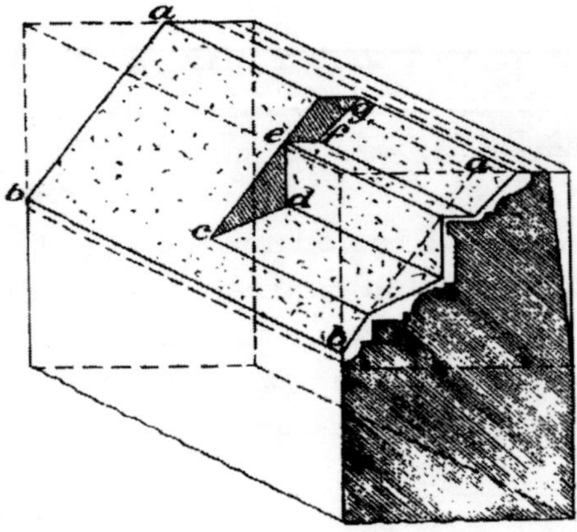

FIG. 5

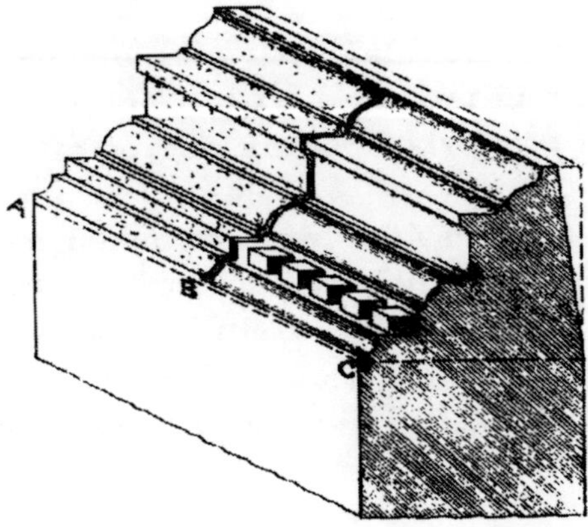

times for extra finish smooth over with the boaster, applying the straight-edge frequently to test the accuracy of working; and lastly, cutting in the dentils.

This method of working applies to all other forms of mouldings.

Fig. 6.—Exhibits the various forms of dressing stone commonly used.

A shews a boasted or chiselled face, sometimes termed droved work. The face is finished with a boaster, and the strokes are generally regular and parallel to each other.

In hard grit stones this face is usually left as finished, and when, as in the case of a building, the whole of the ashlar and plain work is chiselled to the same angle of inclination, the effect is pleasing.

In softer stones a finished face is formed by rubbing the boasted face with sand and water, and removing all chisel marks; it is then called plain ashlar.

B shews ashlar with tooled face.

This is formed with a broad tool, or wide boaster, by a regular succession of strokes, parallel to each other, extending across the whole width of stone, and when finished shews a series of flutes or channels, thus,  the size of flutes depending on the texture of the stone.

Considerable skill is required in tooling neatly, and the tooling is somewhat costly, the surface having first to be worked to a boasted face.

C shews ashlar with pick or pecked face, and tooled margin.

This is produced with a point, or in the case of granite with the pick, and can be worked to any degree of fineness.

D shews ashlar with punched rock face, and tooled margin.

This is similar to the last mentioned, but much coarser. In producing it, the punch is driven in almost vertical to the face until the stone bursts out, leaving a series of cavities. When regularly done it looks well, and is very effective, and for large work it gives the appearance of boldness and solidity.

E shews ashlar with broached face, and tooled margin.

This is produced with a point, which forms a furrow with rough ridges, and is worked across the stone to the required angle.

F shews ashlar with rusticated face, and tooled margin.

This is worked with small chisels and points, and sunk down about half an inch, leaving a plain narrow margin on face; the pattern is irregular, but easily adapted to any space.

G is a rebated or rustic quoin, with vermiculated face.

This is cut out with small chisels, and has the appearance of being worm-eaten.

Fig. 7.—To set out the ENTASIS, or SWELL, of a COLUMN.

Draw the centre line or axis, and set off the height of column, *L K*, and top and bottom diameters, *O P*, *N M*. Divide the column into four equal parts. The first part, to *A*, will be continued straight, and of the same diameter as at bottom. Divide the remaining three-fourths of column, from *A* to *K*, into any number of equal parts (in this example four), as at *B C D K*. At *A*, with radius *F* or *G*, draw the semicircle *F G*. Now project the top diameter *O P*, cutting the semicircle at *4 4*, and divide the arc of semi *F 4*, into four equal parts, as at 1, 2, 3, 4, answering to the number of divisions in column, and draw lines parallel to *F G*, as 1 1, 2 2, 3 3, 4 4; at *b b*, *c c*, *d d*, set off diameters 1 1, 2 2, and 3 3, respectively.

Bend a flexible rod to the points *O*, *d*, *c*, *b*, *F*, and draw the curved line, which repeat on opposite side from *P* to *G*, giving the required entasis.

Fig. 8.—Shews another method of setting out the entasis of columns, by a curve known as the conchoid of Nicomedes. This is preferable to the former method, and the result is more graceful and regular.

The height of column and bottom and top diameter being determined, draw centre line *H G*, and line *E J* at right angles to the same; set off the bottom semi-diameter, *A B*, from *D*, the extreme point of top diameter, cutting the centre line at *E*. Then from *D*, through *E*, produce the line to *F*, cutting base line at *C*, and from this point, *C*, as a centre, draw through the axis of column any number of lines, as *a*, *a*, *a*, &c., on each of which from the centre line towards the circumference set off the distance *A B*, as *a b*.

Through the points *D*, *a*, *a*, *a*, &c., draw the curve, by aid of a flexible rod, giving the entasis required.

This curve may be also struck with a trammel, which gives a continuous line, and is the most perfect of any system adopted.

The base perpendicular and hypothenuse being obtained by the preceding method, take three wood straight-edges, as *G H*, *B J*, and *D F*; fasten *G H* and *J B* together; at *H* plough a groove in middle of *G H* from top to bottom, and at the point *C* on the rule *J B* fix a pin; then on the rule *D F* set off the distance *D E*, equal to *A B*, the bottom semi-diameter of column, and at the point *E* fix a button, whose head must be exactly fitted to the groove made in *G H*, in which it is to slide; and at the other extremity of the rule *D F* cut a slot right through from *F* to *L*, the length being not less than the difference between *C E* and *C B*, and of sufficient size to allow the slot to pass evenly the pin fixed at *C*.

The trammel being thus completed, place the rule *G H* so that the middle of groove is directly over the centre line of column, move the rod *D F* along the groove *G B*, and with its point *D*, on which is fixed a pencil, describe the continuous curve from *D* to *A*, thus giving the required entasis.

To diminish or enlarge a Section Mould.

Fig. 9.—Shews section of a cornice mould, which it is proposed to diminish to the height of a given line, *c d*, and the projection of the same diminishing in like proportion.

Draw the vertical line *a b*, and produce horizontal line of mouldings on to same; with *a b* as base, erect an isosceles or equilateral triangle, *a o b*, and on this set off the given height, *c d*; from *a b* draw the lines of mouldings converging to apex *o*, cutting the given line *c d*, which is proportionately divided by it.

For the projection: On line *g b* draw the triangle *g h b*, and project vertical lines from points in the moulding, and draw converging lines to apex, *h*. The line *e f* is obtained by finding a fourth proportional, namely, as *a b* is to *c d*, so is *g b* to *e f*. This may be solved by geometrical construction or by calculation. Transfer divisions from *c d* and *e f*, Fig. 9, to *c d* and *e f*, Fig. 10, produce the lines to intersections, and draw in the mouldings.

The above principle will apply to any description of mouldings, and any number of points in the members may be obtained similarly.

MASONRY—DETAILS

FIG. 9

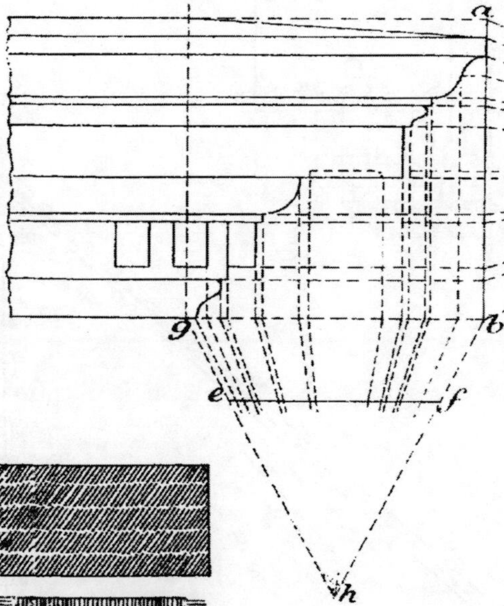

FIG. 10

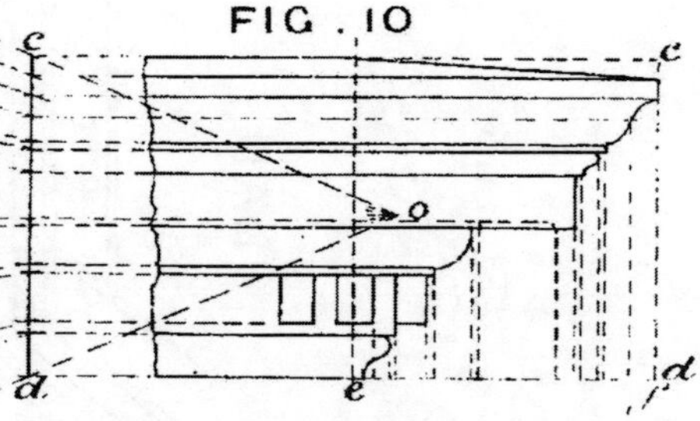

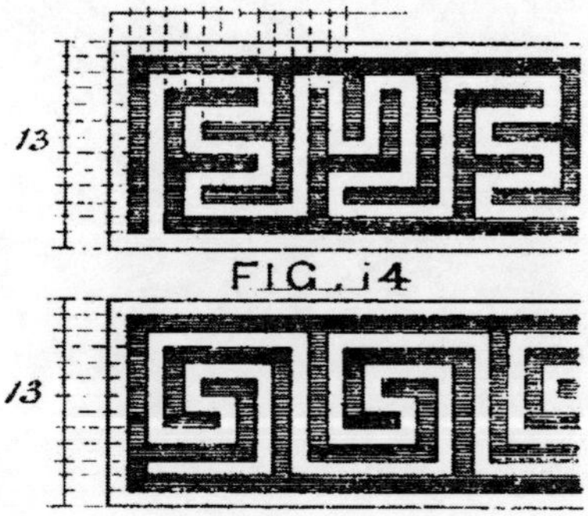

13

FIG. 14

13

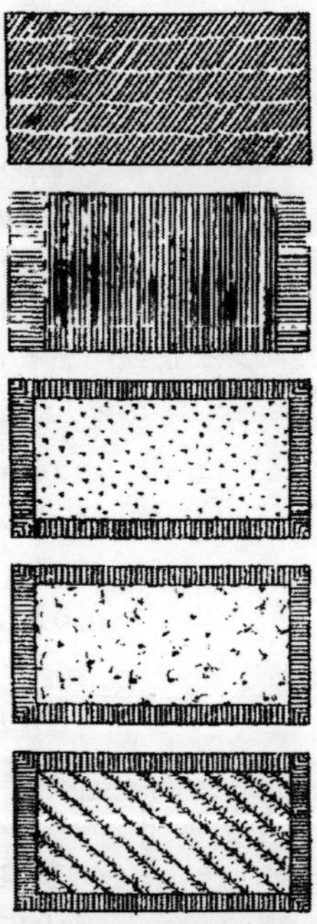

A

B

C

D

E

F

G

FIG. 6

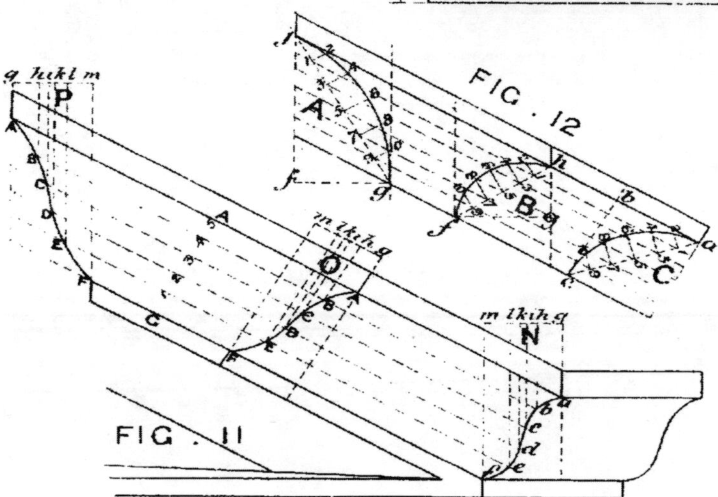

FIG. 11

FIG. 12

MASONRY—DETAILS

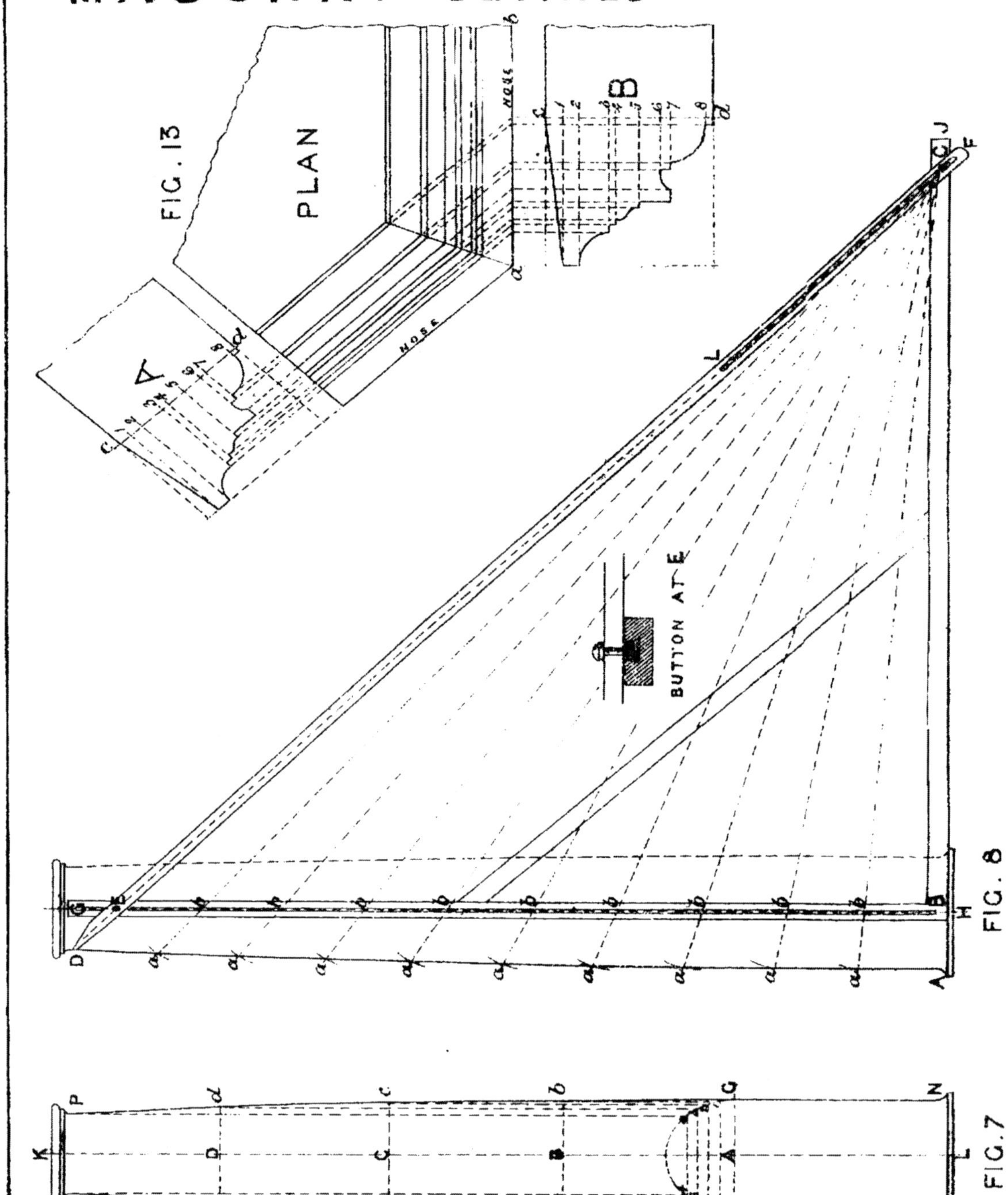

Raking Moulds.

[Raking is a term applied to such members of a building as are inclined from the level or horizontal, and frequently occur, especially in pediments, &c.]

Fig. 11.—To find the RAKING MOULD of the CYMA RECTA, or OGEE, in a pediment.

Let *N* be the given section of horizontal mould. Divide the distance from *A* to *G* into any number of parts, as 1, 2, 3, 4, 5, and draw lines through these points parallel to *Aa*, cutting *N* at *b*, *c*, *d*, *e*, and at *a*, *b*, *c*, *d*, *e*, *f*, erect perpendiculars, as *g*, *h*, *i*, *k*, *l*, *m*. At *O* draw a line parallel to the nosing, and transfer the distance *g*, *h*, *i*, *k*, *l*, *m* from *N*, and from these points project lines at right angles to the nosing, cutting raking lines, 1, 2, 3, 4, 5, at *A*, *B*, *C*, *D*, *E*, *F*. Through these points of intersection draw the section of cyma recta raking mould. This section will form a true mitre at *N* and *P*.

The section of ogee, as in that of a broken pediment at *P*, is obtained similarly.

Fig. 12.—To find the RAKING MOULD of a CAVETTO, or HOLLOW.

Let *C* be the given section. Draw a cord line from *a* to *c*, and divide it into any number of equal parts (in this example six), or divide the square line from *c* to *b* into the same number, and lines drawn through these divisions parallel to rake will equally divide all chord lines. Draw ordinates at chord lines *a c*, *f h*, and *g j*, and set off 1 2, 3 4, 5 6, &c., and through the points 2, 4, 6, 8, at *A* and *B*, draw the curve giving the true sections.

All other sections of mouldings are obtained in a similar manner.

To produce a Stretching Mould, or Elongated Section of Square Mould.

Fig. 13.—Shews plan of octagonal angle, the square section of moulding being given at *A*.

To find the section to apply on line *a b*, project lines of section *A* on to plan and produce them through to line *a b*, and project these lines at right angles to the same. Set off the height and lines 1, 2, 3, 4, 5, &c., on *d c* at *A*, and transfer to *d c* on *B*, and produce them through. The intersection of these lines will give points in the section, and for the contour of the mouldings, any number of points may be projected in the same manner, and the mould thus completed.

This section applies also to the mitre of a right angle.

Fig. 14.—Shews two examples of the Grecian fret, or key pattern.

These are produced by dividing the height into any number of equal parts, and the horizontal line into the same divisions; draw the lines through, intersecting each other, forming small squares, and then trace the pattern, the bands and sinkings being of equal width.

PLATES XII., XIII., XIV., XV.—STAIRCASES.

The *tread* of a step is the upper or horizontal surface, and the *riser* is the front vertical face or upright portion of the step. The *soffit* is the under surface, and in spandrel steps is inclined from the horizontal. The *nosing* is the front edge of the tread and riser, and is either square or moulded.

Flyers are straight steps with parallel edges.

Winders are steps with converging edges on tread, and parallel edges on riser, and generally a twisting surface on soffit.

For general purposes, the tread of a step should not be more than twelve inches, nor less than nine inches, and the rise of a step should not be more than seven inches, nor less than five and a half inches.

The proportion usually adopted, is any two numbers between the above sizes which, multiplied together, produce sixty-six: namely, a twelve-inch tread by a five and a half-inch rise equals sixty-six, or $11 \times 6 = 66$, and again $11\frac{1}{2} \times 5\frac{3}{4} = 66$. This, however, may be slightly modified—as, for instance, a ten-inch tread and a six and a half-inch rise equals sixty-five—but the rule may be relied upon as safe in working to.

A staircase easy of ascent, and in other respects desirable, is one in which all the steps are flyers, and having quarter or half-space landings.

Long straight flights with more than twelve steps before reaching a landing should be avoided.

Where there is a deficiency of room or space, winders have to be introduced; and these, if properly arranged, need not interfere with the ease of the ascent.

In setting out, for the purpose of making the moulds, the first point to be considered (the plan being satisfactory) is the width of the tread and the rise of the steps; these are best obtained by measuring the length and width of the well-hole, and the height from floor to floor, from the actual work if practicable, and then dividing out the dimensions thus obtained into the number of steps on deal rods, or it may be also found by calculation. The height rod is called the storey rod, and this and the other rods are afterwards used in the fixing of the stairs.

Fig. 1.—To set out a Spandrel Step Mould.

Draw a line *F B*, and line *B C* at right angles to same, and on *F B* set off *A B* the width of tread, and on *B C* the height of rise. From *A* to *C* draw a diagonal line cutting tread and rise at their extremities, and draw parallel to it line *E D* for soffit, of a sufficient depth proportioned to the strength of the stone, which in this example is put at two inches. For the back rebate, set off from *A* to *F* one and a quarter inches, and from *F* draw line square with soffit to *E* ; for the front rebate draw line from *C* to *G* square with the rise and set off one and a quarter inches, and from *G* draw line square with soffit to *D*, thus forming a birdsmouth, the exact reverse of the back rebate.

Allow one-twelfth of an inch for joint, which cut off from the mould as shewn by double line at *C G D*.

A moulding or astragal nosing is added on to front of riser when necessary.

Fig. 2.—Shews plan of a stair generally considered to be a good type.

It starts with two curtail steps and four flyers reaching a quarter-space landing, then eleven more flyers, reaching a half-space landing, and five flyers to the top landing.

The setting out of this requires no explanation.

Fig. 3.—Shews part plan of stair with winders.

Fig. 4.—Is a development of the plan of stair shown in Fig. 3.

The stairs should be set out to full size, and on a large board or platform, and it may be here noted that the riser lines only are essential to the setting out, both on plan and section, the moulded nosing being seldom shewn.

Begin with the plan and draw the wall lines *C D E*, and lines *F G H* for the quoin ends, draw centre line *A B*, and on this line from No. 13 to 20 divide out the winders equal to the width of tread of the flyers, dividing the quoin ends into the same number of parts.

These need not be equal in size, and a better result will be obtained if the ends are a little graduated from the flyers to the angle winder each

STAIRS

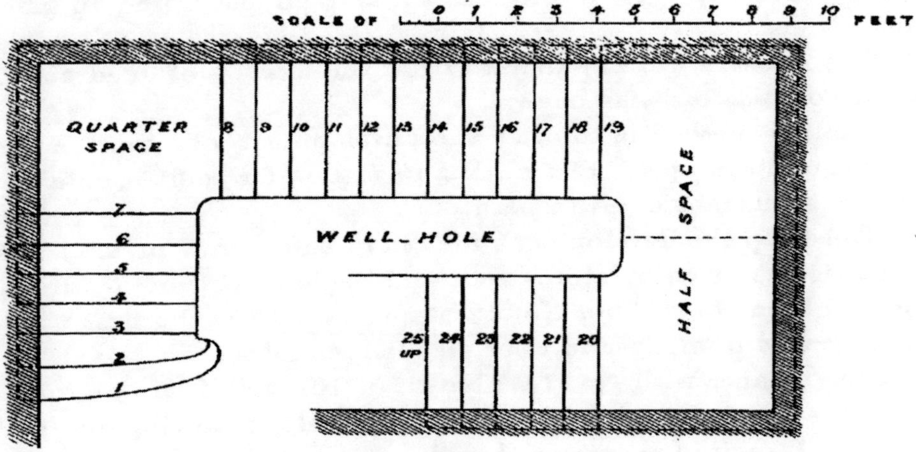

FIG. 2

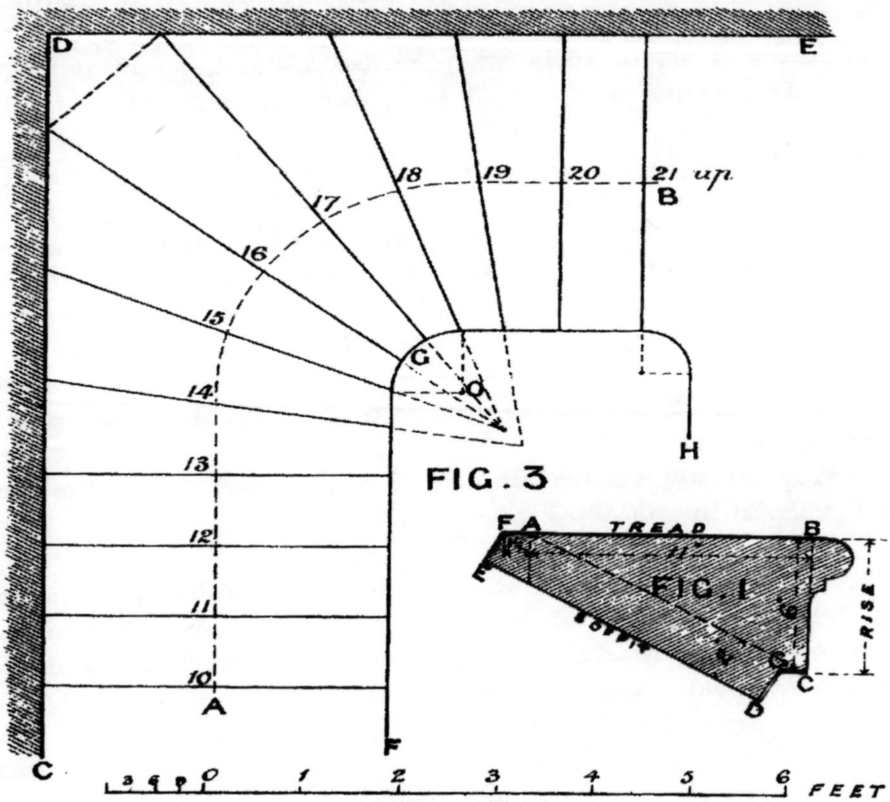

FIG. 3

SCALE TO FIG. 3.

way, in order to get a good tread and an easy line to the soffit and handrail.

The winders will not radiate from the centre of quadrant *O*, but at a distance outside of it, as shewn.

Another method is to draw the development of quoin end, and adjust the ends of steps upon this, until a good line for soffit is obtained, the riser lines are then transferred to plan.

To set up the development for quoin ends, draw parallel lines on board for the rise as given by storey rod, and begin at bottom by drawing No. 10 step, and then No. 11 and No. 12 steps. No. 13 is the first winder. Set off the exact size from riser to riser on plan and draw on board, proceeding in the same manner with No. 14. Nos. 15, 16, and 17 are segmental on plan. Set off the developed size of each respectively, following on with Nos. 18, 19, &c., till each is drawn, so that the distance from riser of No. 10 to riser of landing No. 21 equals the distance of quoin ends on plan, when unfolded or stretched out in a straight line.

For the development of the wall end, set out similarly to the preceding by taking the distance of each winder on the wall line of plan, and setting up the same on board. No. 16 is taken across the corner and not into the angle; with this exception the wall end is stretched out in a straight line.

The soffit has now to be considered. Begin by drawing an easy curved line, taking up with soffit of flyer No. 11 and finishing with soffit of landing No. 21, keeping the rebates about the same size as the ordinary steps; this it is not always possible to do, but the size of rebate is not of so much importance as that of having a good soffit line. The rebates to winders are in every instance of the same square section as the flyers, but in some cases may be less in depth or greater, according as the soffit line cuts through them. A small reverse should be made from the development for guidance in working each.

For drawing the soffit a flexible lath or rod is used, by means of which an easy and graceful line is obtained.

Fig. 5.—The bed moulds for winders are made of deal laths about two inches wide by half an inch thick, nailed together as shewn in sketch. The mould is scribed on the tread of the stone to be worked, allowance being made for the back rebate, and also for the tailing into wall, both of these dimensions being figured on the mould.

Fig. 6.—Shews a well-hole mould, usually made of sheet zinc, used for guidance in drawing the segmental quoin ends.

STAIRS

SCALE OF FEET

FIG. 4

DEVELOPMENT OF QUOIN END AND WALL END

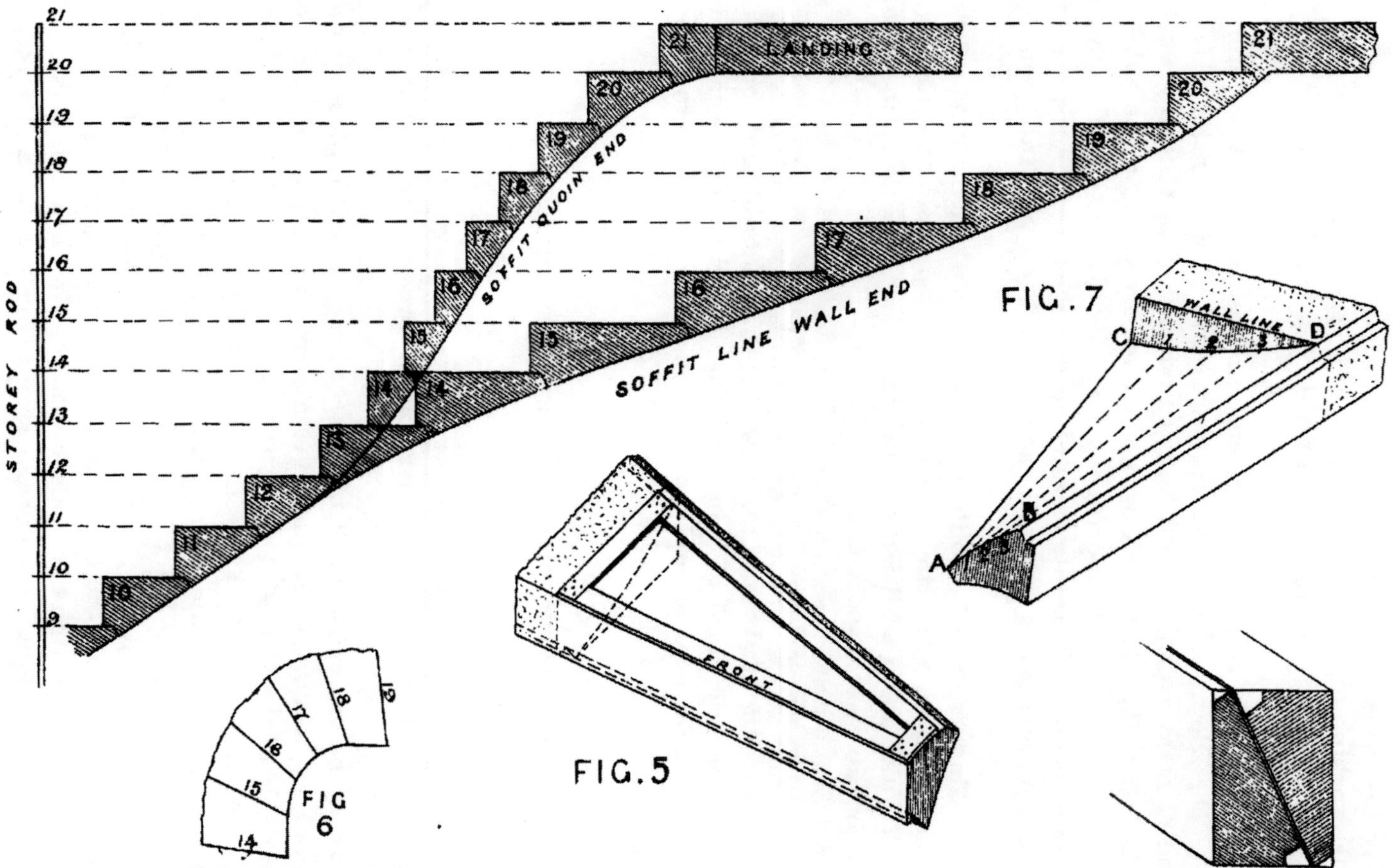

FIG. 7

FIG. 5

FIG 6

WELL-HOLE MOULD

FIG. 17

Fig. 7.—Shews sketch of soffit of winder.

The working of the winder is plain straightforward work with the exception of the soffit, which is a twisted or warped surface.

Cut in draft as *A B* on quoin end and sink draft to templet at wall end as *C D*. Point off superfluous waste and divide drafts *A B* on quoin end, and *C D* at wall end, into four equal parts, as 1, 2, 3; work straight drafts from 1 to 1, 2 to 2, and 3 to 3; these are again to be subdivided and straight drafts worked to corresponding divisions at each end, until the whole soffit is finished to a true winding surface.

The square seating at wall end is left on for a good fixing into wall.

A winding stair with moulded nosing is worked in precisely the same manner as the foregoing, the only difference being in the nosing, the projection of which is an addition to the plain riser, the riser lines, rebates and soffits being in every case identical.

A point which should not be lost sight of in setting out stairs, is to see that sufficient head room is allowed; this should not be less than six feet six inches from nose of steps to soffit of flight over,—that is to say, the soffit line of flight over should not cut below an arc described by a radius of six feet six inches, taken from the nose of either of the steps beneath.

Fig. 8.—Shews the plan of a winding staircase in a circular well, supported by a solid newel in the centre, the newel being worked on each step.

Fig. 9.—Is a sectional elevation of the winding staircase shown in Fig. 8.

It may be known to most of our readers, that if a piece of paper of the shape of a right-angled triangle be wound round a cylinder, the hypothenuse (or long side of the triangle) will generate a curve winding round the cylinder in the form of a spiral. This curve is called the helix.

The soffit line of the stairs winding round the well, and line winding round the newel, is the helix, and the soffit contained between these lines forms a true helical plane; the development therefore of each end of the step is a straight line on the soffit, so that no setting up on section is required. The plan must be laid down on the board full size, the treads being divided out equally, and each step being similar and alike, one mould

STAIRS

FIG. 9

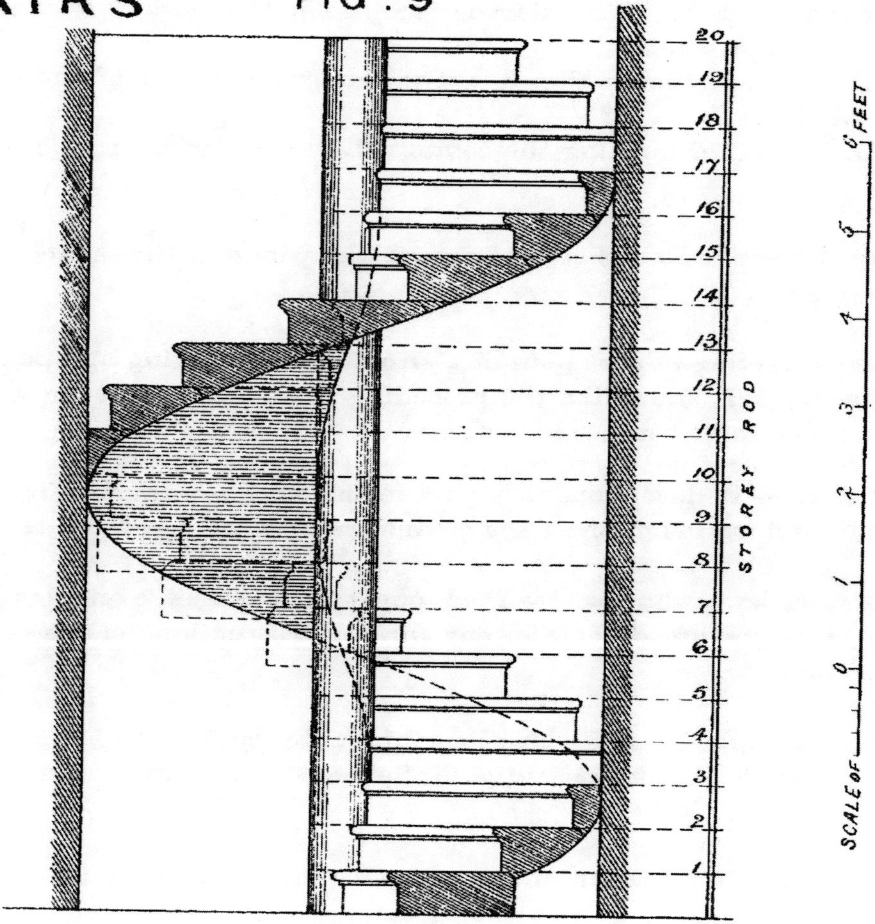

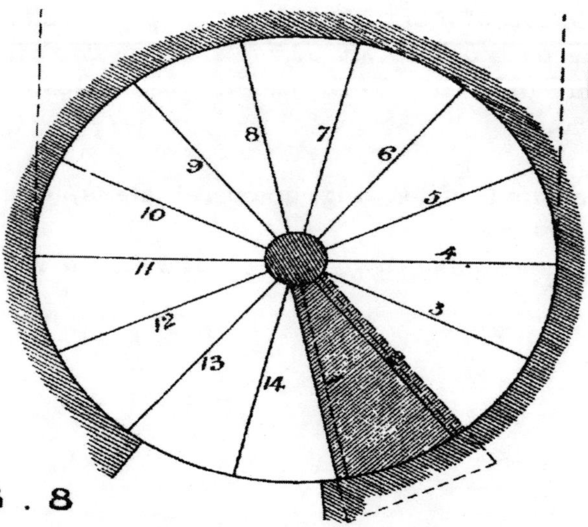

FIG. 8

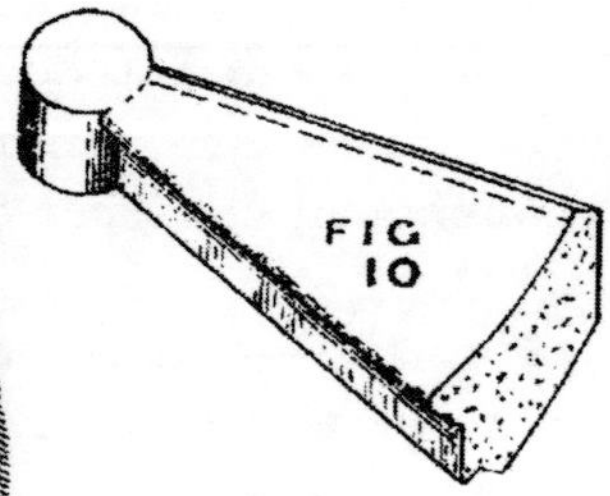

FIG 10

will do for the whole. The starting step is not generally worked on the soffit, but is kept solid.

The hatched line on Fig. 8 shews the extreme size of the bed mould of each winder.

The method of working the soffits will be similar to that described in Fig. 7.

Fig. 10.—Shews a sketch of one of the winders, the newel forming a portion of each.

Fig. 11.—Shews part plan of a circular stair, having an open newel or central well; this stair, like the preceding Figs. 8 and 9, is an example of the helix, the soffit being a helical plane.

Fig. 12.—Is development of part of the circular stair of Fig. 11, shewing quoin and wall end, the lines of soffit to each being straight.

The student who has worked out the previous examples of stairs, will not, it is presumed, require any further instruction on the setting out and working.

Figs. 13 and 14 are elevations of quóin ends, and sections of two forms of bracketed stairs suitable for good buildings, such as hotels, mansions, clubs, &c.

Fig. 15.—Is a section of solid square steps, suitable for warehouses, workshops, &c., where great strength is required.

Fig. 16.—Shews section of a simple form of steps, consisting of treads and risers in separate pieces, worked out of two inch or two and a half-inch stuff. These are chiefly used for back stairs, area steps, &c., and are inexpensive in construction.

Fig. 17.—Shews method of sawing spandrel steps, one out of the other, so as to economise stone.

The treads of winders are also sawn in a similar manner.

STAIRS

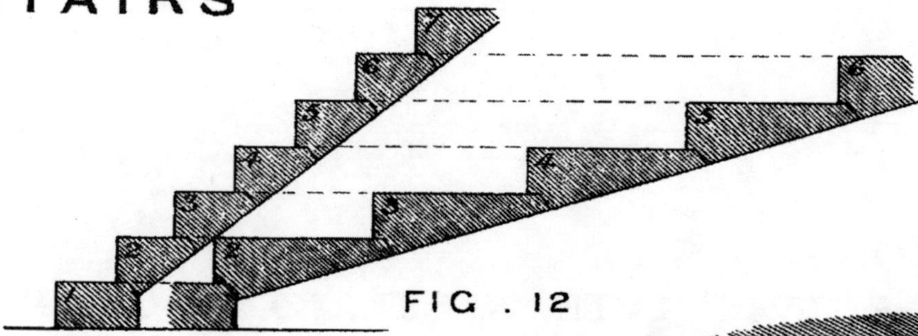

FIG. 12

FIG. 15

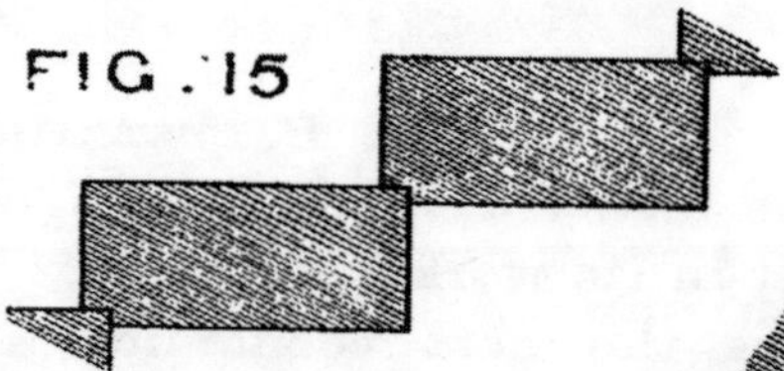

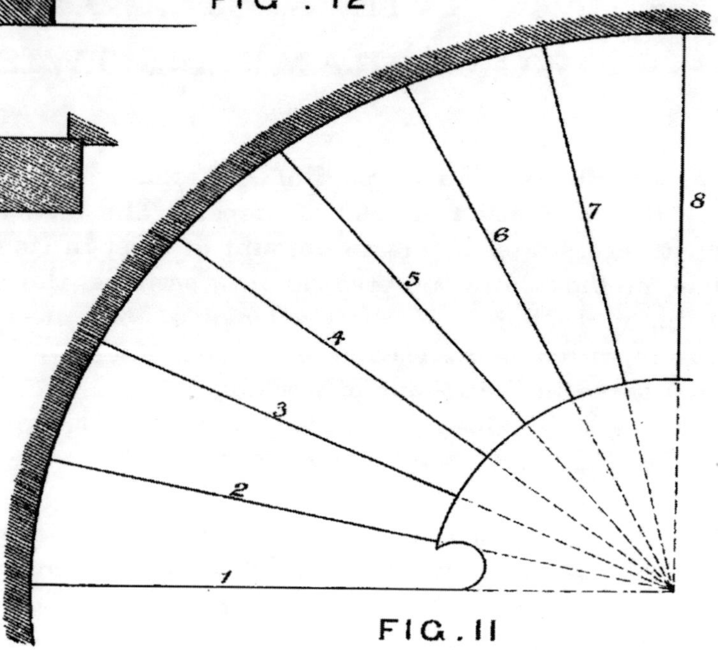

FIG. 11

FIG. 13

FIG. 14

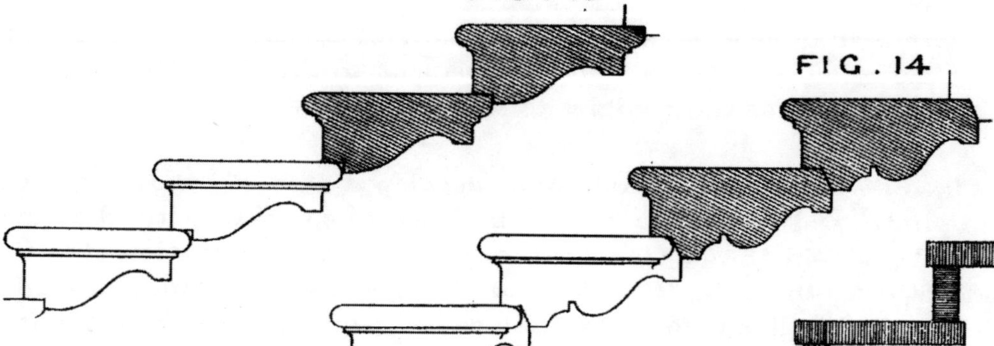

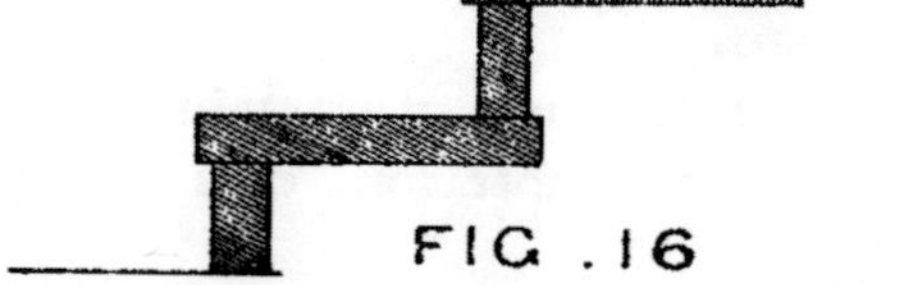

FIG. 16

SCALE TO FIG. 13. 14. 15. 16.

Plates XVI., XVII., XVIII., XIX.—CIRCULAR WORK (RAMP and TWIST).

Fig. 1.—Shews plan of part of a Terrace Stair, with Balustrade following the inclination or rake of steps. The balustrade being circular on plan, it necessitates a certain amount of twist in its working.

[The method here adopted is not, perhaps, the most economical as regards material; but it is comprehensible, and more true in form when worked than with a complication of moulds and bevels, and the material is more than saved in the labour of working.]

Begin by laying down the plan full size on a large board or platform, carefully dividing the space for balusters equally.

Fig. 2.—Set up the elevation to developed line of convex or outside face of plinth—that is to say, the line *A B C* on plan (Fig. 1), when stretched out or unfolded in a straight line, is equal to or of the same length as the horizontal line *A B C*. The line of inclination will be a helical line, as the steps are of equal tread and rise; therefore the plinth starts with a straight line parallel to the nose of steps.

On elevation set off the joints (convenient to the size of stone) for the plinth and capping at right angles to the line of rake.

Fig. 3.—Set up the elevation to developed line of concave or inside face of plinth, and set off the joints which are to coincide with the outside joints. To obtain these, transfer the joints from the elevation (Fig. 2) of outside face to the plan (Fig. 1), and produce the joint lines through to inside face by the lines radiating from centre, and re-transfer to the inside elevation.

The method of drawing the section of steps is shown by the dotted lines and the notation, this being similar to the plan.

BALUSTRADE RAMP & TWIST

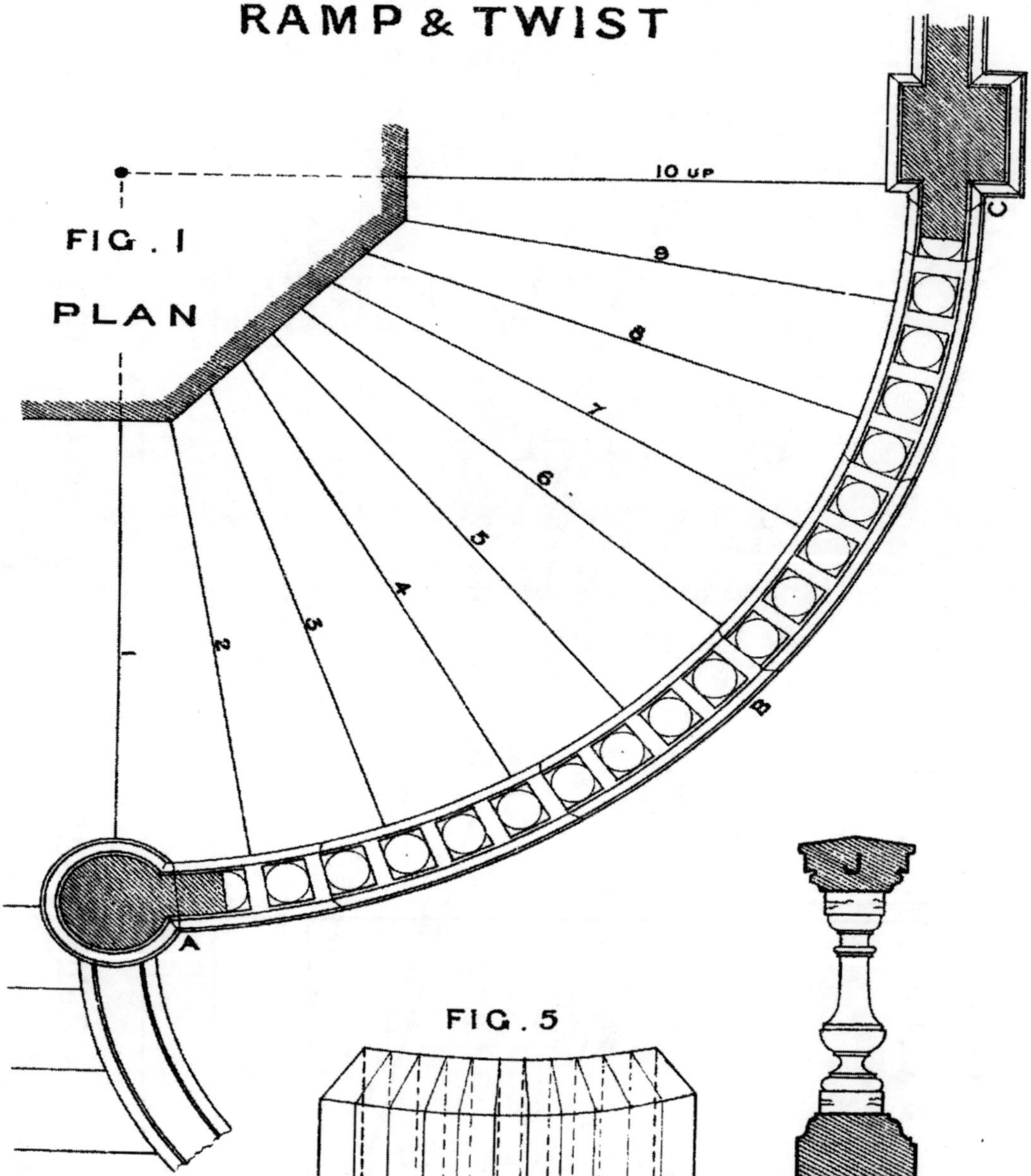

FIG. I

PLAN

FIG. 5

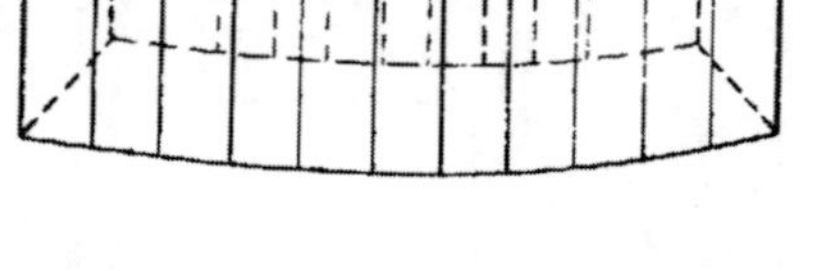

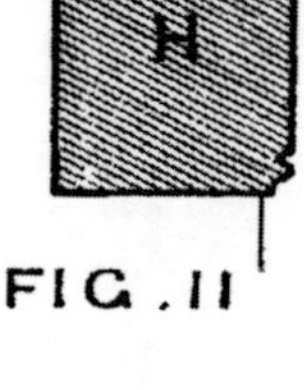

FIG. II

SCALE TO FIG. 1. 2 & 3.

BALUSTRADE RAMP & TWIST

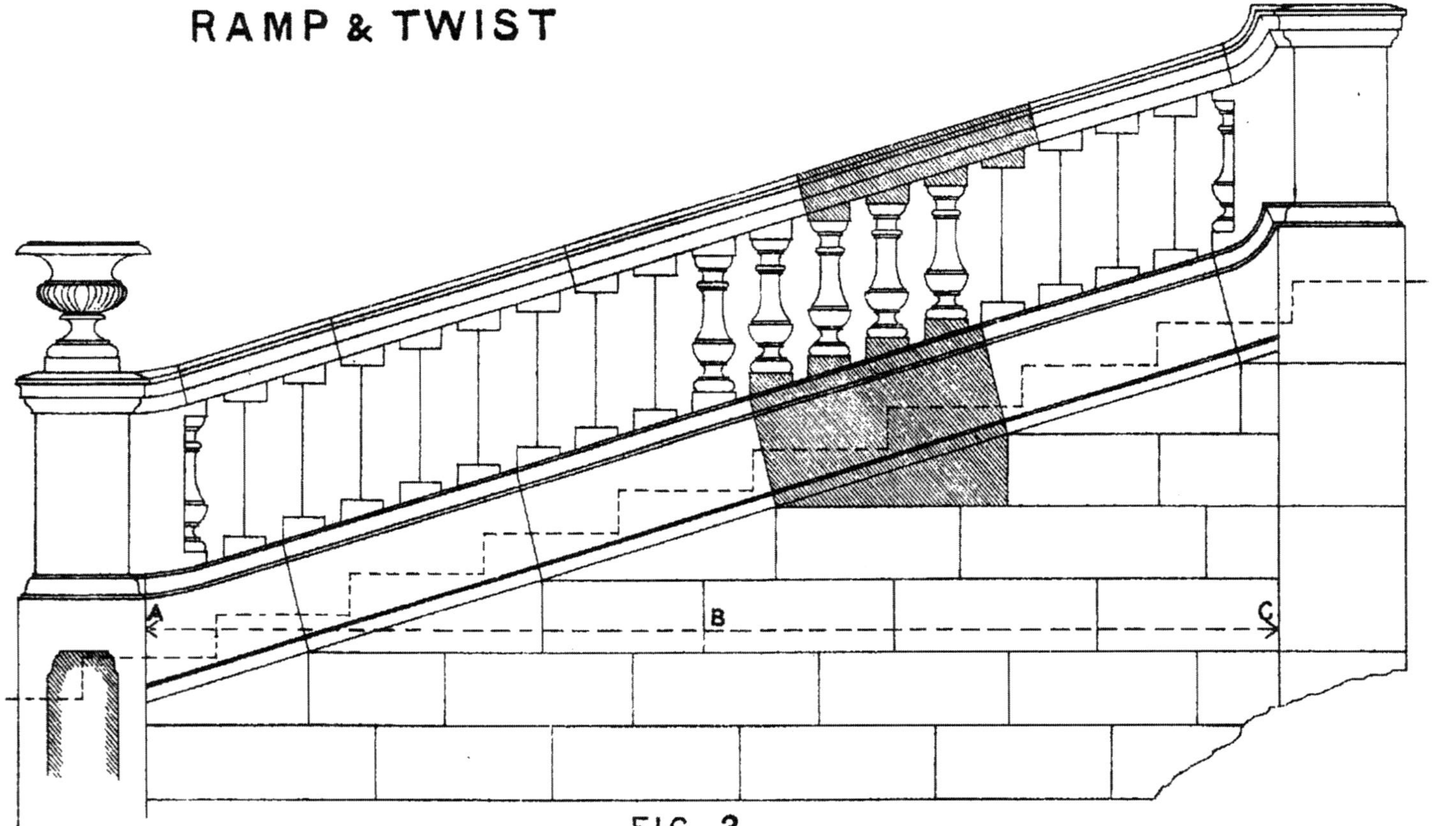

FIG. 2

DEVELOPMENT OF OUTSIDE ELEVATION

For the purpose of illustrating the making of the moulds and the working of the stones a plinth block and length of capping are taken, as shewn by hatched lines on Figs. 2 and 3. The details are given to a larger scale.

To work the Plinth Block.

The block of stone required to work the plinth block will be rectangular in shape, of the extreme length of the bed mould; and the width will be equal to the distance across the chord line, and the height will be that of the face moulds.

Fig. 4.—*A* Shews bed mould of the plinth.
B Shews face mould of convex or outside face.
C Shews face mould of concave or inside face.

Begin by working the bottom bed to a true plane; then work the top bed parallel to it as a surface of operation, and taken to the height of the face mould. Scribe the bed mould in on each bed, care being taken to bone the points through so that the moulds are perfectly out of twist; proceed to work the concave and convex surfaces. For guidance in working this to a true form radiating lines are marked on the beds taken from the mould, and the straight edge is applied on the face to drafts coinciding with these. At this stage the stone is a true segment of a hollow cylinder, as shewn in Fig. 5. Now apply face mould *B* (Fig. 4), to convex face, and face mould *C* (Fig. 4), to concave face, and scribe them in to their respective shapes; work the joints through, and scribe in the section mould *H* (Fig. 11).

The top bed, or surface of operation, is now done with, except at the high corner which forms the bed of the baluster seating. Point off the superfluous waste down to the top of the other baluster seatings, and clean through the beds and sides of these from outside to inside face, as shewn by sketch Fig. 6.

Next gauge the distance taken from the bed or section mould of seating of baluster to the convex and concave faces, and work the same, thus completing the baluster plinths.

For guidance in working the ogee raking mouldings, a bending strip or thin lath, and one or two small reverses cut to section of moulding, will be all that is required, and the stone is finished as in sketch (Fig. 7).

Each of the other plinth stones are worked similarly.

BALUSTRADE

RAMP & TWIST

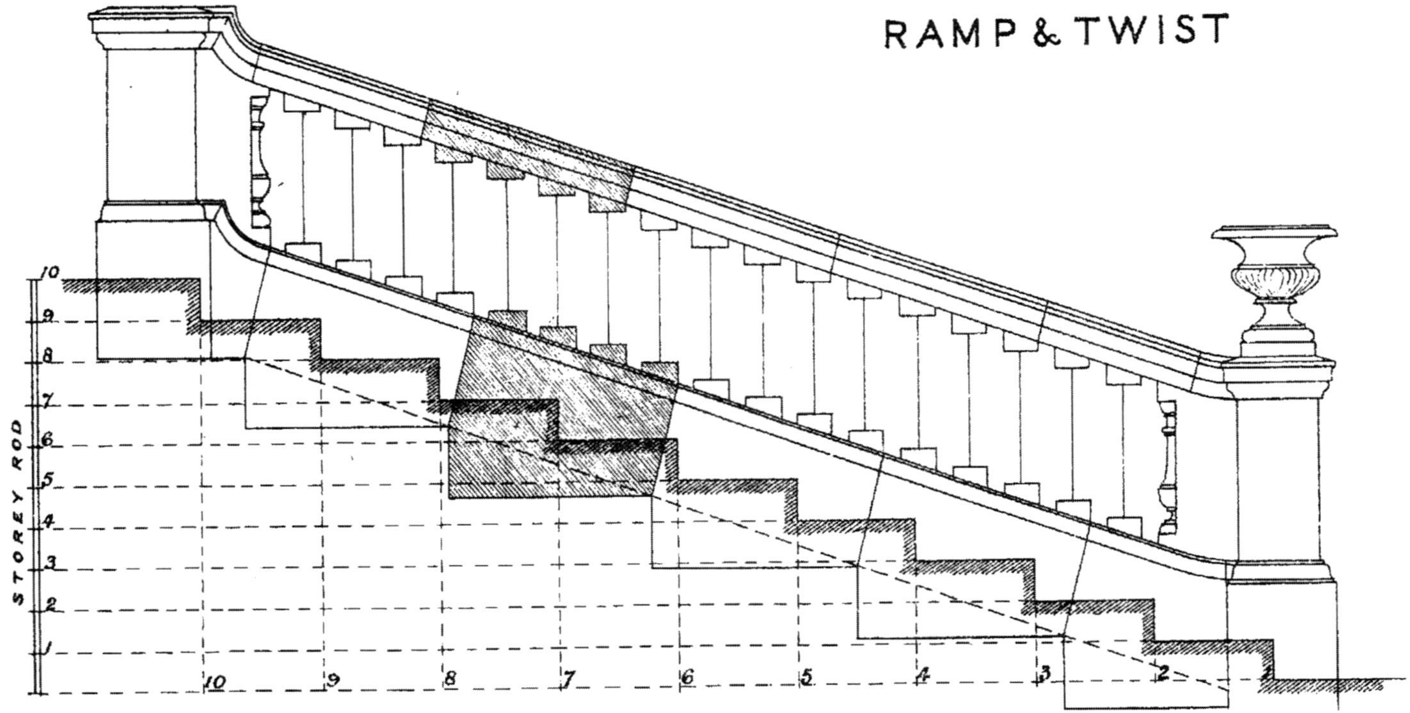

FIG. 3

DEVELOPMENT OF INSIDE ELEVATION

SCALE 0 1 2 3 4 5 6 FT

FIG. 4

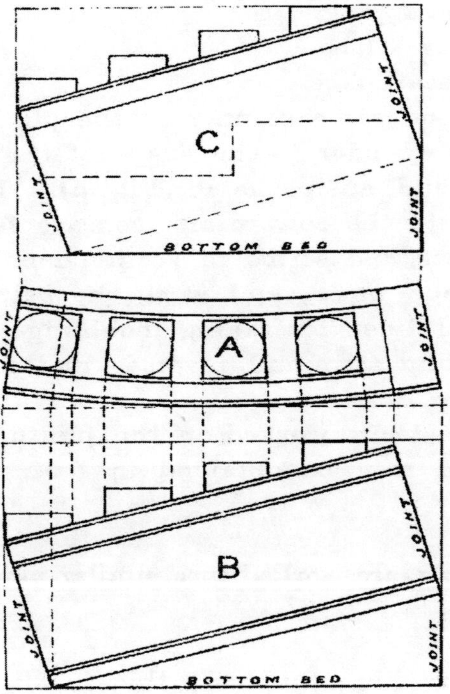

FIG. 8

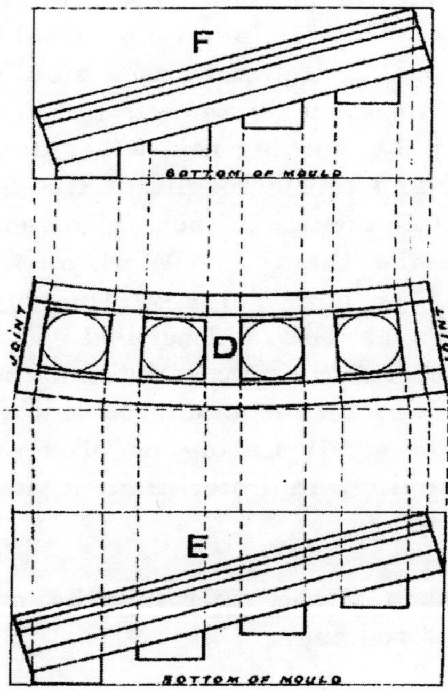

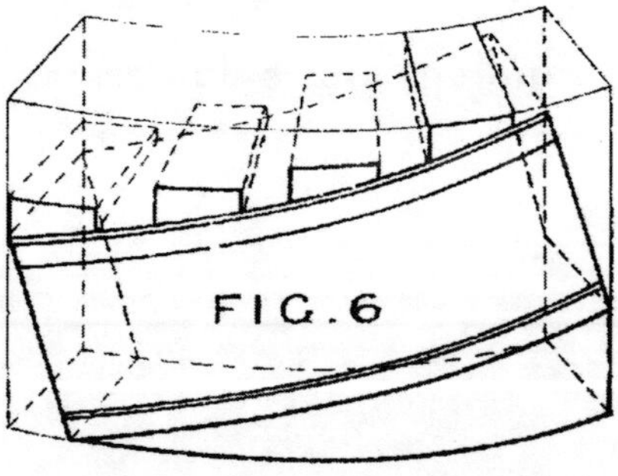

FIG. 6

FIG. 9

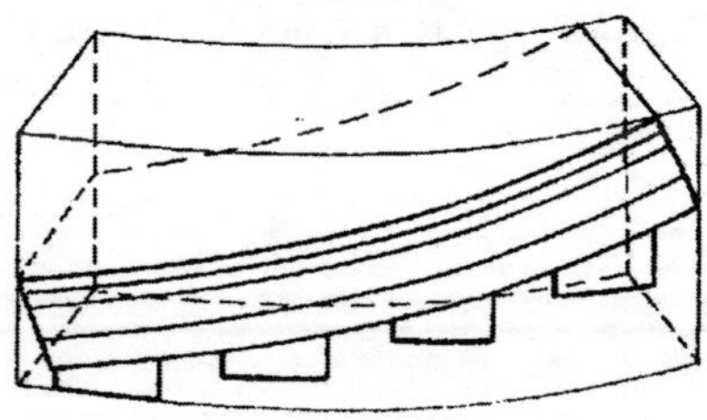

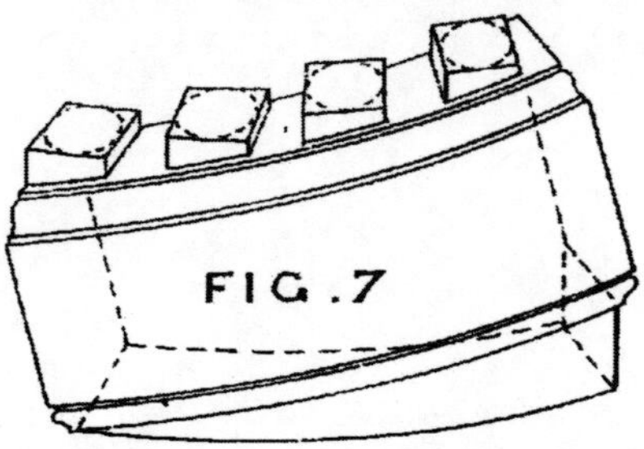

FIG. 7

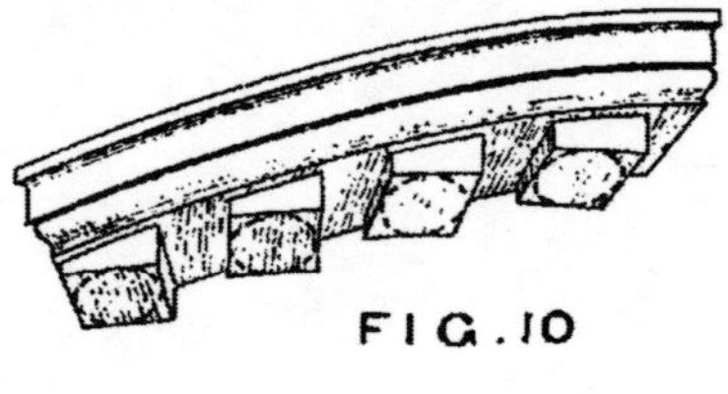

FIG. 10

SKETCH OF FINISHED PLINTH

SCALE FOR DETAILS

To work the Length of Capping.

Fig. 8.—*D* Shews bed mould of the capping.
E Shews face mould of convex face.
F Shews face mould of concave face.

This stone is worked in precisely the same manner as the plinth—namely, by working first a segment of a cylinder to the shape of the bed mould and to the height of the face mould, as in sketch (Fig. 5). Then apply face moulds *E* and *F* respectively to the convex and concave faces, and scribe them in. Work off the joints, and scribe in section mould *J* (Fig. 11); next point off the superfluous waste, and work the baluster seatings as before described. Trammel lines for raking mouldings and work them through, assisted by a bending strip and reverses, and finish by working off the saddle-back weathering.

The small seating or plinth of baluster is worked on the plinth and the capping, in order that a level bed may be obtained in fixing the baluster.

Each of the other lengths of capping are worked in a similar manner to the foregoing.

Fig. 10.—Is sketch of length of capping finished; this is slightly tilted up, so as to shew the baluster plinths.

Fig. 11.—Shews section of the plinth, capping, and baluster.

Plates XX., XXI., XXII., XXIII.—ARCHES.

CIRCULAR ON PLAN, OR ARCHES OF DOUBLE CURVATURE.

To describe the construction of a Semi-circular Arch in a Cylindrical Wall, the development of which on convex or outside face is a semi-circle, and on concave or inside face is a semi-ellipse, the soffit radiating to a centre at springing, and the crown of the arch level or at right angles to the vertical face of the wall.

Fig. 1.—Shews plan of the arch, *B C D* being the opening, the arch radiating to *O*, the centre of the cylinder.

To set up the Elevation on the Development for the Face Moulds.

Fig. 2.—Develop the segment *A B C* of convex face (Fig. 1), setting out the length on springing line as *A B C* from *C* as the centre ; erect a perpendicular as centre line, and describe with *C B* as radius half of the semicircle. Set off the joints radiating to the centre *C* corresponding to the number of arch joints required, which in this example is seven. The square bonding *d a, f b, g c* of vertical and horizontal joints may be of varied sizes. The radiating joints (here shewn) are made equal in length from the soffit, and for this purpose from the centre *C* describe a quadrant, cutting the joints at *a b c*.

To find the Development of Concave Face.

Fig. 3.—Divide the quadrant *B K* (Fig. 2), into any number of equal parts—in this example seven—and draw the ordinates 1, 2, 3, 4, 5, 6, projecting the same on to the springing line, and transfer these to the segment line *B C* on plan (Fig. 1) as 1, 2, 3, 4, 5, 6, and from these points draw radiating lines from the centre *O*, cutting the segment *B′ C′* at 1′, 2′, 3′, 4′, 5′, 6′ ; draw the developed length of *B′ C′* on springing line (which is also equal to *C′ D′* and is half of the inside face) from *C* to *D′* ; transfer 1′, 2′, 3′, 4′,

5′, 6′ from Fig. 1, and draw the ordinates of equal height to those of Fig. 2, cutting Fig. 3 at 1^a, 2^a, 3^a, 4^a, &c., through the points 1^a, 2^a, 3^a, 4^a, &c.; draw the half of semi-ellipse, which gives the curve of the arris to the soffit.

The length of the joints in Fig. 3 is determined in the same manner as in Fig. 2—namely, by means of ordinates. One joint is here given as an example:

From *A* No. 2 *A* (Fig. 2) drop a perpendicular cutting the springing line at 2 *C*; and from 2 *C* to 2 transfer to 2 *C* and 2 on the segment line of plan (Fig. 1), and draw radiating lines from 2 *C* to the centre *O*, cutting the segment *A′ C′* at 2 *d*; transfer the distance from 2 *d* to 2′ on to the springing line (Fig. 3). Set up ordinate and make equal in height to *a* on Fig. 2, and from 2 *A* to *A′* (Fig. 3) draw joint line, which also radiates from the centre *C*.

The moulds required for working each arch block are a bed mould and two face moulds (one to the convex and one to the concave face); these are already set out on plan and in developed elevations, but now require separating.

As an example, No. 1 *A* (Fig. 2) is the springer. For the bed mould take *A B* 2 and *A′ B′* 2′ from plan (Fig. 1), and transfer to 1 *C* (Fig. 4).

The dotted line *B B′* shews the line of the soffit on the bottom bed, the line *a a′* the line of the arch joint on the top bed, *A A′* the line of radiating vertical joint, and 2 2′ the line of arris of the arch joint. This gives the plan of a segment of a hollow cylinder to the extreme size of the stone.

No. 1 *A* (Fig. 4) is the face mould for convex face, No. 1 *B* (Fig. 4) is the face mould for concave face, and both of these are transferred from 1 *A* and 1 *B* (Figs. 2 and 3) with the addition of the square line 2 2 and 2′ 2′.

The stone for the arch block should be large enough to work the bed mould square through; if there is a "wanty" corner in the rough block, this may be arranged for in the corner where the stone has to be cut away for the soffit or the top joint.

Work the two beds bottom and top parallel to each other and of the height of the face mould, scribe in the bed mould No. 1 *C* on both beds (to be correct this should be boned in), the vertical joint *A d* being at right angles to the bed. Next work the convex and concave faces through, and also the radiating joint *A A′*, the block at this stage being a portion of a hollow cylinder similar to sketch (Fig. 7).

ARCHES *CIRCULAR ON PLAN*

DEVELOPMENTS

HALF CONVEX (OUTSIDE) — HALF CONCAVE (INSIDE)

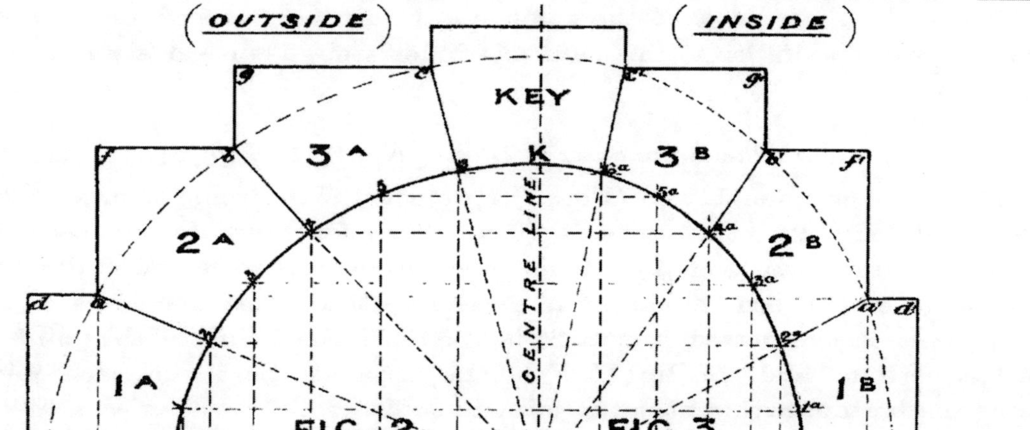

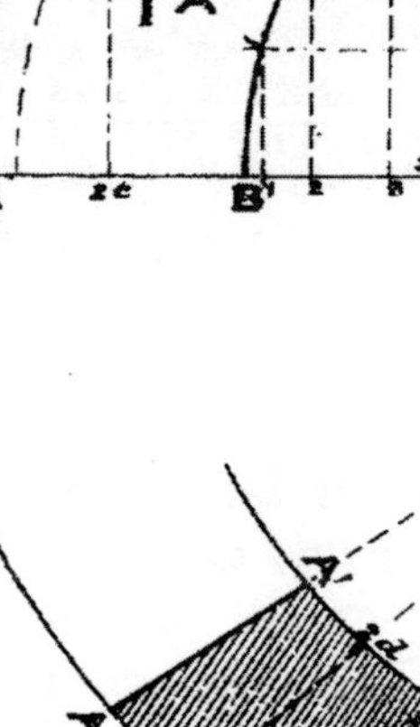

FIG. 8

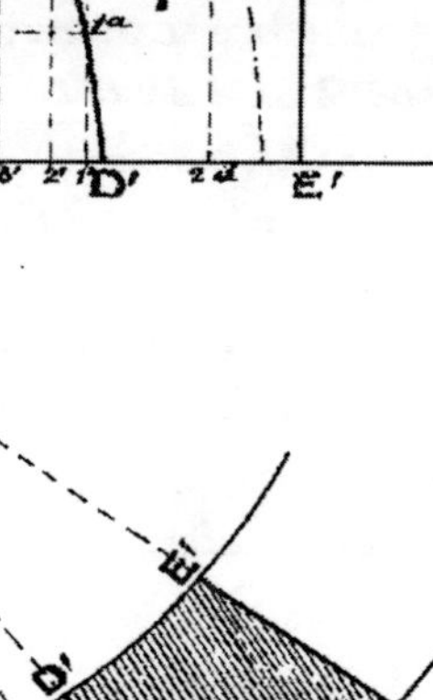

FIG. 7

Now scribe in the face moulds 1 *A* on the convex and 1 *B* on the concave faces (Fig. 4); next work the arch joint *a e* through (this will have a slight twist); and, lastly, for the soffit cut in a draft *B e* on convex and *B′ e′* on concave faces, and work the surface through, thus completing the springer.

It may be observed that the soffit is a winding or warped surface, and it will be worked similar to the soffit of winder step, as previously described on page 38.

To work the Second Arch Stone, No. 2 A (Fig. 2).

For the bed mould 2 *C* (Fig. 5), project the extreme points *a* and 4, No. 2 *A* (Fig. 2) on to springing line; transfer these to the segment line *A C* on the plan (Fig. 1). This gives from 2 *C* to 4 and 2 *d* to 4′, which encloses the bed mould; *a a′* is the vertical joint and arris of the arch joint *a* 2, the dotted line 2 2^a is the horizontal line of the joint on soffit at bottom, and the line *b b′* is the arris at the top of arch joint, 4 4*a* is the bottom arris of the top joint to soffit.

No. 2 *A* (Fig. 5), is the face mould for the convex face, and No. 2 *B* (Fig. 5) is the face mould for the concave face; both of these are transferred from 2 *A* and 2 *B* (Figs. 2 and 3), with the addition of the square line 4 *b*, 4 *C*, and 4 1, 4 2.

Work the top bed first *f b*, 4 *b*, and take the bottom bed *a* 2, 4 *C* parallel to the top and of the height of the face mould (this is a surface of operation, all being cut away except arris 2 2 *a*, which must be kept true across the bed). Scribe the bed mould No. 2 *C* (Fig. 5) on both beds. Now work the two faces convex and concave through, and the radiating joint *a a′* square with the top bed, bringing it again into the shape of a portion of hollow cylinder, as in sketch (Fig. 7).

Scribe the face mould 2 *A* on the convex and 2 *B* (Fig. 5) on concave faces. Work the arch joints *a* 2 and *b* 4, and for the soffit cut in the draft 2 4 on the convex and 2 *a*, 4 *a* on concave faces, and work through as previously described.

The other arch stone 3 *A* and keystone are worked in a similar manner, the general principles of working being the same.

Note.—The radiating joint lines on the developments (Figs. 2 and 3) to be geometrically correct should not be straight, being slightly curved. This is apparent on cutting a cylinder by a right line obliquely, the development of which is a compound curve; but in this case the curve is so

FIG. 4

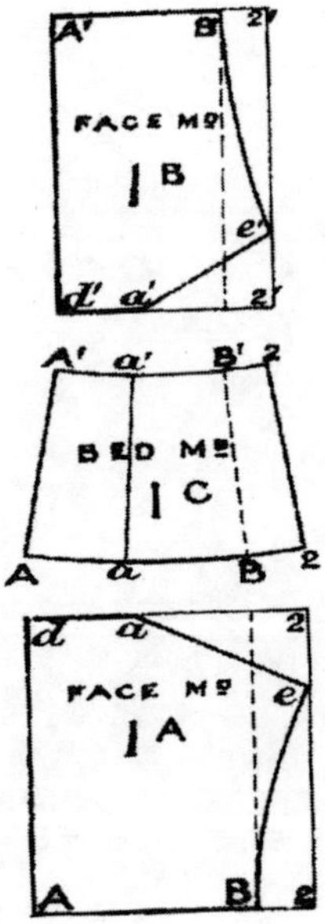

FIG. 5

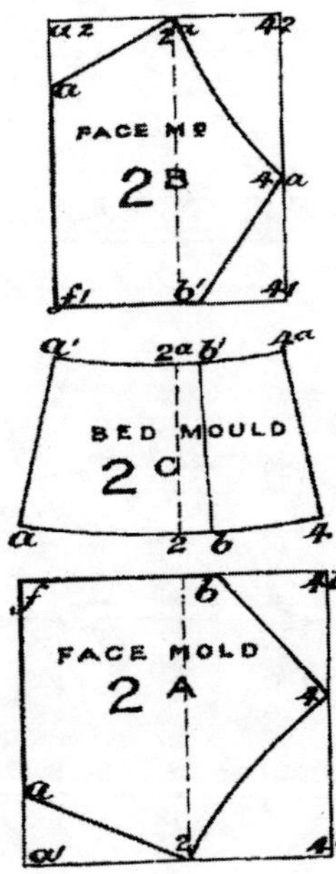

FIG. 6

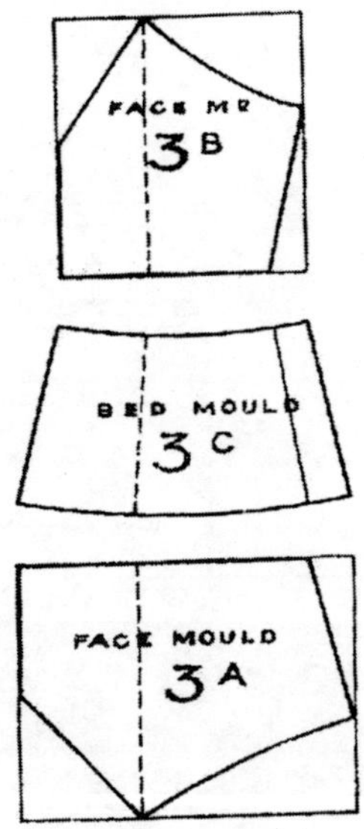

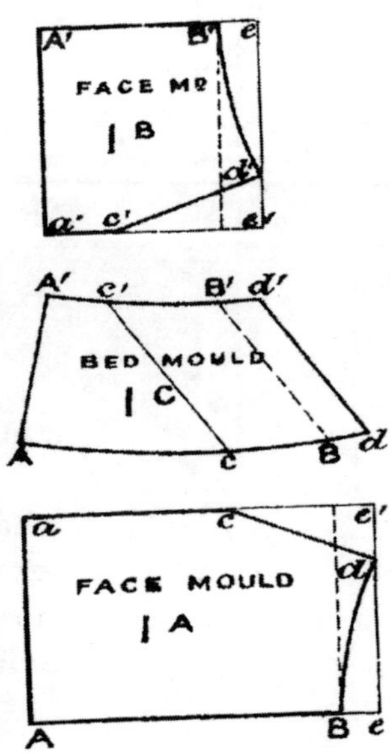

FIG. 12

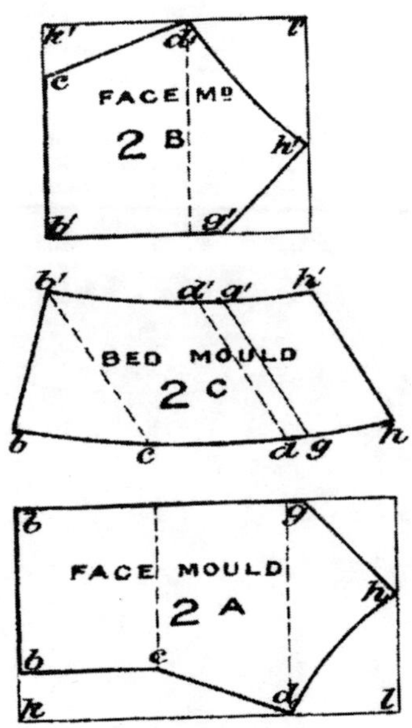

FIG. 13

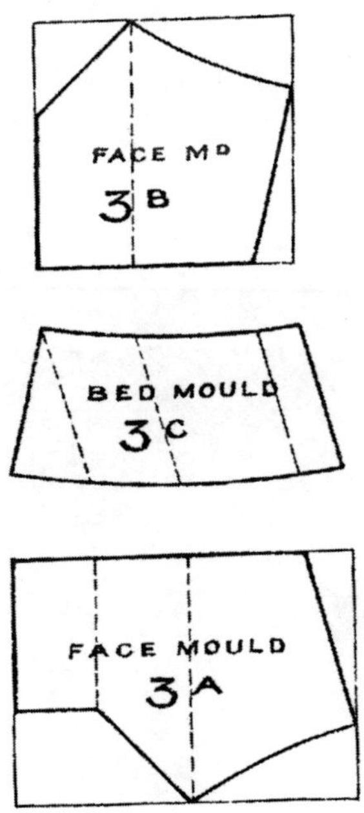

FIG. 14

ARCHES *CIRCULAR ON PLAN*

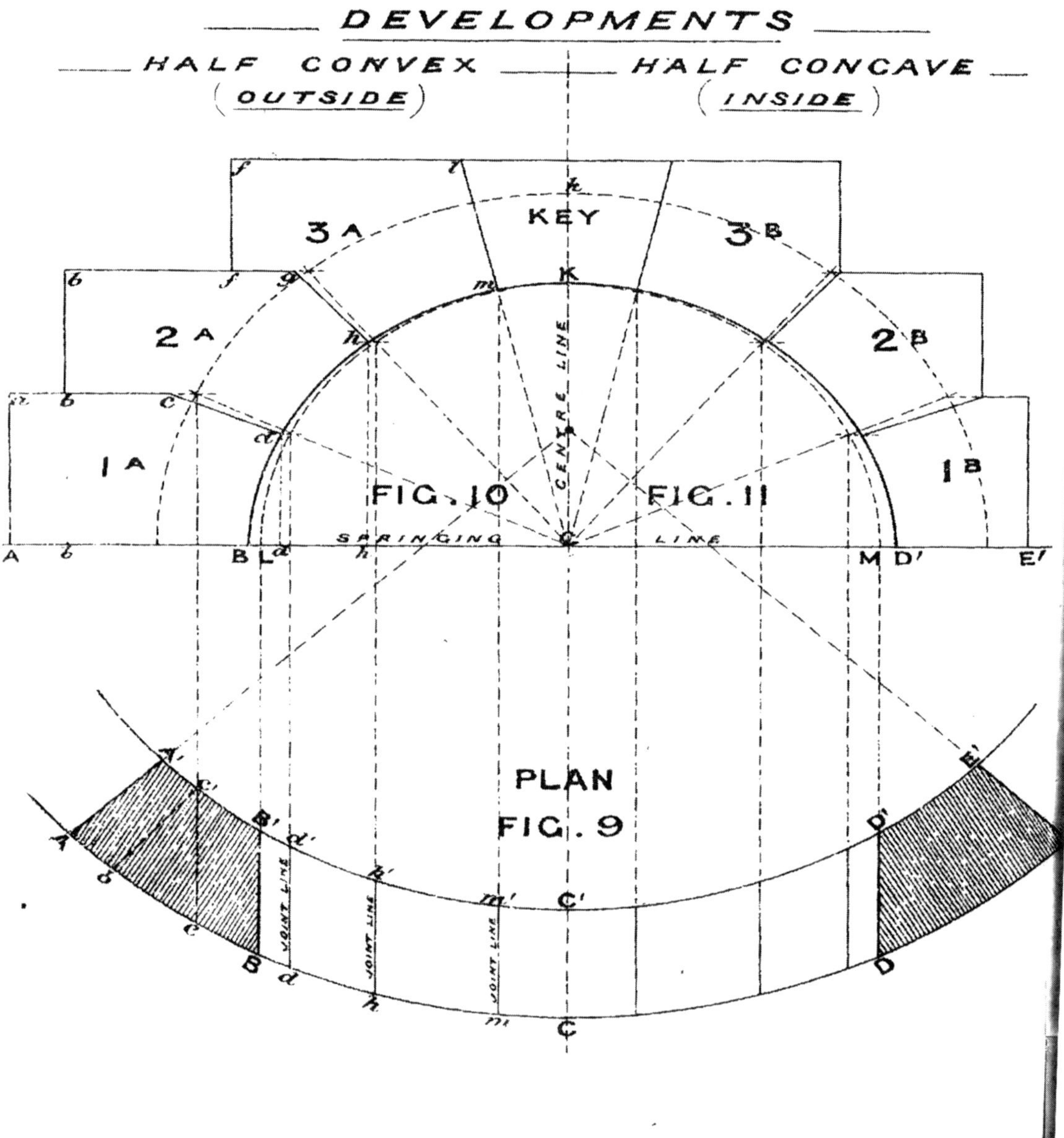

slight as to be scarcely perceptible, and need not in the present and the following example be taken notice of.

To construct a Semi-circular Arch in a Cylindrical Wall, whose line of soffit on the plan is parallel to the axis, the axes of the two cylinders intersecting each other at right angles.

Fig. 9.—Shews the plan of the arch, *B C D* being the opening.

Figs. 10 and 11 are the developed elevations.

In order to prevent confusion with Figs. 9, 10, and 11, and to make matters easier of explanation, three diagrams are here shewn containing Fig. 15, Figs. 16, 17, and Figs. 18, 19, these being slightly exaggerated to shew more clearly the working.

Let Fig. 15 be the plan of segment of cylinder, with the semi-cylinder penetrating the same at right angles to the axis at *a e*, *b d*.

Let Fig. 16 be the square section of the quadrant of cylinder, and divide this into any unequal number of equal parts corresponding to the number of arch stones required in Figs. 10 and 11, which in this example is seven, as 1, 2, 3, 4, 5, 6, 7, and project on to the segment line *a c b* on plan (Fig. 15), as *C* 6, 5, 4, 3, 2, 1; transfer this to the springing line *a b*, 1, 2, 3, 4, 5, 6, 7 (Fig. 17), which is now the developed line; erect ordinates, and make them equal in height to the ordinates of the square section, as 1′, 2′, 3′, 4′, &c.; draw line through the intersecting points 1′, 2′, 3′, 4′, &c., giving the curve required on the development at the point of penetration for the outside or convex face of cylinder.

For the development of the inside or concave face, let Fig: 18 be the square section, divided into seven equal parts, projecting the ordinates as before. Transfer from Fig. 15 1^a, 2^a, 3^a, 4^a, 5^a, 6^a, 7^a to the springing line (Fig. 19), erect ordinates and make them equal in height to those of square section at 1, 2, 3, 4, &c., and through the intersecting points 1^a, 2^a, 3^a, 4^a, &c., draw the line giving curve required at the point of penetration for the inside or concave face of cylinder.

For the joints, draw radiating lines at 2, 4, 6 (Figs. 16 and 18), and to make them of equal length draw a quadrant line with radius of the square section as *f g h*, project *f g h* on to plan (Fig. 15) as *f g h*, and transfer to the springing line (Figs. 17 and 19); erect ordinates at *f g h*, making equal in height to those of the square section. Next draw the joint lines *h* 2′,

ARCHES *CIRCULAR ON PLAN*

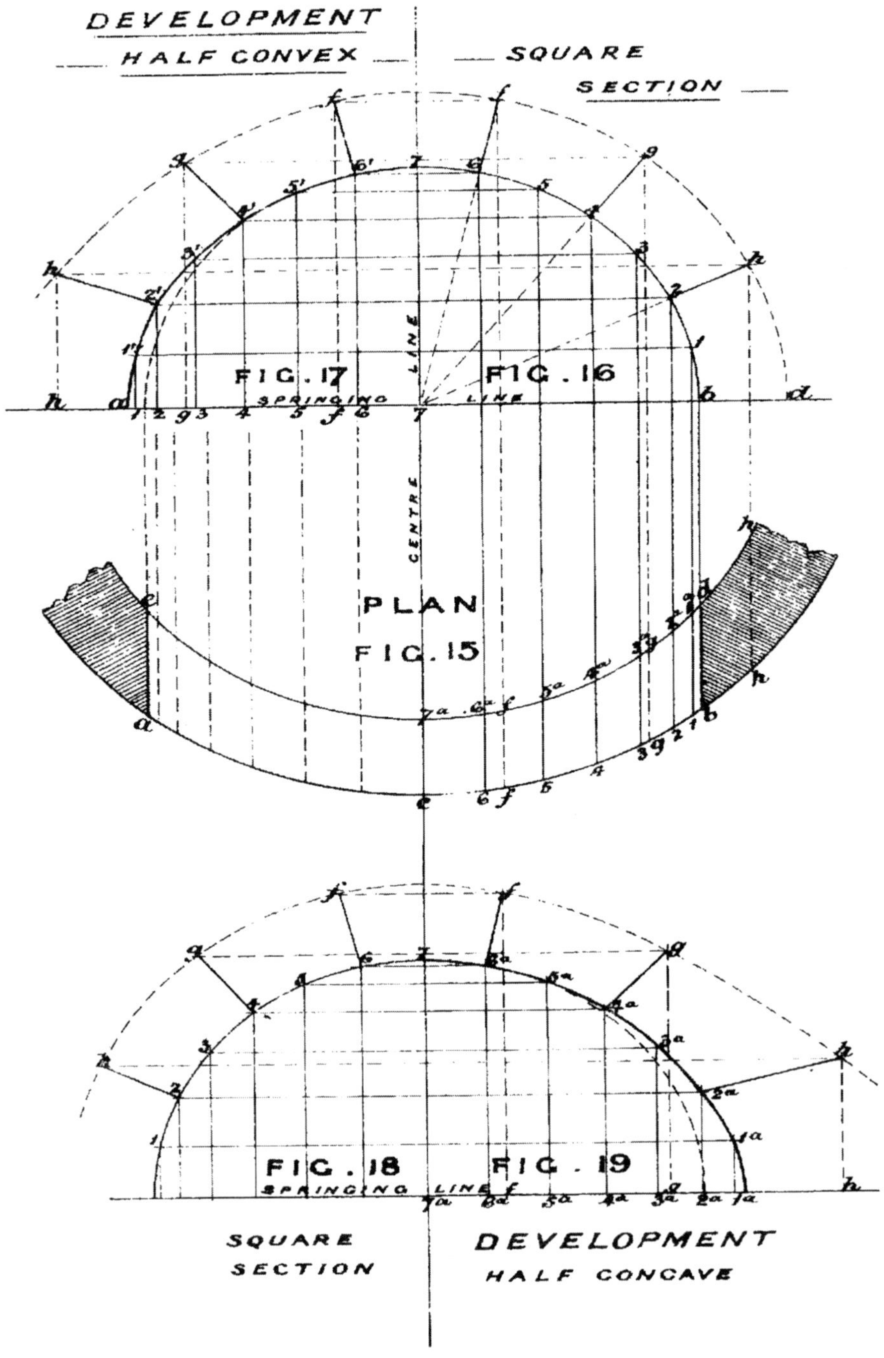

$g\ 4'$, $f\ c'$ on Fig. 17, and $h\ 2^a$, $g\ 4^a$, and $f\ c^a$ (Fig. 19); the developed length of joint is thus obtained.

To set up the Elevation on the Developments for the Face Moulds.

Figs. 10 and 11.—Let *A E′* be the springing line, *C K* the centre line, and *L K M* dotted line the square section of the cylinder whose centre is *C*. For the development *B K D* proceed as previously described, and divide into any number of equal parts for the arch stones required—which in this example is seven—and draw the joints; the square bonding *a b*, *b f*, *f l* may be set out at will, but should be set out from the inside or concave face, so as to obtain a parallel arch joint.

The joint *c b′*, No. 2 *C* (Fig. 13), which is the arch joint cutting out to the vertical joint *b′*, illustrates this.

The moulds for working each arch block are a bed mould and two face moulds. These are already set out on plan (Fig. 9) and elevations (Figs. 10 and 11), except the addition of a square line to the extreme size.

To work the springer:

For the bed mould take *A c*, *B d* from the plan (Fig. 9) and transfer to 1 *C* (Fig. 12); the dotted line *B B′* is line of the soffit on the bottom bed, the line *c c′* is the line of joint on top bed, the line *d d′* is the line of arris of the arch joint in soffit, and the line *A A′* is the radiating vertical joint. No. 1 *A* (Fig. 12) is the face mould for convex face, and No. 1 *B*, Fig. 12, is the face mould for concave face; both of these are transferred from 1 *A* and 1 *B* (Figs. 10 and 11), with the addition of the square line *e e′*.

Work the two beds (bottom and top) parallel to each other, and of the height of the face mould. Scribe the bed mould No. 1 *C* (Fig. 12), on both beds, and work the two faces convex and concave through, and also the vertical joint *A a*, which must be at right angles to beds; this will form a portion of a hollow cylinder similar to sketch Fig. 7. Now scribe in the face moulds 1 *A* and 1 *B* (Fig. 12), on the convex and concave faces respectively, and work the arch joint *c d* through and for the soffit, cut in arrises to the lines, and work drafts parallel to the bed *B B′* until the whole of the soffit is finished.

In this arch the soffit is not a winding surface.

To work the Second Arch Stone No. 2 A (Fig. 10).

Let No. 2 *C* (Fig. 13) be the bed mould, project the extreme points *b h*, No. 2 *A* (Fig. 10), on to springing line *A C*. This being a developed face it will require folding back on to the segment line *A C E* of plan (Fig. 9), as *b d h*, and transfer this to No. 2 *C*, which gives the bed mould.

No. 2 *A* (Fig. 13) is the face mould for convex face, and No. 2 *B* (Fig. 13) is the face mould for concave face, and both of these are transferred from 2 *A* and 2 *B* (Figs. 10 and 11), with the addition of the square line *l*.

Work the two beds (bottom and top) parallel to each other, and to the height of the face mould. The bottom bed is worked as a surface of operation for the application of the bed mould, and it is all cut away except the arris *d d′*. Scribe the bed mould 2 *C* (Fig. 13) in on each bed, and work the two faces convex and concave through, and scribe in the face moulds 2 *A* and 2 *B* (Fig. 13).

Work the vertical joint *b b* square with either the top or bottom beds, and work the bed *b c* and joint *c d*; then joint *g h*, and, lastly, soffit *d h*.

Fig. 14.—Nos. 3 *A*, 3 *B*, and 3 *C* are the face moulds and bed mould of the third arch stone, and together with the keystone are projected and worked in precisely the same manner as the foregoing Nos. 1 and 2 stones.

It will be advisable for the student to work small models, which should be constructed to scale in plaster, clay, or other soft material. The moulds for these models may be cut out of stout drawing paper, and in their application will be found the best method of obtaining knowledge of these subjects.

Plates XXIV., XXV., XXVI.—SKEW ARCH AND NICHES.

To construct a Semi-circular Arch Rib, the oblique angle of which does not extend more than ten or twelve degrees from a right angle, the joints being parallel to axis, and in the same planes.

This is not a difficult problem, as the arch within these limits may be set out and worked as a right arch; but beyond these a different principle of construction is necessary.

The archivolt and arch ribs to coffered vaulting at the entrance to Burlington House, Piccadilly (about 20 feet span), and the archivolt at entrance to the Criterion Restaurant, Piccadilly, which are similar to the above, were set out by the writer, and worked as herein described.

Fig. 1.—Shews the elevation of the arch, which is a semi-circle.

Fig. 2.—Shews the plan of the arch, *B G* and *D J* being the opening, *B D* and *G J* the inclination or angle of skew, *E* and *F* the centres, *A* and *H* the outer face line of the arch, and *C K* the inner face line of the arch.

There is no difference in the outer and inner faces of the arch, both being alike, but the terms are here used for purpose of explanation.

Project *A C*, *B D* and *G J*, *H K* from the plan to the springing line (Fig. 1), as *a c*, *b d* and *g j*, *h k*, with *e* as centre, and *e a* and *e b* as radius, describe the semi-circles *a o h* and *b m g*, for the outside face, and with *f* as centre, and the same radius, describe the semi-circles *c p k* and *d n j*, for the inside face. For the joints, divide the arch into any convenient number of equal parts—in this example seven—as *q r s t u v* on line *b m g* of intrados, and with the same divisions repeat on the line *d n j* as *q′ r′ s′ t′ u′ v′*; from the centre *e* draw radiating lines through these points, and produce to the outside curve or extrados for the outside, and for the inside of the arch; repeat the same from the centre *f*. It will be observed that the direction of joints is perfectly horizontal, the

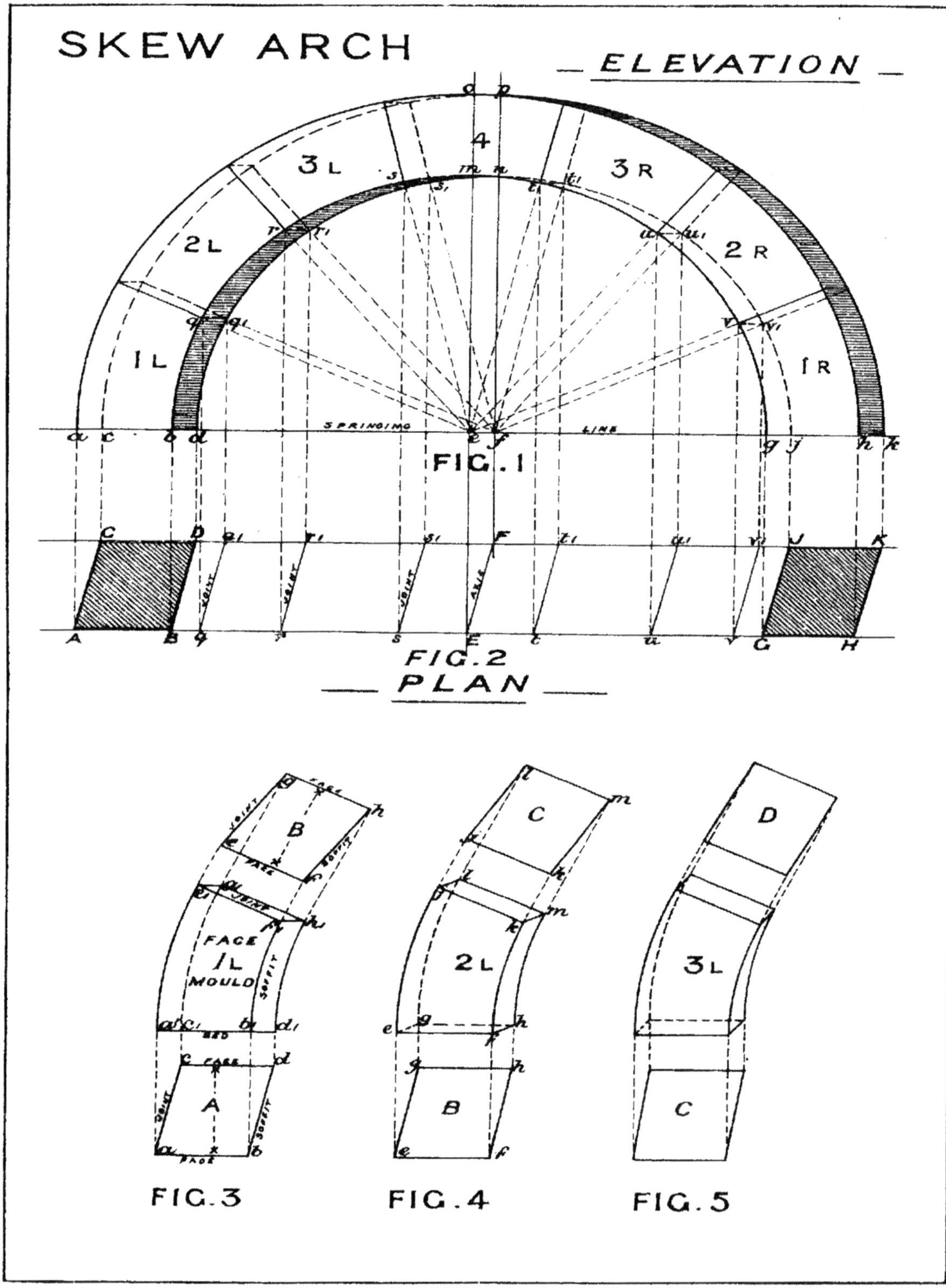
SKEW ARCH
ELEVATION
4
3L
3R
2L
2R
1L
1R
SPRINGING LINE
FIG. 1
JOINT
AXIS
FIG. 2
PLAN
B
FACE
JOINT
SOFFIT
FACE /L MOULD
BED
A
C
2L
D
3L
FIG. 3
FIG. 4
FIG. 5

lines *q q′*, *r r′*, *s s′*, &c., being level; the radiating lines and joints are also parallel to each other, and are therefore in the same plane.

This is all the setting out required, with the exception of the joint moulds.

To work the Arch Stones.

Fig. 3.—Let No. 1 *L* be the face mould of the springer and *A* and *B* the joint moulds.

The face mould 1 *L*, is transferred from the elevation Fig. 1, and the bottom bed or joint mould *A*, from plan (Fig. 2); for the joint mould *B*, draw a line parallel to joint *e′ f′*, and project *e′ f′* and *g′ h′* as *e f* and *g h*, of an equal and parallel thickness, as *X X* at *A* and *B*.

Work *a′ b′ e′ f′* outside face of springer No. 1 *L*, to a plane surface, and *c d g h* inside, face parallel to it; scribe the face mould in to extreme size on each face as *a′ d′ e′ g′ h′*; scribe in the segment line *f′ b′* giving arris of soffit on outside face (this may be done by drawing the mould back, as *h′ d′* is the same segment and also the same length as *f′ b′*).

Work the bottom bed *A* which is horizontal, and square with the vertical face, and scribe in the bed mould as *a b c d*, which will coincide with the lines on the face mould: now work the top joint *B*, this from the outside face will be full of the square, or, in other words, it makes an obtuse angle with the vertical face. This, however, is given by the face mould, as *e′ f′* is line of joint on the outside, and *g′ h′* on the inside.

Scribe in the joint mould *B* as *e f g h*, and work the soffit *b′ d′ f′ h′* through, as in a right arch, and finish with the back joint *a′ c′ e′ g′*.

Fig. 4.—No. 2 *L* is worked similar to No. 1 *L*; the top joint mould *B* of No. 1 is the bottom joint mould of No. 2, and the top joint mould *C* of No. 2 is the bottom joint mould of No. 3, and so on,—this is self evident. The bevels of these joints are found by projecting the points of the face mould, as *j k l m*, &c., as before described.

Begin by working the two vertical faces *e f j k* and *g h l m* parallel to each other, scribe in the face mould No. 2 to the extreme size as *e f h j l m*, and work both joints *B* and *C*; the top joint *C* is full of the square, whilst the bottom joint *B* is slack of the square from the outside face, the amount of the obtuse and acute angle being given on the face mould.

Fig. 5.—No. 3 *L* and the key-stone are worked precisely similar to the foregoing.

One set of moulds for one half of the arch only is required, as the four face moulds and the four joint moulds will work the complete arch:

being a plain arch without mouldings, the stones are reversible; this is apparent on looking at the elevation, but should there be an architrave moulding on one face, a mould to each stone is then required.

To construct a SPHERICAL NICHE in a straight wall with horizontal splay beds, and with vertical joints.

Figs. 6 and 7.—Shew the elevation and plan of the niche.

Let *A E* be the face line of the niche on plan (Fig. 7), *B D* the opening and *C* the centre; with *C B* or *C D* as radius, and *C* as centre, describe a semi-circle *B K D*, which is plan of extreme size of inside of niche; project *A B C D E* to the springing line on elevation (Fig. 6), as *a b c d e*, and at *c* erect perpendicular for the centre line. With *c* as centre and *c b* or *c d* as radius, describe the semi-circle *b k d* for the outer curve, and divide this into five equal parts as at *f g h i*; from *c* draw radiating lines through these points of division, cutting the horizontal bed at *l m n o*, giving the joints, the bevel of which will be continued horizontally round the niche as at *f i* and *g h*. For joints to the plan draw ordinates at *f g h i* and *l m*, &c., and project them on to line *A E* on plan (Fig. 7), as *F G H I* and *L M*, &c.; at *L F M G* describe the semi-circles, giving the horizontal line of splay joints. For dividing joints on the plan, take the second course first and divide the line of semi-circle *F Q I* into four equal parts as *P Q R*, and from *C* draw radiating lines through these divisions, producing them on to the line *L N O*, which gives the joints. The springers 1 *L* and 1 *R* in the first course will require to be about half the depth of others in the same course, in order to break the bond (as will be seen by reference to the plan); therefore, on the line *B K D*, set off say little more than half for the two springers as *B S* and *D V*, dividing the remainder into three equal parts as at *S T U V*, and draw the lines through, radiating from the centre to the back, giving the joints in the bottom course.

The top course No. 3 is in one stone, and to prevent any tendency to slip out of its place forward, the upper part of bed may be kept square; this would require notching on the inside, as *M M* 2 and *N M* 2 on the plan, and *m* 4 4 and *n* 5 5 on the elevation.

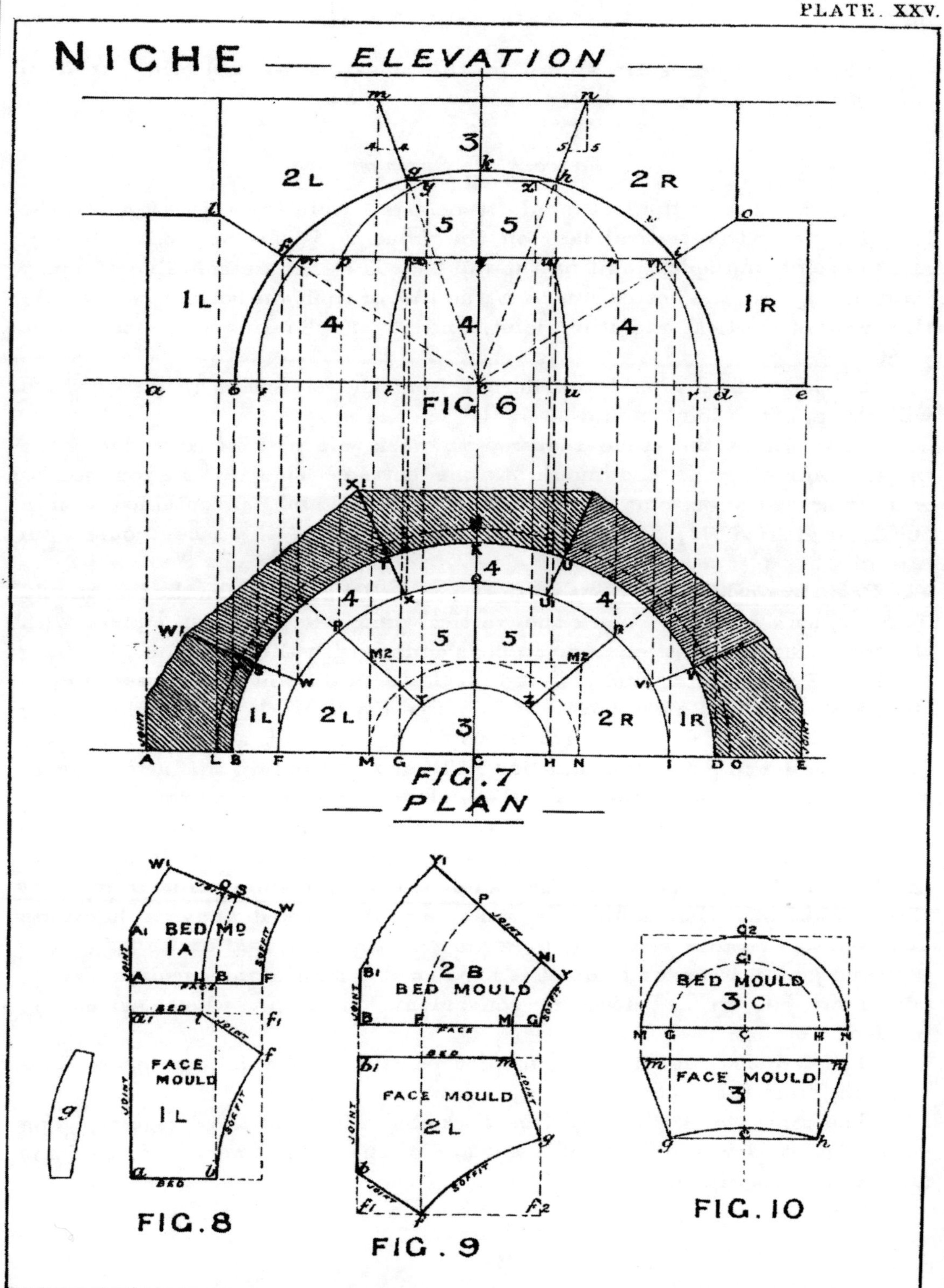

FIG 6

FIG. 7
PLAN

FIG. 8

FIG. 9

FIG. 10

The vertical joints are shewn on the elevation by projecting up from the plan, as shewn by the dotted lines *w p x q*, &c.

To work the Springer.

Fig. 8.—1 *A* is the bed mould transferred from the plan (Fig. 7), the line *A F* being the vertical face on the front, *F W* the horizontal line of arris of soffit and splay joint on the top bed, *L O* the outside line of splay joint on top bed, the dotted line *B S* the line of soffit on bottom bed, *W W′* the line of vertical radiating joint, and *A A′* the line of vertical face joint.

1 *L* is the face mould transferred from the elevation (Fig. 6), which will also apply as joint mould at *W W′*

The form of the stone required to work this will be a wedge-shape prism, containing the bed mould to the extreme size on the top bed as *A F W W′* ; the bottom bed is a little smaller, and is contained within the lines *A B S W′*, and of the extreme height of the face mould from *a* to *a′*.

Begin by working the front vertical face *A B F*, and scribe the face mould 1 *L* on, as *a b f l a′*. Work the vertical joint *A A′* as *a a′* square with the front face, and bottom and top beds square with the front face, scribing on the bed mould 1 *A*, and also the inside vertical joint *W W′*, scribing in the face mould as *a b f l a′*. It is necessary to work the whole of the top bed, although a portion from *l* to *f* 1 will be cut away for the splay joint, in order to get horizontal line *F W* at *f*; to obtain this arris, square down the concave line from *F* to *W* to the depth at *f*, or a draft from *F* to *W*, may be worked by the aid of a templet. This being done, trammel the line *f* parallel to *f* 1, giving the arris line required; the line *L O* is marked on the top bed with the templet, and the splay joint from *f* to *l* then worked off. The soffit now remains to be worked : cut in the drafts *B S* on the bottom bed and *F W* on the top bed, and drafts *b f* on the face and joint; a convex templet is used as at *g* for the intermediate drafts, which are cut in as close as convenient, until the whole surface is worked.

The templet *g* must not be applied parallel to the joints, but to lines radiating from the centre.

The three No. 4 stones will be worked similarly to the foregoing; one vertical joint is worked first as a surface of operation, instead of the front face as in the springer.

NICHE — ELEVATION —

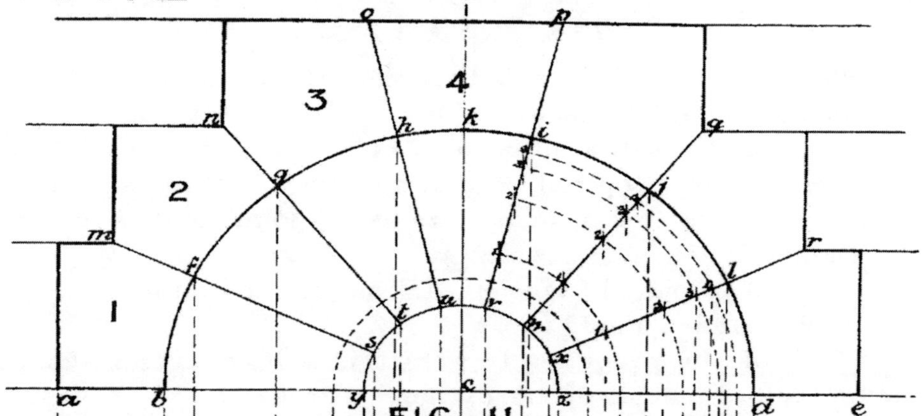

FIG. 11

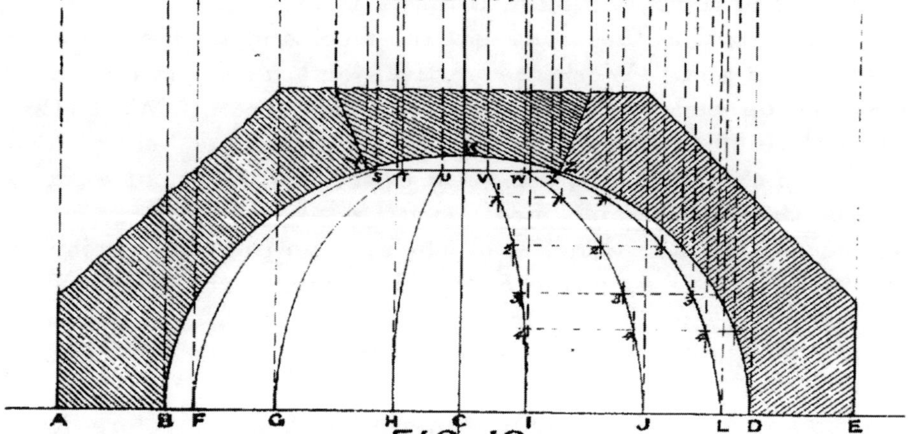

FIG. 12

— PLAN —

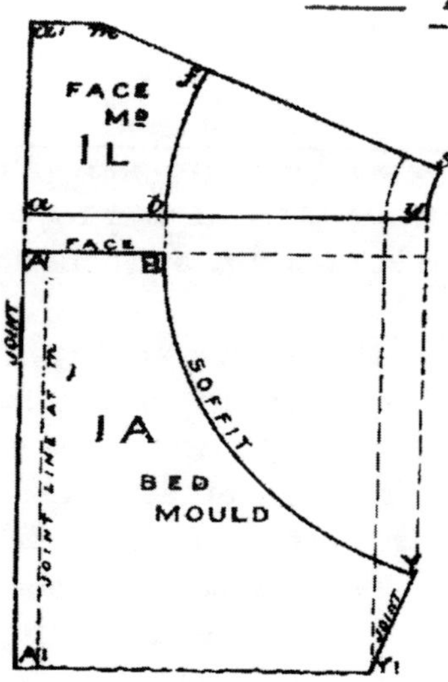

FIG. 13

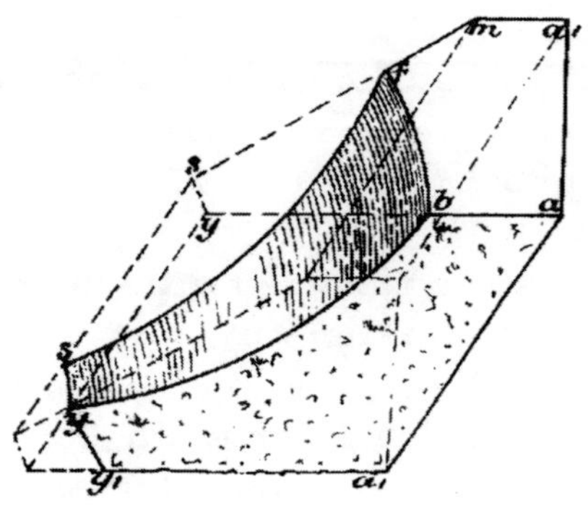

FIG. 14

To work No. 2 L Stone.

Fig. 9.—2 *B* is the bed mould transferred from the plan (Fig. 7), the line *B G* being the vertical face on the front, and *G Y* the horizontal line of the arris of soffit and the splay joint on the top bed, *M M′* the outside line of the splay joint top bed, the dotted line *F P* the line of soffit on bottom bed, *Y Y′* the line of vertical radiating joint, and *B B′* the line of vertical face joint.

2 *L* is the face mould, transferred from the elevation (Fig. 6), which will also apply as joint mould at *Y Y′*.

The form of stone required to work this will be a wedge-shape prism, containing the bed mould, to the extreme size as *B G Y Y* 1, and of the extreme height of the face mould, from *f* 1 to *b* 1.

Begin by working the front vertical face, and scribe the face mould 2 *L* on as *b* 1 *b f g m*. Work the vertical joint *b b′* square with the front face, also the top bed, and scribe the bed mould on. Work the bottom bed as a surface of operation; the only part required being the arris of the splay joint, and soffit *F P*, the rest of the bed being cut away.

This is the easiest and most accurate way of working, but the bed need not necessarily be worked as a whole, a portion only being required, sufficient to obtain the arris line *F P*; in this case the soffit *F G* should be worked after the arris line is drawn on the bed, by a convex templet made from *f* to *g*, and the splay joint is worked from a bevelled templet made from *g f b*.

The remaining portion of the stone is worked as before described to springer.

The two No. 5 stones are worked similarly.

To work the Key-stone No. 3.

Fig. 10.—3 *C* is the bed mould transferred from the plan (Fig. 7), the line *M N* being the vertical face on the front, *M C* 2 *N* the top line of the splay joint, and *G C* 1 *H* the line of arris of soffit, and the splay joint on bottom.

No. 3 is the face mould transferred from the elevation (Fig. 6).

Begin by working the vertical face *M N*, scribing in the face mould as *g h m n*. Work the top bed through square with the face, scribing in the bed mould, also the bottom bed parallel to the top at extreme points *g* and *h*, and with a templet scribe *G C H* the arris of the soffit and the splay joint. Work the joint round to the splay lines, then the soffit by cutting in the draft *g c h* on the front, and with a convex templet made from *C* to *C* 1, complete the surface.

The niche need not be jointed as here shewn, for much depends on its size, and the size of the stone convenient to use, but the general principle of working will be the same.

To construct a SPHERICAL NICHE in a straight wall, with joints radiating from the centre.

Figs. 11 and 12.—Shew elevation and plan of the niche.

Let *A E* be the vertical face line of the niche on the plan (Fig. 12), *B D* the opening, and *C* the centre. With *C B* or *C D* as a radius, and *C* as a centre, describe the semi-circle *B K D*, which is the plan of extreme size of the inside of niche, and project *A B C D E* to the springing line *a e* on the elevation (Fig. 11), as *a b c d e*. At *c* erect a perpendicular for the centre line, and, with *c* as centre and *c b* or *c d* as radius, describe the semi-circle *b k d* for the outer curve. With *c y* as a radius and *c* as the centre, describe a semi-circle for the centre stone, which may be of any convenient size. Divide the semi-circle *b k d* into seven equal parts as *f g h i j l*, and through these points of division from *c* draw radiating lines cutting horizontal beds at *m n o p*, &c., and the centre stone at *s t u v*, &c., which gives the joints. Draw ordinates from *f g h i*, &c., and project on to the line *A B* as *F G H I*, &c., and repeat the same at *s t u v*, &c., on the line *Y Z*, giving joint lines on the plan: to determine points in the curve of the soffit for templets, the dotted lines at the right hand of the niche shews how they are obtained. The dotted segment line from 1 to 1, 2 to 2, 3 to 3, &c., on elevation will be the section of curve at corresponding points on the plan at 1 1, 2 2, 3 3, &c., and also gives the points in the line of curve for the joints on plan, although the last named is not necessary for the setting out or the working.

To work the Springer 1 *L.*

Fig. 13.—1 *A* is the bed or joint mould transferred from the plan (Fig. 12), the line *A B* being the front vertical face, *B Y* the line of soffit, *Y Y* 1 the splay joint, and *A A* 1 the vertical face joint.

No. 1 *L* is the face mould transferred from the elevation (Fig. 11).

The form of stone required will be that of a wedge-shape prism (as in sketch, Fig. 14), containing the face mould to the extreme size as *a′ a y s m.*

Begin by working the bed or joint *a b y*, keeping the segmental line

B Y fair for arris, and scribe the bed mould 1 *A* on. Work the vertical face and scribe in the face mould 1 *L*, and the other bed *m f s*, scribing in the bed mould 1 *A*. Work the vertical joint *a a′*, and top bed *a′ m*, and lastly, the soffit, the working of this being guided by one or two templets made from 1 1, 2 2, &c.

The remaining stones are worked similar to the foregoing, keeping in mind the principle that the stone is contained within the wedge-shape prism, thus making it easy of comprehension.

PLATES XXVII., XXVIII., XXIX.—CYLINDRICAL VAULTING.

To obtain the PROFILES or CURVATURE of a GROIN.

Fig. 1.—Let *A B C D* be a rectangular plan, its vault to be intersected by two semi-cylinders.

Bisect the line *H J*, and with *F* as a centre, describe the semi-circle *G H J* (the given section), which divide into any number of equal parts in this example 12, and project ordinates **1 2 3 4 5**, &c., through the springing line *H F J* on to the diagonal line *A E D* as 1′ 2′ 3′ 4′ 5′, &c. Erect ordinates perpendicular to the diagonal, and make them equal in height to those of semi-circle *G H J*, and through the points of intersection draw the semi-ellipse, which is the curve of the groin.

The outer profile *K L M* is obtained in the same manner, namely, by projecting ordinates from the diagonal, and making them of equal height to those of semi-circle, and tracing semi-elliptic curve through the points of intersection.

These profiles may also be obtained by means of an elliptic trammel, taking *A D* and *K L* respectively as the major axes, and *E N* and *M O* as the minor axes, and drawing semi-ellipses by a continuous curve.

To obtain the PROFILES for the ANNULAR GROIN.

Fig. 2.—Let *A B C D* be the given plan.

Produce *A C* and *B D* until they meet in the point *X*, which is the centre of the radiating vault; bisect the line *A C* and *B D* at *E* and *G*, and describe the two semi-circles *A J C* and *B D H* the given section; divide the diameter of either semi-circle as *A C* into any number of equal parts—in this example 10—the last division from 1 to *A* and 9 to *C* may be

FIG. 1

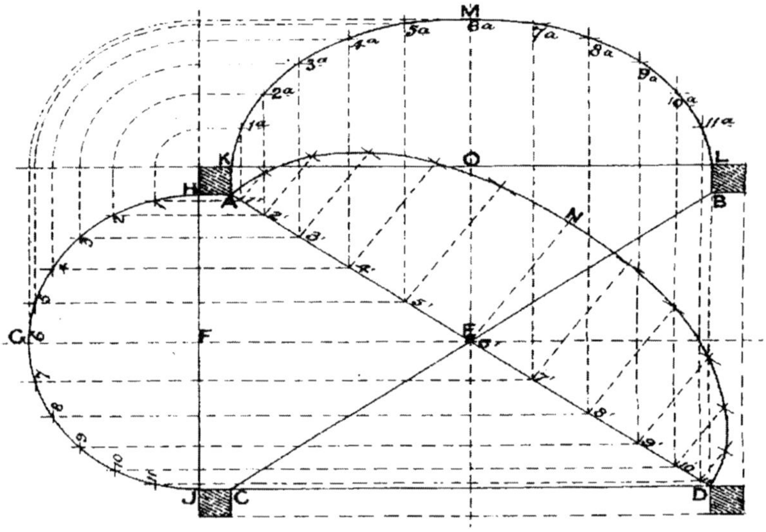

FIG. 2

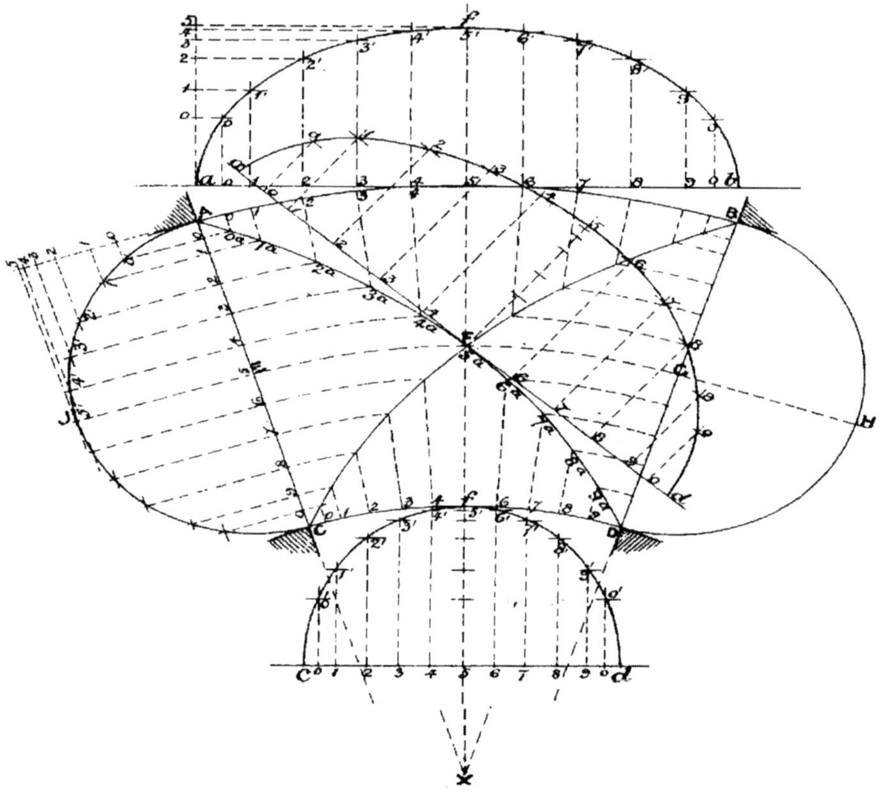

again divided as at *O*, and erect ordinates as *O* 1 2 3 4 5, &c., cutting the semi-circle at *O′* 1′ 2′ 3′ 4′ 5′, &c.; at the centre *X*, with radius *O* 1 2 3 4 5, &c. on the diameter *A C*, describe concentric arcs to the diameter *B D*. Divide the segmental line *A* 5 *B* into the same number of equal parts as the diameter *A C*, as *O* 1 2 3 4 5, &c., and from these points draw radiating lines from centre *X*, intersecting the above arcs at O^a 1^a 2^a 3^a 4^a 5^a, &c., and through the points of intersection draw the curve, giving the plan of groins *A F D* and *C F B*.

To describe the outer and inner profiles, develop segmental line *A* 5 *B* as right line *a b*, and *C f D* as right line *c d*, and transfer the divisions *O* 1 2 3 4 5, &c.; erect ordinates as *O′* 1′ 2′ 3′ 4′ 5′, &c., equal in height to those of the semi-circle *A J C*, and through the points *O′* 1′ 2′ 3′ 4′ 5′, &c., draw the curve which gives the true sections.

To find the profile on the diagonals *A F′ D* and *C F B*, develop line *A F′ D* as right line *a F′ d*, and transfer divisions O^a 1^a 2^a 3^a 4^a 5^a, &c. on the same, erect ordinates, and make them equal in height to those of the semi-circle *A J C*; through the points of intersection draw the curve, giving the true section at the mitre of groins, when bent or worked, so as to stand on the curve *A F D* on the plan.

To construct a RECTANGULAR VAULT, intersected by two semi-cylinders, crossing each other at right angles, and of equal height, each course of Stone being level and parallel to the axes of the Cylinders.

Fig. 3.—Let *A B C D* be the springing of the groins, *A E D* and *C E B* plan of the groins or intersection of cylindric surfaces, *F H G* is a section of the soffit or intrados whose profile is a semi-circle, and *I K J* a section of the outside or extrados, both of which are concentric semi-circles. The form of this section determines the shape of the groin and outer profile. *L M N* and *O P Q* are sections respectively of the intrados and extrados of the semi-elliptic profile, the curves of which are found by the method described in Fig. 1.

To obtain the joints, divide the semi-circle *I J K* into any unequal number of equal parts (convenient to the size of the stones), in this example 13, and draw the arch joints radiating from the centre *R* as *a′ b′ c′ d′ e′ f′*, &c. From the joints on the soffit, as *a b c d e f*, &c., project lines on to the plan, cutting the diagonal line *A E*—*C E* at *a b c d e f*, &c.; and, from these points of intersection, project lines on to the semi-ellipse *L M N* for intrados, and project points from the extrados *I J*, to the

VAULTING — CYLINDRICAL

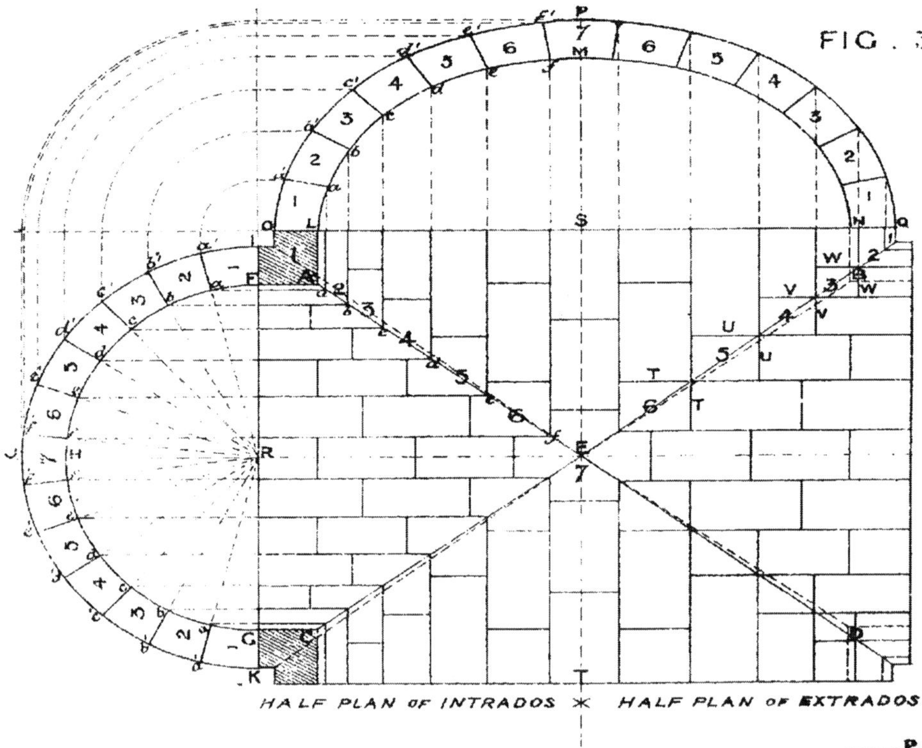

FIG. 3

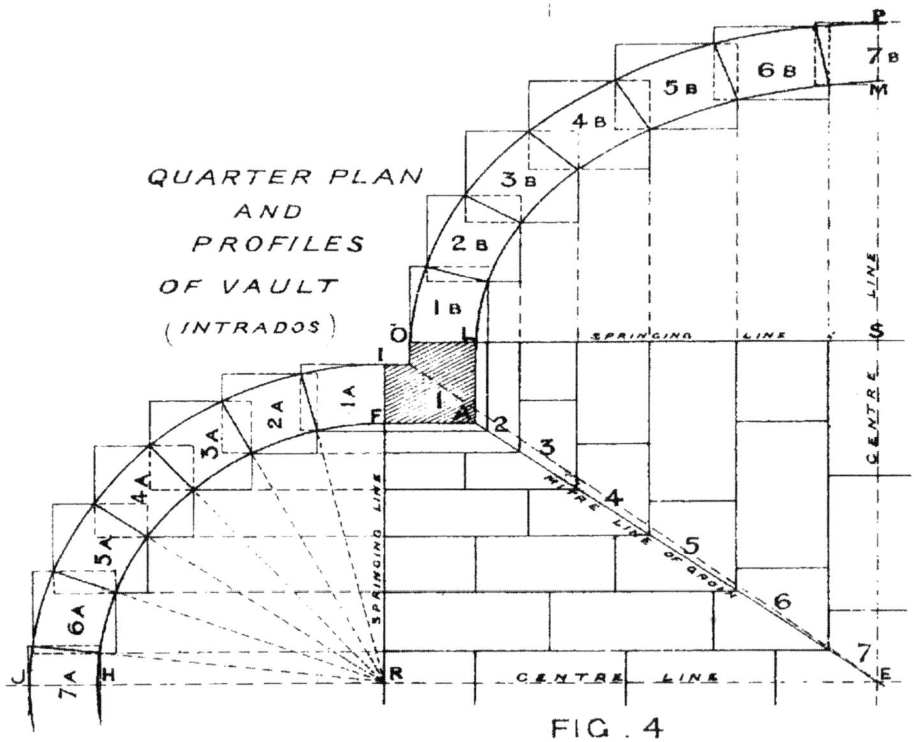

FIG. 4

VAULTING — *CYLINDRICAL*

FIG. 10

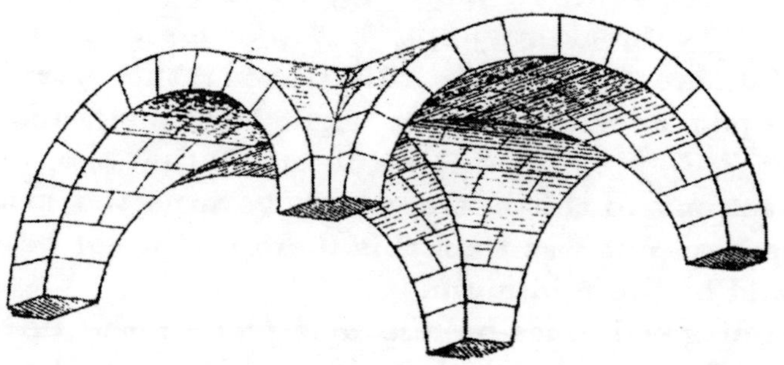

— *SKETCH OF VAULT* —

FIG. 5.

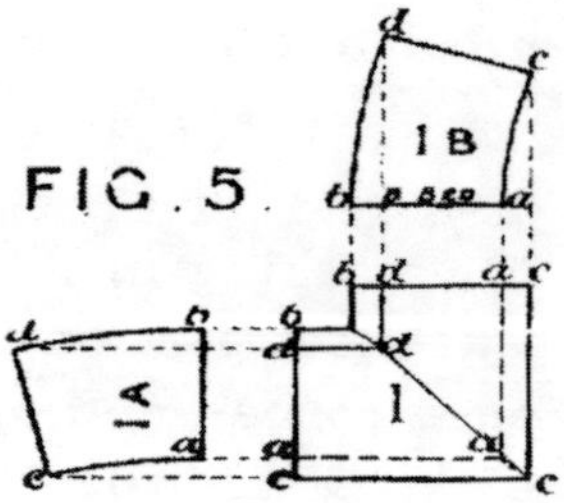

FIG. 6.

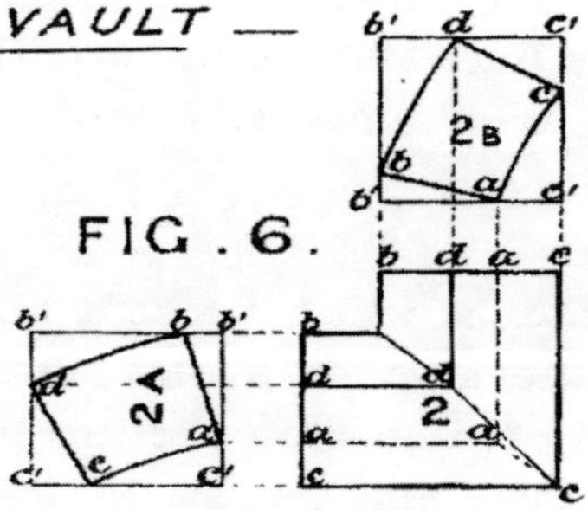

FIG. 5A

FIG. 6A

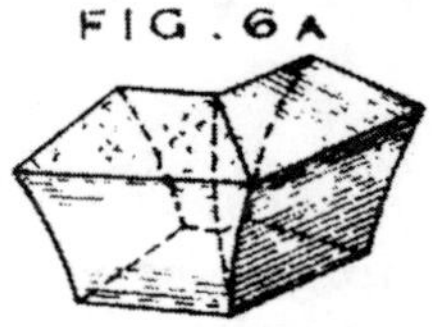

FIG. 6B

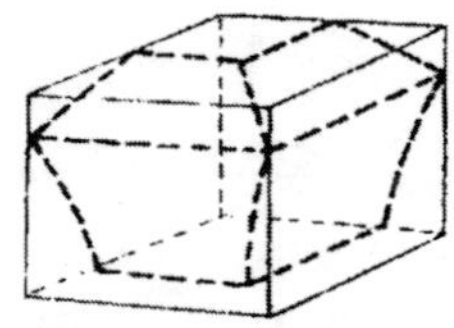

FIG. 9

FIG. 7A

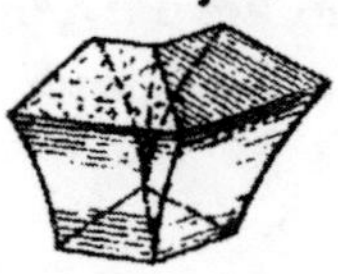

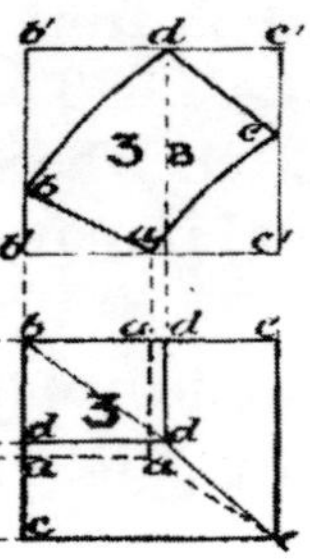

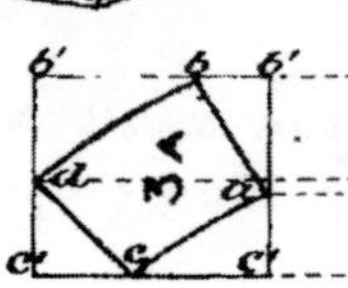

FIG. 7

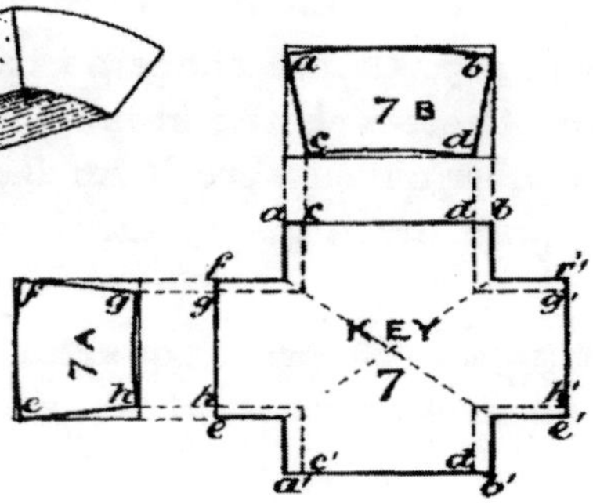

FIG. 8

extrados *O P*, and draw the joint lines through, which gives the direction and position of joints.

The vertical cross joints in vault may be drawn at pleasure, care being taken to "bond" by breaking joint, but the angle quoins of the groin must be treated differently, and for this reason: the extrados of the arch is set out on the plan as shewn on the right hand half, and; by noting the joints 3 4 5 6 at *T U V W*, it will be observed that the vertical joints of the groins are set out to the mitre, which governs the size on the soffit. If the stones were set out less than this there would not be so good a bed, as this size should be the minimum.

The dotted diagonal lines on the half plan of the intrados shew the mitre on the extrados, and the dotted diagonal lines on the half plan of the extrados shew the mitre of the groin on the intrados. Although the extrados is here shewn apparently as a finished face, yet in practice it is not so, as it is generally left rough, and stepped out as a seating for concrete.

The stones which present any difficulty in the working in this form of vault are the angular groins, and these are the weakest part of the vault, on account of each stone acting to some extent as a corbel, and one corbel standing upon another, as indicated by the sketch (Fig. 10). Therefore care must be taken in working them true to shape and form.

The stones in other portion of the vault may be worked as those in a right arch.

The easiest way of working either of the groin stones is to take a block cubical in form, and containing it, as shewn in Fig. 6 B; and, although in stones No. 3, 4 and 5, there is a little waste attached to this method, yet it gives the best results, and is more correct in shape when worked than by using bevels. The danger of using bevels is in the application of them, that is to say, should there be the least deviation from the actual position in applying the bevel, the stone would not be true. This would not be of so much consequence were it an isolated block, but where it is surrounded by others, and forming a cylindric surface, it is of importance.

Fig. 4.—Shews a quarter plan and profiles of the vault to a larger scale, for the purpose of shewing more clearly the working of the groins;

in actual work this is all that is necessary to set out, as the set of moulds of one groin will work the three others if "handed," that is worked in pairs.

Fig. 5.—Is the springing stone. No. 1 is the bed mould, 1 *A* and 1 *B* the joint moulds.

Begin by working the bottom bed, this being horizontal, and scribe on the bed mould; next work the two vertical faces or joints *c a d b*, and scribe in the joint moulds 1 *A* and 1 *B*, then the top splay joint *c d*, and lastly the curved soffit, care being taken to keep the mitre true.

Fig. 5A.—Shews a sketch of this stone finished; the working of this differs very little from that of an ordinary arch stone.

Fig. 6.—Is the second stone. No. 2 is the bed mould, and 2 *A* and 2 *B* the joint moulds.

Work the two beds parallel to each other, and of the extreme height of the joint mould from *a* to *d*, as surfaces of operation; labour need not be thrown away on these beds, as they may be roughly chiselled over and at the same time true: the mason should know just where to put the work that is necessary, in some cases, perhaps, a couple or three straight drafts being all that is required. This done, scribe in the bed mould No. 1 on the bottom and top bed. Work the vertical joints *c a d b*, scribing in the joint moulds 2 *A* and 2 *B*. The position of these moulds is given by the circumscribing rectangle, coinciding with the lines on the bed mould; next work the splay beds, and then the curved soffit guided by a convex templet, keeping the mitre also true.

Fig. 6A.—Shews a sketch of the stone when finished.

Fig. 6B.—Shews a sketch of the same contained within the circumscribing prism.

Fig. 7.—Is the third stone. This is worked precisely as the last named in Fig. 6.

Fig. 7A.—Shews a sketch of this stone when finished.

Fig. 8.—Is the key-stone No. 7.

In working this stone commence on the soffit plane, the points *a b* and *e f* and points opposite these being in this plane, which may be taken as a surface of operation. Scribe in the bed mould No. 7; the dotted lines *c d* and *g h* shew the finished arris on the soffit. Work the two joints *a b* and the two joints *e f* at right angles to the plane, and scribe in the joint moulds 7 A and 7 B, then the splay joints *a c*—*f g*, &c., and lastly the concave surfaces *c d* and *g h*. The mitres of intersection being here very obtuse must be carefully worked.

Fig. 9.—Shews a sketch of one of the ordinary arch stones between the groins, which is worked similar to that of a right arch.

Fig. 10.—Shews a sketch of the vault.

Plates XXX., XXXI., XXXII., XXXIII.—DOMES AND PENDENTIVES.

The Dome may be generally described as a convex roof or vault, covering a circular elliptical or polygonal area.

The Pendentives are the corbellings resting on the internal angles of piers, and support the dome.

Fig. 1A.—If a hemisphere or other portion of a sphere, *a b a*, be intersected by vertical planes, *a d c*, equidistant from its centre, the angular or spandril portion, *e e*, between the boundaries of the planes are pendentives.

Fig. 1.—Shews half plan of square area, covered by dome and supported by pendentives.

Fig. 2.—Shews sectional elevation of the dome and pendentives, taken through the centre line *E F* on plan.

For the making of the moulds, and working of this vault, a quarter plan only is required to be set out full size; but in order to shew it more clearly the half is here given.

Begin by setting out on the plan (Fig. 1). the rectangle *A B E F*, the line *E F* being the centre line, and the line *C D* being the transverse centre line. The semi-circle *E D F* is the half of inscribed circle, forming wall line of cornice and dome.

Set out the archivolt on impost caps at *A* and *B* as shewn by hatched lines, which gives the span or opening of arches, and project on to springing line of section (Fig. 2).

At *c* as centre, with *c g* or *c h* as radius, describe semi-circle *g j h* for soffit, and semi-circles concentric to this for lines of mouldings forming archivolt. The arch at crown *j k* must equal in height the width at spring-

DOME AND PENDENTIVES

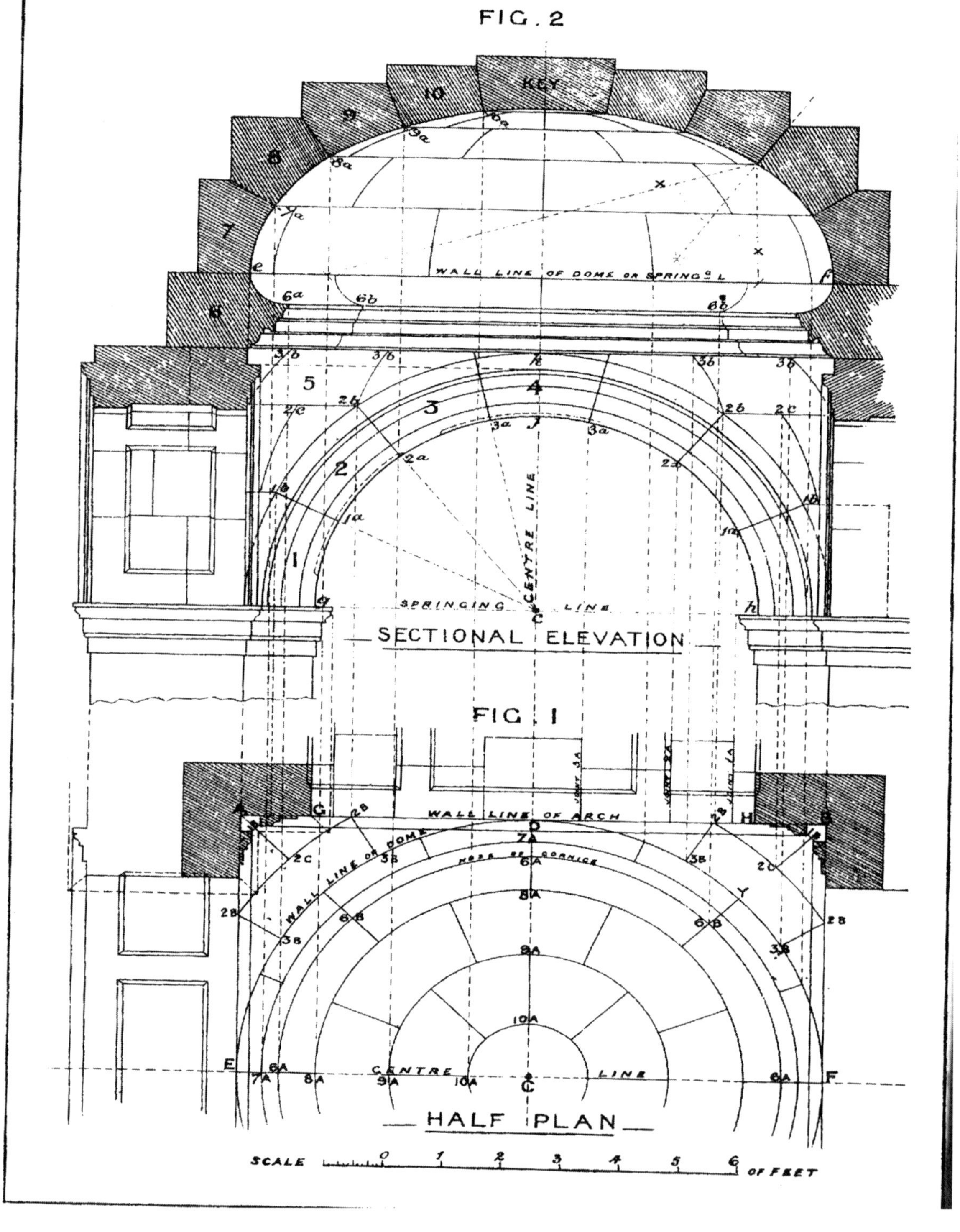

ing *A G*, Fig. 1, so that the corbelling of pendentives start exactly in the angles at *A* and *B* on springing line at top of impost cap.

Divide the arch into any number of equal parts—in this example 7—and draw joints radiating from centre *c* as 1^a 2^a 3^a &c. ; at extremities of joints as 1 *b* 2 *b* draw horizontal lines for beds (these are better if worked in conical or splay beds, but as it takes more material they are generally horizontal as shewn at Fig. 3). Project 1 *b*, 2 *b* on to wall line of arch on plan, fig. 1, and with *C* as centre describe arcs 1 *B*, 2 *B*, giving line of curvature of horizontal joints in pendentive. The vertical joints may be drawn in at will, but are here shewn as at 1 *B*, 2 *B*, 3 *B*.

It will be observed that the arch is panelled on soffit, and is shewn on section by a chamfer, the detail being too small to shew a moulding.

Set up the section of cornice No. 6 and project nosing on to plan (Fig. 1) as 6 *A*. For vertical joints divide cornice into 8 parts, this being a convenient number for stones in the dome, and also breaking joint with those in pendentives.

Draw in the joints which radiate from the centre *C* (Fig. 1) at 6 *A*, 6 *B*, and project on to the section (Fig. 2).

The wall line of the cornice, *e f*, Fig. 2, is the springing line of dome, and equals the width *E C F* on centre line of plan (Fig. 1).

On the line *e f* set up the curvature of dome, which is a semi-ellipse, and may be struck with the trammel or the curve may be traced through points in the inter-section of lines.

For the joints divide the dome into any convenient number—in this example 9—as Nos. 7, 8, 9, 10, &c., and draw radiating lines perpendicular to the tangent of the curve, as at 7^a, 8^a, 9^a, &c. ; see construction as shewn by dotted lines *X X*.

Project 7^a, 8^a, 9^a, &c., on to plan (Fig. 1), and, with *C* as centre, and 7 *A*, 8 *A*, 9 *A*, &c., as radii, describe semi-circles which give horizontal lines in splay joints of dome.

For the vertical joints follow divisions of joints in cornice, the same number (eight) being required in each course, breaking joint, as shewn on plan and section.

Fig. 3.—Is a section on the centre line, shewing corbelling out of the pendentive taken across the diagonal from *B* to *Y* on the plan (Fig. 1), the radius of which equals the distance from *C* to *B*, and the projection *B′*, *Y′* equalling *B*, *Y* on the plan (Fig. 1).

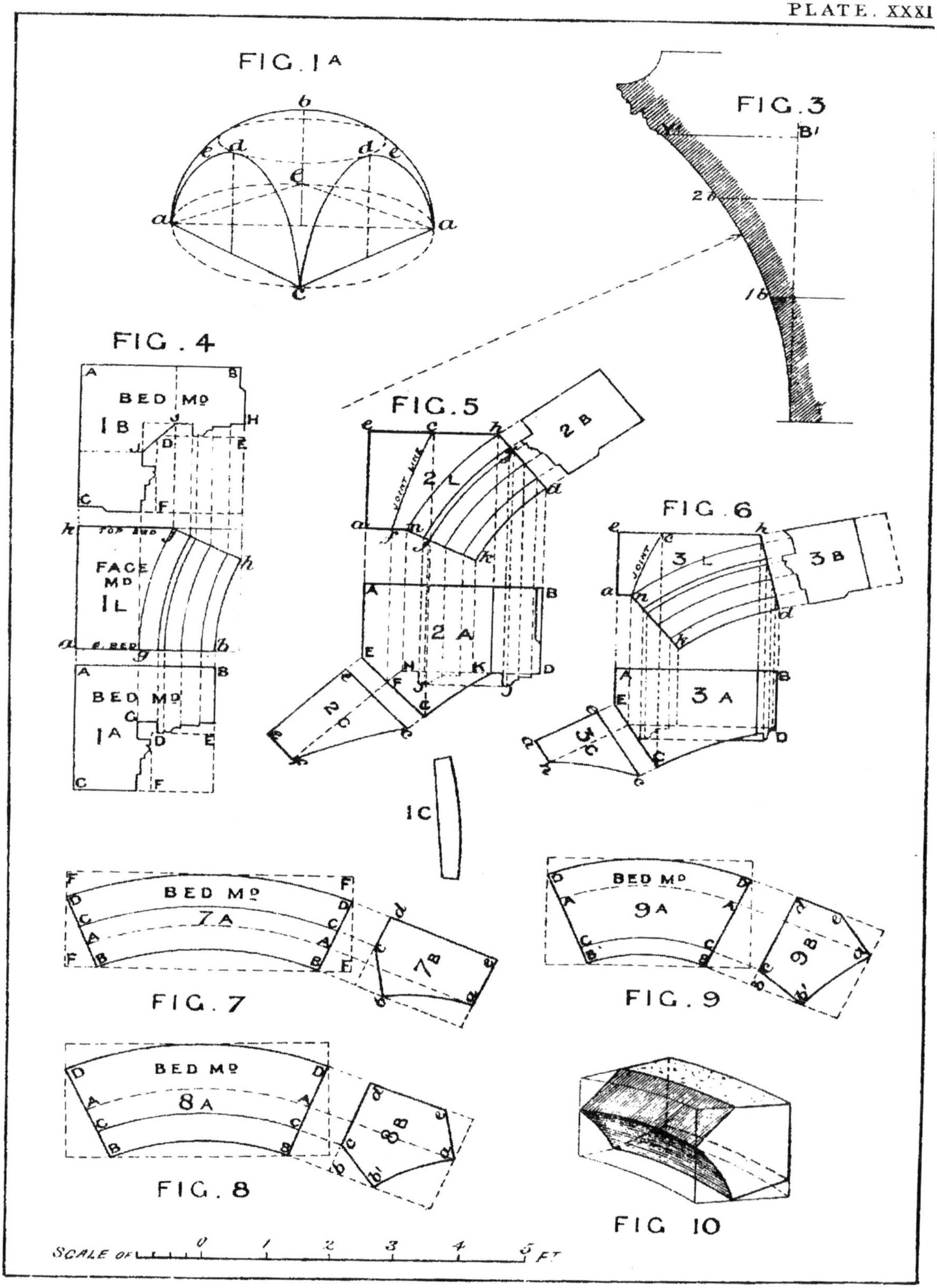
FIG. 1A
FIG. 3
FIG. 4
BED Mº
1B
FACE Mº
1L
TOP BED
BED Mº
1A
FIG. 5
JOINT LINE
2L
2B
2A
2C
FIG. 6
JOINT
3L
3B
3A
3C
1C
BED Mº
7A
7B
FIG. 7
BED Mº
9A
9B
FIG. 9
BED Mº
8A
8B
FIG. 8
FIG 10
SCALE OF
0
1
2
3
4
5 FT

To work the Double Springer No 1.

Fig. 4.—1 *A* is the bottom bed mould, 1 *B* is the top bed mould, and 1 *L* is the face mould.

The stone will require to be cubical in form, and the size of bed mould 1 *B*, and of the height of face mould 1 *L*.

Work the bottom bed and scribe in bed mould 1 *A*; work vertical joints *A B* and *A C* square with the bottom bed, and apply face mould 1 *L* to each joint and scribe in; next take the top bed *k j* parallel to bottom bed. Work out the check *D E F* right through, keeping the nosing of moulding fair or clean, and apply part of face mould 1 *L* coinciding with the moulds marked on vertical joints *A B* and *A C*, which gives the soffit line *h b*, the splay joint *j h* and the nose and mitre line of the archivolt.

Work the splay joints *j h* and scribe in the archivolt, which is part of the bed mould 1 *A*; next the soffits and panels and archivolt mouldings guided by convex templets; lastly, work the small concave portion of pendentive, which starts imperceptibly at the angle *G* on the bottom bed, and increases to *J J* on the top bed.

The convex templet 1 *C* gives the curvature in the centre from *G*—1 *A*, to *D*—1 *B*. An obtuse mitre is formed on each side where the spandrel intersects the archivolt, and is shewn by the segmental line *j g* on the face mould 1 *L*.

It will be observed that the archivolt on the bed mould 1 *B* is foreshortened, but 1 *A*, being a square section, is used on all arch joints.

To work No. 2 Arch Stone.

Fig. 5.—No. 2 *A* is the bed mould, 2 *L* the face mould, 2 *B* the joint mould of arch, and 2 *C* the joint mould of a portion of the pendentive.

This stone will require to be the size of the bed mould, and of the extreme height of the face mould 2 *L* from *k* to *h*.

Begin by working the top bed *e c h*—2 *L*, and scribe in bed mould 2 *A*, as *A B C D E*. Work the vertical joints *A B* and *E C* square with top bed, and scribe in the face mould 2 *L*, and joint mould 2 *C* respectively; point off vertical side *A E*, and rough out section of pendentive *c f* from joint *E C* on to face line *N K*, and work draft through at *J J* for nosing. Apply part of face mould *h d f n k*—2 *L*, coinciding with the face mould marked in on vertical joint *A B*, and work the splay joints *h d*—*n k*, and bottom bed *a n*. Scribe in archivolt mould 2 *B* on joints *h d* and *n k*, and run the moulding through; clean in portion of pendentive *c f*—2 *C* intersecting with archivolt and forming obtuse mitre on the segment line *n* to *h*, and lastly, work panelled soffit.

Fig. 6.—No. 3 arch stone is worked in a similar manner to the foregoing No. 2 (Fig. 5).

No. 4, the key-stone, needs but little explanation, it being worked similarly to that of a right arch, with the exception of the mitre of the pendentive, which is here very obtuse and loses itself at *k*.

The section mould at each joint is 3 *B* (Fig. 6), taken to the dotted line.

Note.—The dotted lines shew the projection of coinciding points in the face and bed moulds of Figs. 4, 5, and 6.

The section of cornice directly under dome is shewn on Fig. 2, No. 6. A bed mould for this is required and also convex templets for the mouldings and fillets, these are obtained from the plan (Fig. 1), 6 *A* being the nose line.

The working of this stone presents no difficulty.

To work the Voussoirs in the Dome.

The shape of stone for working one of these is first, a rectangular prism, of the extreme length of the bed mould 7 *A* (Fig. 7), as shewn by circumscribed dotted lines *F F*, and of the height of joint mould 7 *B*, and second, that of a segment of a hollow cylinder, as shewn in sketch (Fig. 10), which contains the finished block.

Fig. 7.—7 *A* is the bed mould, and 7 *B* the section or joint mould of springer, or first stone in dome.

Begin by working the bottom bed *a e*—7 *B*, and scribe on the bed mould 7 *A*, the dotted line *A A* being the wall line on bottom bed, which must be worked fair to preserve the arris *a*. Work the joints *B D* square with the bed, and scribe in the joint mould 7 *B*. Work off the top bed *c d* and splay joint *c b*, a convex templet giving the arris *B B*, and lastly the concave surface of intrados *a b*.

The back *D D* is left rough.

Fig. 8.—To work the second stone in dome No. 8. 8 *A* is the bed mould, and 8 *B* the section, or joint mould.

Work the top bed, *b c d*—8 *B*, and scribe in bed mould, 8 *A*, to the extreme size, as *D D*, *B B*, the dotted line *A A* being the horizontal arris of joint and soffit at *a*; the line *C C* top line of splay joint *c*; and the line *B B* the horizontal arris of joint and soffit at *b* 1.

Work the joints, *B D* square with the top bed, and scribe in the joint mould, 8 *B*; at points *B B*, at depth *b* 1, work a concave draft, and draw the horizontal line of joint and arris of soffit. Next work off the splay joint *c b′*, also the splay joint *a e*, and lastly the concave surface of intrados.

The back, *D D*. is left rough.

Fig. 10.—Shews a sketch of this stone completed.

It may be mentioned that the stones Nos. 2 and 3 (Figs. 5 and 6), previously described, are worked to one hand; for the opposite hand, the same moulds and templets will do, if reversed.

No. 5 (Fig. 2), is a plain spherical stone in the pendentive, and is worked similarly to those in the dome, as above described.

To construct a Spheroidal Dome, with an aperture at the apex or top. The bed-joints are conical surfaces, and terminate on the extrados and intrados, in horizontal circles. The vertical joints are contained within a plane, which intersects with the axis of the dome.

Fig. 11.—Shews half-plan of the dome.

Fig. 12.—Shews section of the dome through the centre.

For the making of the moulds, and working this dome, a quarter only is necessary to be set out full-size, but in order to shew it more clearly the half is here given.

Begin by setting out on the plan (Fig. 11), the centre lines, *A C A* and *C K*. With *C* as a centre and *C A* as radius, describe the semicircle *A K A*, giving the extreme boundary of exterior surface, or extrados of dome. The thickness of the dome having been determined as *A B*, with *C* as centre and *C B* as radius, describe the semicircle *B B*, as shewn by the dotted line, giving the extreme boundary of interior surface, or intrados of

DOME

FIG. 12

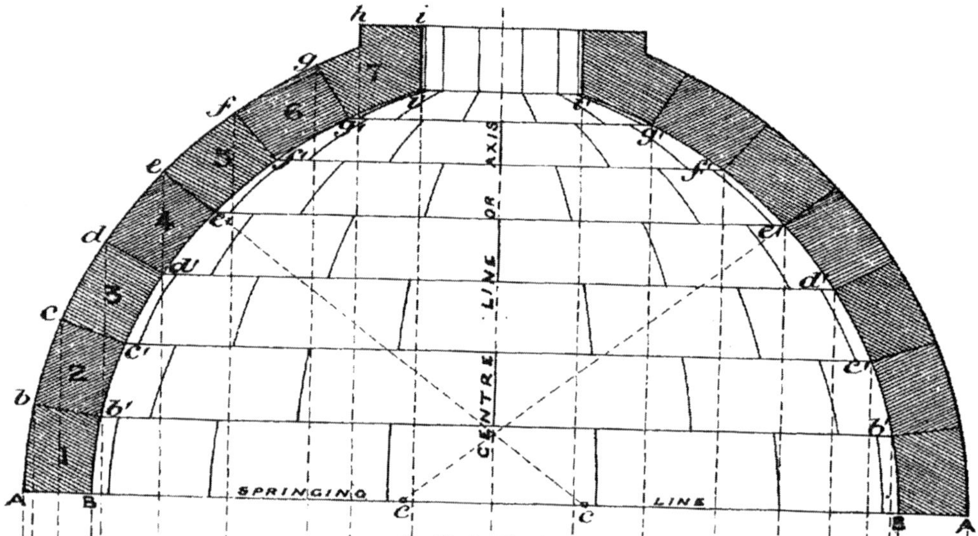

— SECTION —

— HALF FIG. 11 PLAN —

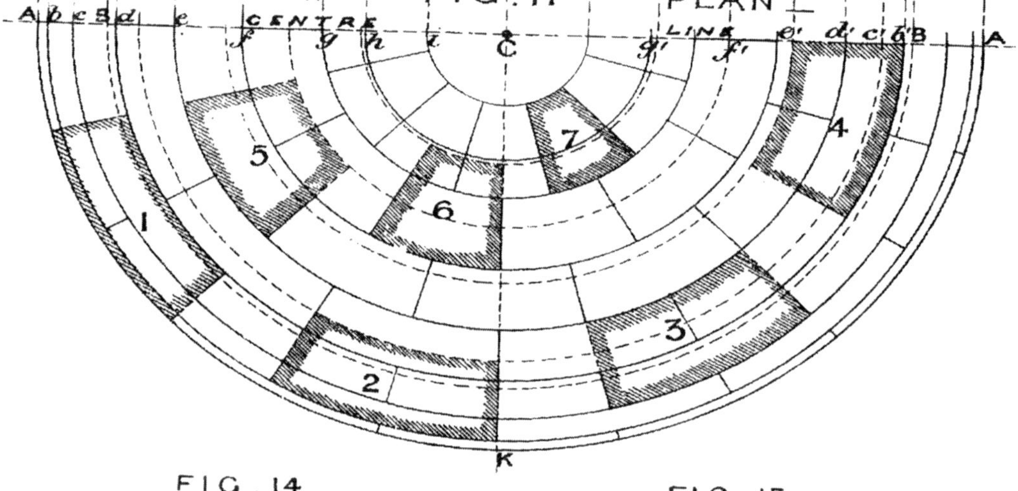

FIG. 14

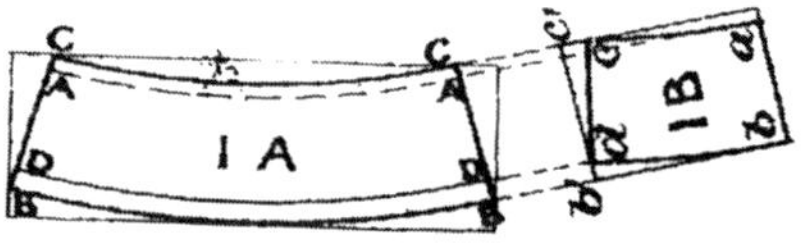

BED Md

FIG. 15

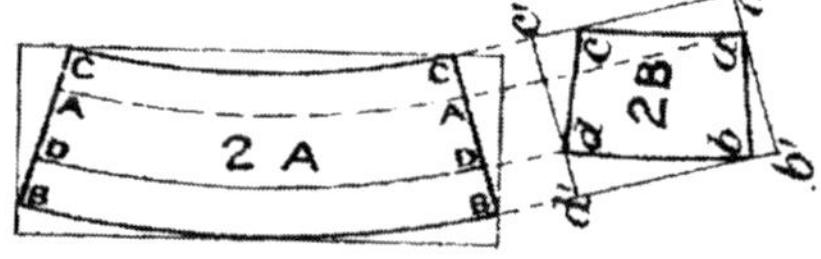

dome. Project lines *A* and *B* to springing line, Fig. 12, and with *c c* as centres set up the section of dome, and divide the same into any number of equal parts for bed-joints as may be convenient (in this example, seven), as *b c d e f g*, and draw radiating lines for the joints from centre, *c*. Project *b c d e*, &c., on to plan (Fig. 11), and with *C* as centre describe semicircles *b c d e*, &c.; the plan of the arris of horizontal bed-joints on exterior is thus obtained. For the arris of horizontal bed-joints on interior surface, project *b c d e*, &c., on to plan, and draw the semicircles *b′ c′ d′ e′*, &c., shewn by the dotted lines on right-hand half.

For the vertical joints each course will consist of the same number of stones (in this example, twelve), breaking joint directly over each other and diminishing in size from bottom to top course. These are set out on the plan.

The stones "hatched in" on the plan (Fig. 11), shew the projection of one voussoir in each course, as 1 2 3 4 5 6 and 7, and, being equal and similar stones, and alike in situation, one bed mould to each course only will be required.

To work the Voussoirs.

The shape of rough block required for working these stones by this method is a rectangular prism of the extreme length of the bed mould, as 1 *A* (Fig. 14), shewn by the circumscribed line, the height being that of the joint mould 1 *B*; and secondly, that of a segment of a hollow cylinder, as shewn in sketch (Fig. 17), which contains the finished block, the arrises only touching the boundaries of the cylinder.

Fig. 14.—1 *A* is the bed mould, and 1 *B* the section, or joint mould, of springer, or No. 1 stone.

Begin by working the bed, *a b*—1 *B*, and scribe in bed mould 1 *A*. Work the joints *B C* square with the bed, and scribe in joint mould 1 *B*. Work the top bed *b′ c′* as a surface of operation, and scribe in the line *D D*, which gives the top line of arris of convex surface and of splay joint. With the templet *C C* at *c* work the horizontal draft, giving the arris of joint and of concave surface. Work the top, *d c*, to lines as given, and the inside concave surface *a c*; and lastly, the outside convex surface, *b d*, using templets made at *a c* and *b d* for guidance.

Fig. 15.—To work the second stone (No. 2).

2 *A* is the bed mould and 2 *B* the section, or joint mould. Work the bottom bed *a′ b′* as a surface of operation, and bed *d′ c′* parallel to it.

DOME

FIG. 13

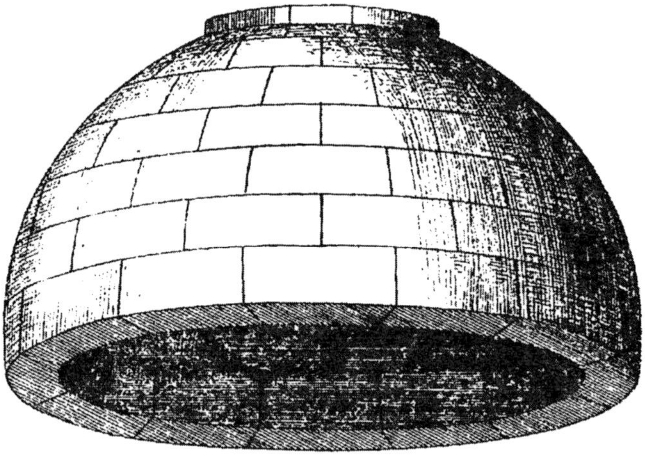

— SKETCH OF DOME —

FIG. 16

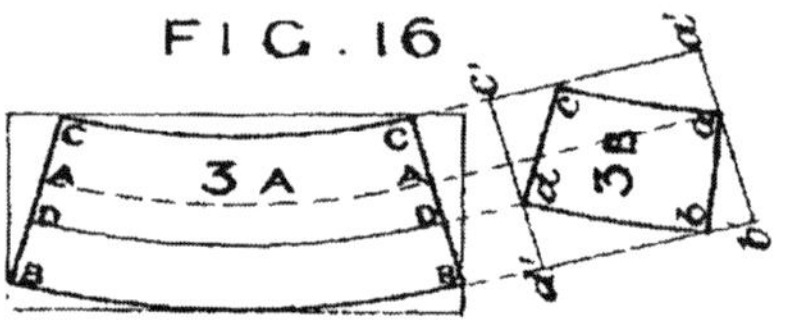

FIG. 17

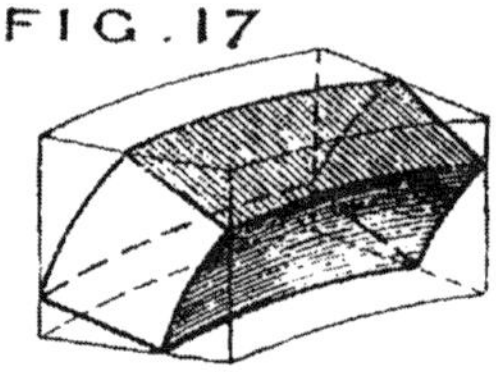

FIG. 18

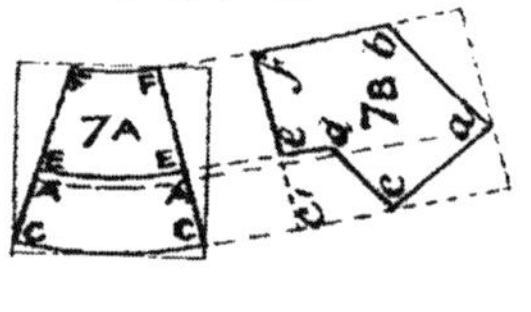

FIG. 19

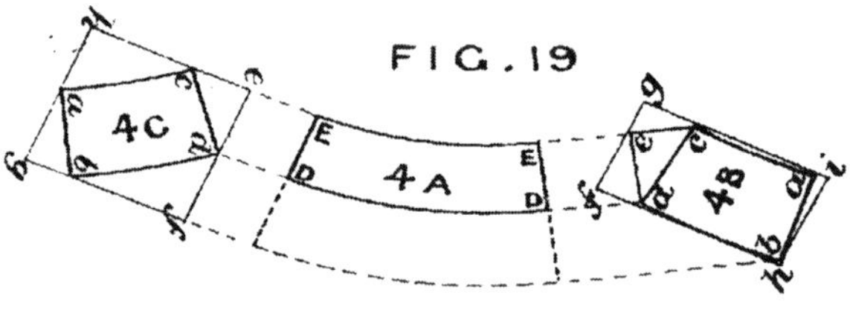

FIG. 20

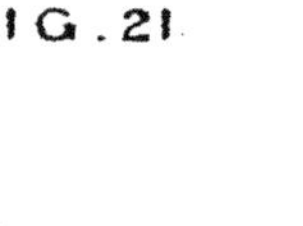

FIG. 21

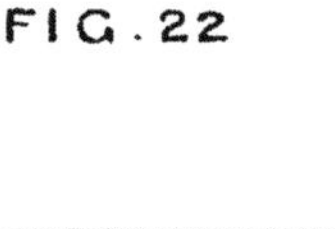

FIG. 22

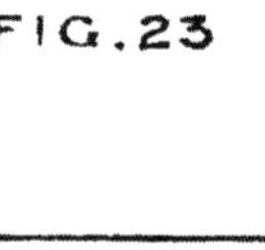

FIG. 23

Labour need not be thrown away on these surfaces, or beds, as the arris, *a a* on one bed and *d d* on the other, is all that is required to be kept fair; the other portion may be roughly chiselled off, and at the same time kept straight. Scribe in the bed mould on both beds, as *B C—B C*, and work the joints *B C* square with same; scribe in the joint mould, as *b a d c*, to each joint. With the templet *C C* at *c* work a horizontal draft, and draw a line parallel to *C′*, giving the arris of joint and of concave surface. With the templet *D D* scribe in line on the top bed, giving the arris of top joint and of convex surface. Work off the splay joint *d c* to the lines thus given. On the bottom bed, with templet *A A* scribe in line, giving the arris of bottom joint and of concave surface. With the templet *B B* at *b* work the horizontal draft, and draw line parallel to *b′*, giving the arris of bottom joint and of convex surface. Work off the splay joint to the lines thus given, and inside concave surface *a c*, and lastly outside convex surface *b d*, using templets made at *a c* and *b d* for guidance.

The stones in the other courses of the dome are worked in a similar manner to those last described, except the top course, or rim.

To work the Rim of Aperture in Dome, being the top, or No. 7, course.

Begin by working the top bed *c′ f*, and scribe in the bed mould 7 *A*. Work the joints *C F* square with bed, and scribe in the joint mould 7 *B*. At *a* work a horizontal draft straight to *a*, and scribe in the templet *A A*, giving the arris of bottom joint and concave surface; then work the bottom joint and spherical surfaces *a b* and *c d e*.

There is some difference of opinion as to the best method of working the voussoirs in a dome, with respect to waste of material and labour. Perhaps for the first and second courses, and also the courses near the apex, no better method can be followed than the one just described, and, as before explained, in reference to vaulting, page 74. This method is simple, gives the best results, and the stones are truer in form when worked than by using a number of bevels. However, another method is here shewn, which saves much material and labour, although greater care is required in the execution.

Another Method of Working the Voussoirs.

Fig. 19.—Let 4 *A* be the bed mould of stone in fourth course of dome. (This being one of the courses in which there is much waste by the previous method of working, and is shewn by section 4 *C*, at line *e f g h*.)

For the joint mould, 4 *B*, transfer No. 4 from section (Fig. 12), as *d c b a*. Draw *e d* parallel and *e c* vertical to the base, or springing line; *f g h i* is a rectangle, circumscribing the mould and giving the size of stone required. When compared to that of 4 *C*, *e f g h*, the difference is at once seen.

Select a stone sufficiently large, so that all the surfaces and arrises are contained within it.

Fig. 20.—Begin by working a plane surface of operation, as *e d*, and apply templet 4 *A*, and scribe in as *D E*, *D E*. Work joints *D E* square with the bed; these require careful working, a portion of the joint being outside the line of square, as at *X X X*, but the one portion of joint having been worked, the other is obtained by means of the straight-edge. Apply joint mould to each joint, as *d c b a*, and scribe in.

Fig. 21.—Shews the next operation of working the convex spherical surface, by the guidance of a bevel, the stock of bevel being applied in the direction of a line radiating from centre *C*, as the joint lines *E D*—4 *A*.

Fig. 22.—Shews the third operation, the line *b* being drawn parallel to *d*; a bevel is used, giving the bottom splay bed, *b a*.

Fig. 23.—Shews the fourth and last operation, the angular portion, *e g d c*, being cut away and bevel used for splay joint; and the concave spherical surface is worked by the guidance of a templet made from *a c*.

It will be observed in the working of this stone that by this method the accuracy of the work depends almost entirely on the first plane surface of operation, and, should any errors occur in applying the bevels from this bed, the stone will not be of the shape and form intended.

The stones in other courses of dome may be worked in a similar manner.

PLATES XXXIV., XXXV., XXXVI., XXXVII.—GROINED VAULTING.

To construct a GROINED VAULT, in four compartments, square on plan, and supported by a central shaft or column, with wall, transverse, and diagonal ribs.

Fig. 1.—Is the inverted skeleton plan of vault, shewing the general arrangement of compartments: *A A* being the wall ribs, *B B* the transverse ribs, crossing the vault at right angles to the wall, *C C* the diagonal ribs, spanning across from corners to the shaft, and *D D* the vaulting surface.

Fig. 2.—Shews the inverted plan of one compartment, or one quarter of the vault, with elevation of the wall, transverse and diagonal ribs, each being of equal height at the apex, and the ridge line of vaulting surface being also level throughout.

For the purpose of making the moulds, and the working of this vault, a small portion of the plan (one-sixteenth only), set out to full size, is all that is necessary, the remainder being a repetition; but, in order to shew the setting out more clearly, a quarter of the plan is here given.

Begin by setting out the wall lines of vault, then the centre lines of wall ribs *A B* and *A C*, the transverse ribs *B D* and *C D*, and the diagonal ribs *A D* and *B C*, and set off on each side of the centre lines the width of their section.

Before proceeding further it is necessary to determine the position of the feet of ribs at the springing; these generally depend on the plan of the abacus of cap, and it is also a matter of arrangement, as well as of taste and design, so that no fixed rule can be given.

In this example the ribs are arranged so that the nosings are equidistant from the point of intersection of the centre line of ribs at *A B C D*, in order that the wall ribs and transverse ribs may be of the same curvature, and also that the opening or span between the nosing of springers may be equal.

GROINED VAULTING

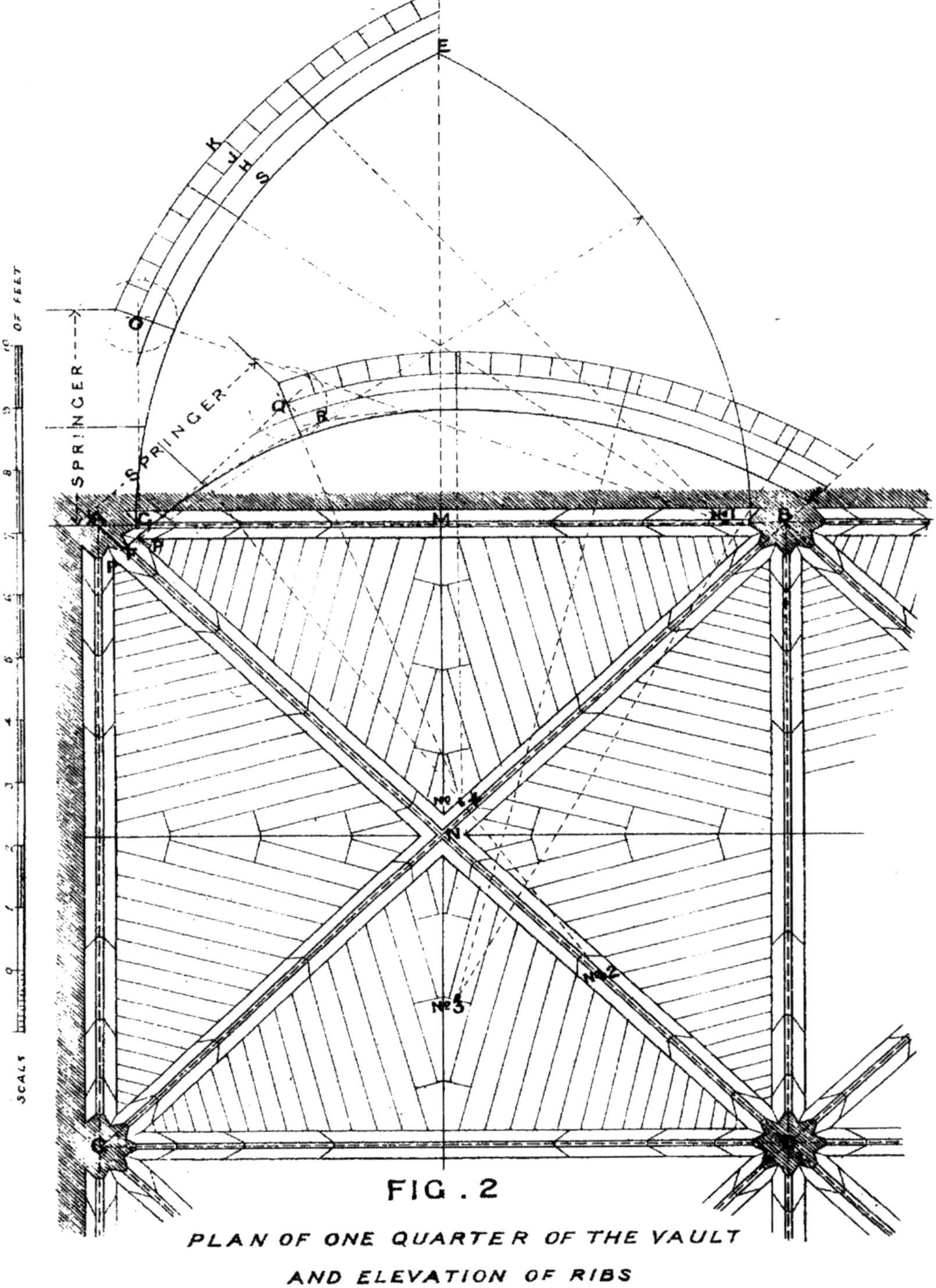

FIG. 2

PLAN OF ONE QUARTER OF THE VAULT AND ELEVATION OF RIBS

Having set out the position of the springers at *A B C D* on plan, the next process is to find the elevation or contour of the ribs. This is generally governed by the wall ribs, which have some opening or arch in the wall below them, regulating to some extent the form of vaulting. In some cases, perhaps, it may be preferable to begin with the transverse or diagonal rib, but this again depends on the shape of the vault.

In this example the contour of the transverse and wall ribs are similar, their span being equal, as before explained.

Begin by drawing the wall rib first. Take the centre line *A B* on plan, and make use of it as a base or springing line. Erect a perpendicular as a centre line at *M* on the plan, and on this set up the height of vault, as at *E*. Let point No. 1 be the centre from which the wall rib is struck, and with this as a centre, and nosing *G* as radius, draw the segment line *S* for the nose of rib on the soffit, cutting the centre line at apex *E*; gauge on the width of members of the rib, from the line of soffit *S* as *H J K*, and with the same centre, No. 1, draw the segment lines through these points, thus forming the wall rib. This is also the elevation of the transverse rib.

The profile of the diagonal rib is now to be obtained, and the first consideration is the shape of vault. If a horizontal section be taken through any one of the compartments, above the springers, and the vaulting, or filling in, between the ribs is rectangular in shape and parallel to the sides, the courses of stone forming the vaulting surfaces are level, and the upper edges of the diagonal ribs, upon which the filling-in rests, are portions of elliptic curves. These curves are obtained by ordinates, the curvature being subordinate to the wall rib; this is sometimes done, but as the elliptic rib entails more work both in the setting out and in the execution, the simpler method of using compound circular curves is generally adopted, and with perhaps better results constructively. The ribs are thus made geometrically regular, while the filling-in surfaces take their chance as it were, and are adjusted to the curvature of the ribs, and although twisting to some extent, yet do not offend the eye, which is guided mainly by the principal lines, and not the surfaces.

Another consideration is the separation of the ribs at one level, at the point where they become fully developed. The more equally the ribs can be grouped together at the springing, without projecting at unequal distances before each other, the better it is for their separation or clearance; the advantage of this being, that the winding in the vaulting surface is much reduced, and is free from that ploughshare-like twist, to which objection is sometimes made. The ribs are also equal in depth and of the same cross section, and the setting out and the working generally are easier. In some cases it may be impossible to do this, and the ribs are then arranged to suit the conditions of the case.

In this example the contour of the diagonal is struck from centres, and these may be varied to suit any adjustment of curvature.

The point at which the feet of ribs is struck should be on the springing line, neither above nor below, for if above the rib would be stilted, and if below an acute angle would be formed with the springing line, neither of which results is pleasing.

Let *A D*, the centre line of diagonal rib on plan (Fig. 2), be the base or springing line for the elevation of rib; produce the centre line *C B*, which is perpendicular to *A D*, as the centre line of elevation, and on this set up, from the base line to the apex of the soffit of rib, the height *N L*, equal to the height *M E* on the elevation of the wall rib. Next in the elevation of wall rib, find the point of clearance, or where the rib separates from the springer, and the full section of rib is obtained; this will be the point in the upper edge of the rib vertically over the point where the sides of the rib intersect at *P* on plan. At *P* erect a perpendicular to the springing line *A B*, cutting the upper edge of rib at *O* in elevation, which is the point of separation, or where the wall rib is fully developed, and clears the springer. Through the same point *P*, erect a perpendicular to the springing line *A D* on the diagonal, and set off the height *F Q*, equal to the height at wall rib of *G O*; the diagonal rib thus clears the springer at point *Q*, the back edge of the rib at vaulting surface.

Two points are already given in the curve of the diagonal rib, namely at *F*, the springing, and at *L*, the apex, but a third is required. Now at point *Q* describe an arc with radius equal to the depth of the rib as at *O*, and it will be at once evident that the arc furnishes a point through which the curve of rib must be drawn. Commence on the springing line *A D*, and find a centre by which the curve may be drawn from *F*, to touch the arc whose centre is *Q*, but as this throws the curve too high, and would make a cripple, find a centre, No. 2, that takes the curve still higher, that is to *R* as shewn by the dotted line. Now find a centre as No. 3, and draw curve to *R* from the apex *L*. An intermediate radius is now required, by which a curve may be drawn touching the arc whose centre is *Q*, and intersecting the other curves Nos. 2 and 3. This is found at No. 4, and the curvature of the diagonal rib thus obtained is easy and graceful, retaining also the pointed form. Gauge on the width of members of the rib from the line of soffit, and with their respective radii draw curves forming the elevation of the diagonal rib.

GROINED VAULTING

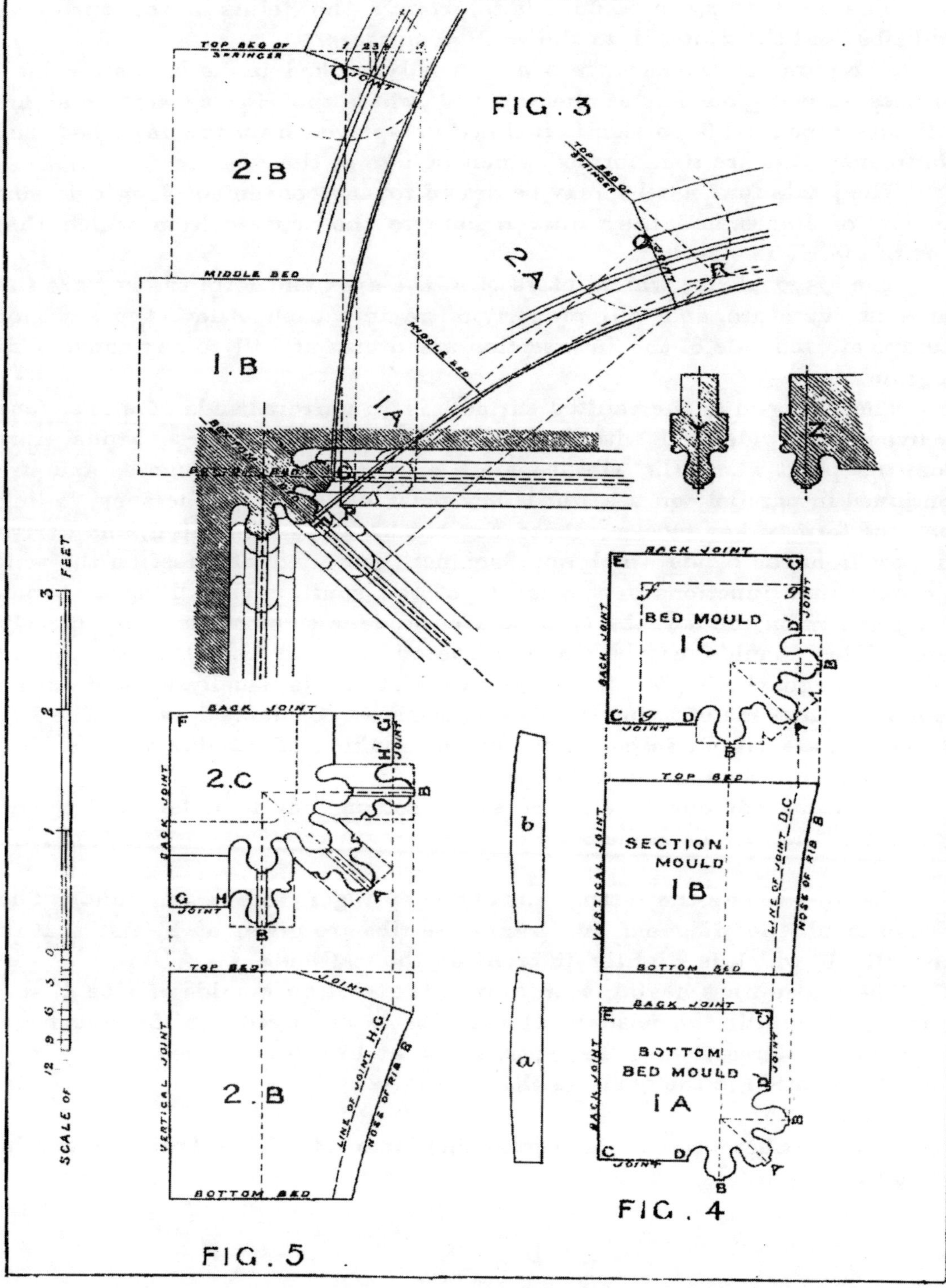

The radii and centres are best found by repeated trials.

The next thing to be done is to arrange the joints of the springers and ribs, and the filling-in to the vaulted surfaces.

The joints of the springers are usually worked in horizontal or level courses, except a portion of the top bed, where the ribs separate and are fully developed; this portion is inclined or splayed from the level bed, and abutment joints are thus formed which radiate to their centres.

The joints for the ribs may be drawn to any convenient length to suit the size of stones, and they must radiate to the centres from which that part of the rib is struck.

The diagonal ribs which intersect at the apex and form the key are the same in curvature, and will properly mitre into each other; the arms or stumps at each side of the intersection are drawn at will to any convenient length.

The filling-in to the vaulted surfaces is in narrow bands of stone, four or five inches wide, and with beds slightly radiating. These bands start from the point where the ribs separate at the top of springers, and are continued in parallel courses until they meet obliquely at the apex, taking then the form of key blocks; these key blocks are rack shaped, and derive support from the bands which abut against them, and also rest on the wall ribs and mitre junctions in the centre of the vault. The filling-in bands being narrow on the face the twist to each stone is so small as to be scarcely perceptible; moulds may be made to these if desired from the elevation of wall and diagonal ribs, but the twist on the stones is usually worked on the scaffold at the time of fixing, this being the most economical way. The key blocks also are simple in construction, the making of moulds and working of the stones presenting no difficulty.

Attention may now be directed to the setting out in detail and to the working of the various stones.

Fig. 3.—Shews the setting out of the springers to a larger scale. The section moulds for diagonal and transverse ribs are given at *Y*, and that of the wall rib, which is slightly different on the wall side, at *Z*.

The centre lines having been drawn, the section moulds of ribs *Y* and *Z* are applied until the position of the ribs is arranged equi-distant from the point of intersection of the centre lines, as before explained.

The notation is the same as that of Fig. 2.

Fig. 4.—Shews the bed and joint moulds of No. 1, or bottom stone in springer.

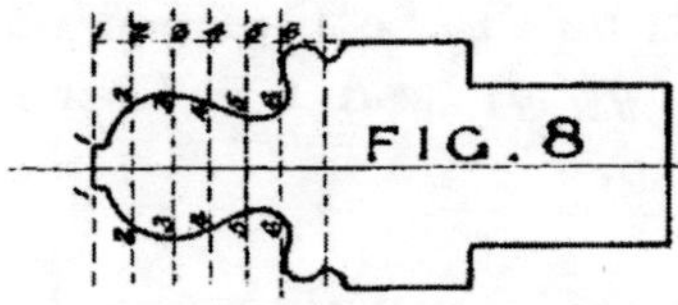

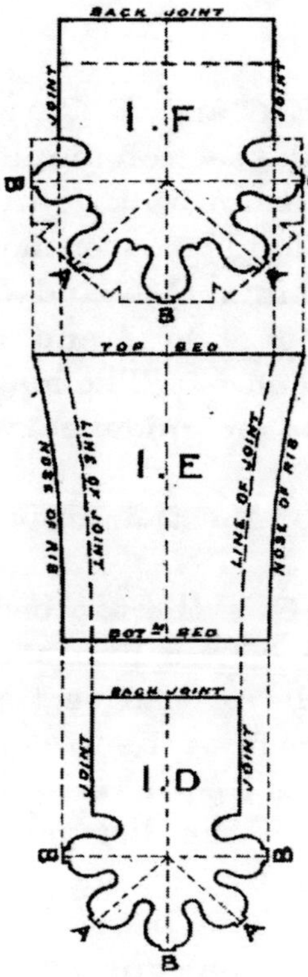

FIG. 6

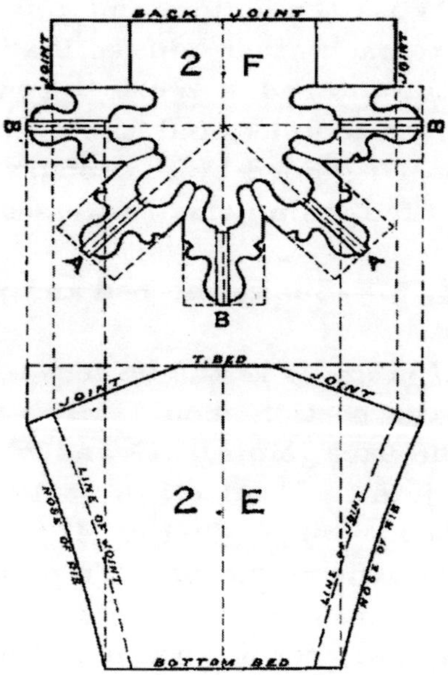

FIG. 7

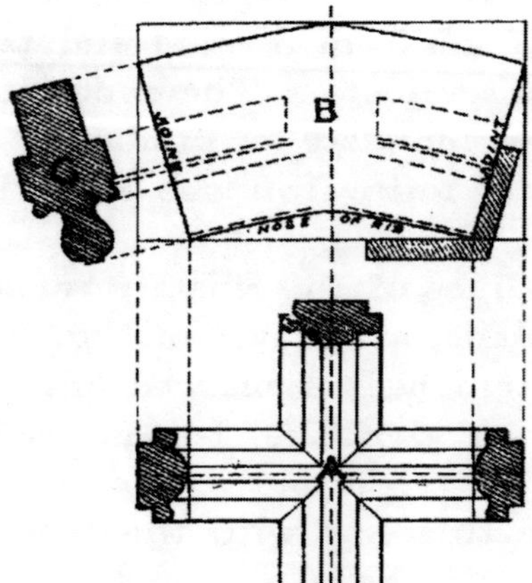

FIG. 9

FIG. 10

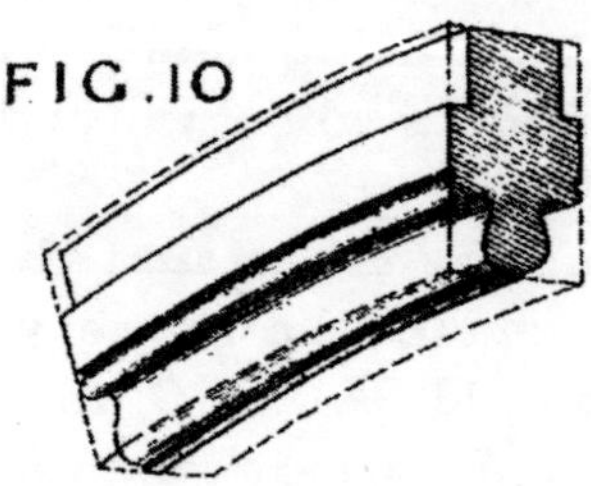

SKETCH OF RIB

1 *A* is the bottom bed mould, 1 *C* is the top bed mould or middle bed (this also will be the bottom bed mould of No. 2, or upper stone in springer at dotted line *g f g*), and 1 *B* is the section mould taken through the centre line of wall rib.

Commence by working the back joints *E C* and *E C′* (which may be taken as surfaces of operation), and scribe on the section mould 1 *B* on each joint. Work the bottom and top beds square from back joint, these being parallel to each other, and scribe in the bed moulds 1 *A* on bottom bed and 1 *C* on the top bed. Work the two concave joints *C D* and *C′ D′*, guided by a convex templet, and the nosing of rib from *A* to *A* and the nosing of ribs *B* to *B*, guided by the convex templets *a* and *b*. The moulding is now to be worked, using small reverses and templets for guidance.

Fig. 5.—Shews the bed and joint mould of No. 2 or upper stone of the springer.

1 *C* (Fig. 4) is the bottom bed mould, 2 *C* is the top bed mould, and 2 *B* is the section mould taken through the centre line of the wall rib. Work the back joints *F G* and *F G′*, and scribe on the section mould 2 *B* on each joint. Work off the bottom bed square from the back joint, scribing on the bed mould 1 *C* (Fig. 4) to the dotted line *f g*; next work off the top bed square from the back joint and parallel to the bottom bed, and the splay joint seating for the wall rib, as given by section mould 2 *B*, also the splay joint for the seating of diagonal rib. The bevel for this may be obtained from 2 *A* (Fig. 3) or the nose line may be squared down from the top bed and the depth gauged on. On the centre lines of the top bed scribe on the section of rib moulds *Y* and *Z*. Work the two concave joints *G H* and *G′ H′*, also the nosing of rib from *A* to *A* and the nosing of ribs from *B* to *B*, guided by convex templets. The moulding is now carefully worked, using small reverses and templets for guidance.

The springers when worked will truly mitre from the springing to the separation of ribs.

Care must be taken that the centre lines of the ribs are vertically over one another, or in the same vertical plane, as shewn in Fig. 5—2 *C*, in which the mould No. 1 *C* for the bottom bed is marked on, and again in Fig. 7—2 *F*, where the mould 1 *F*, for the bottom bed, is also marked on.

The moulds should always be made this way with the sections vertically over one another.

It will be observed in the bed mould 2 *C* (Fig. 5) that although the moulding to ribs is given it is only approximate, and cannot be worked to accurately, because it is here foreshortened, and consequently a little distorted. This may be seen by reference to Fig. 3, the plane at 1, 2, 3, 4, 5 being that to which the mouldings are projected from the splay joint. The position of nosing, however, is correctly given, starting square down at the depth of the splay joint from the horizontal bed.

The section of the rib moulding at the middle bed, or at any horizontal line of the springer, may be obtained by projection. Divide the square section of the rib into any number of parts as in Fig. 8 at 1 2 3 4 5 6. Set off these points on the elevation of the rib, and from the centre draw the segmental lines through, cutting the horizontal line or bed; transfer these points of intersection to the centre line of the rib on plan, and draw lines through square from the centre line, and make them equal to 1 1—2 2—3 3, &c., of square section, and draw the curves through these points, giving the true section at horizontal level.

Fig. 6.—Shews the bed and joint moulds of springers of No. 1 or bottom stone at *B* and *C* on the plan (Fig. 2).

1 *D* is the bottom bed mould, 1 *F* is the top bed mould, and 1 *E* is the section mould taken through the centre line of wall rib *B B*.

Fig. 7.—Shews the bed and joint moulds of No. 2 or upper stone of springers at *B* and *C* on the plan (Fig. 2).

1 *F* (Fig. 6) is the bottom bed mould, 2 *F* is the top bed mould, and 2 *E* is the section mould taken through the centre line of wall rib *B B*.

The moulds for the central springer at *D* on the shaft are identical with the last-named (Fig. 6 and Fig. 7). The centre line at *B B* being half of the mould, this half scribed on the stone and then reversed for the other half, gives a completed whole.

These last-named springers are worked precisely as those already described, the same templets as before being used for the nosing of ribs and concave joints.

Fig. 9.—Shews the bed and section mould of the key-stone at the intersection of the diagonal ribs. *A* is the bed mould, *B* is the section mould, taken vertically through the centre, and *C* is the section mould of the rib.

Work a plane bed as a surface of operation, and scribe in the bed mould *A* on the soffit. Work off the splay joints to bevel, and scribe in the section mould of rib *C* on each joint; work out the square checks on each side of ribs, and cut the nosings to a concave shape, guided by convex templets. Now run the mouldings in on each stump to their intersection, forming mitres, cut off the back if required, and take out the rebate for vaulting surfaces.

Fig. 10.—Shews a sketch of the rib.

The working of this requires but little description, it being treated as a simple arch stone. A plane surface is first formed; on this the face mould is scribed, and the joints which radiate from the curve of the soffit are then squared through, and the section mould of rib is scribed in on each joint. The stone is next worked to a parallel thickness, the rebate for vaulting surface being taken out and the moulding run through, guided by convex templets and reverses.

Fig. 11.—Shews a sketch of part of the vault.

GROINED VAULTING

FIG. II

SKETCH OF PART OF VAULT

FIG. I

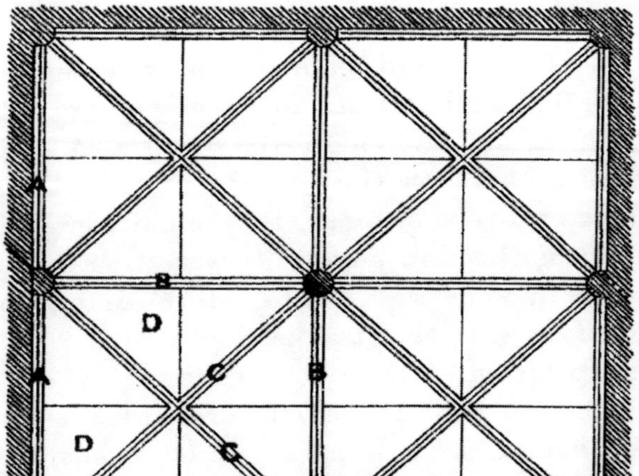

PLAN OF VAULT

Plates XXXVIII., XXXIX., XL., XLI.—GROINED VAULTING.

(Continued.)

To construct a Groined Vault, square on plan, with wall, diagonal, intermediate and ridge ribs.

This vault is somewhat different to the one previously shewn on pages 89 and 90, in having intermediate ribs, ridge ribs, and bosses.

Ornamental bosses are introduced into these vaults, as it is not possible to nicely mitre the mouldings of the ribs, at the intersection of the apex or ridge, on account of the differing inclinations of the ribs. The mouldings, therefore, die into the bosses, and the difficulty is got over. The bosses also give strength and richness to the vault.

Fig. 1.—Is the inverted plan of vault, shewing the general arrangement of ribs, *A A* being the wall ribs, *B B* the diagonal ribs, *C C* the intermediate ribs, *D D* the ridge ribs, and *E* the vaulting surface, or filling in, and *F* the bosses.

Fig. 2.—Shews the inverted plan, of one quarter of the vault, with elevation of the wall, diagonal, intermediate, and ridge ribs, each being of equal height at the apex, and the ridge ribs being also level throughout.

For the purpose of making the moulds and working the vault, only one quarter is necessary to be set out, the remainder being a repetition. Begin as previously described on page 89 by setting out the wall lines of vault, then the centre lines of wall, ridge, intermediate, and diagonal ribs, and draw circles for bosses, at the intersection of ribs.

Determine the position of the feet of ribs, at the springing line, as shewn at Fig. 3. The noses of these ribs are arranged so as to touch a segmental line (the abacus of cap upon which the springer rests being segmental). Gauge off on each side of the centre lines the width of ridge, intermediate, diagonal, and wall ribs; the first three are equal, but the

GROINED VAULTING

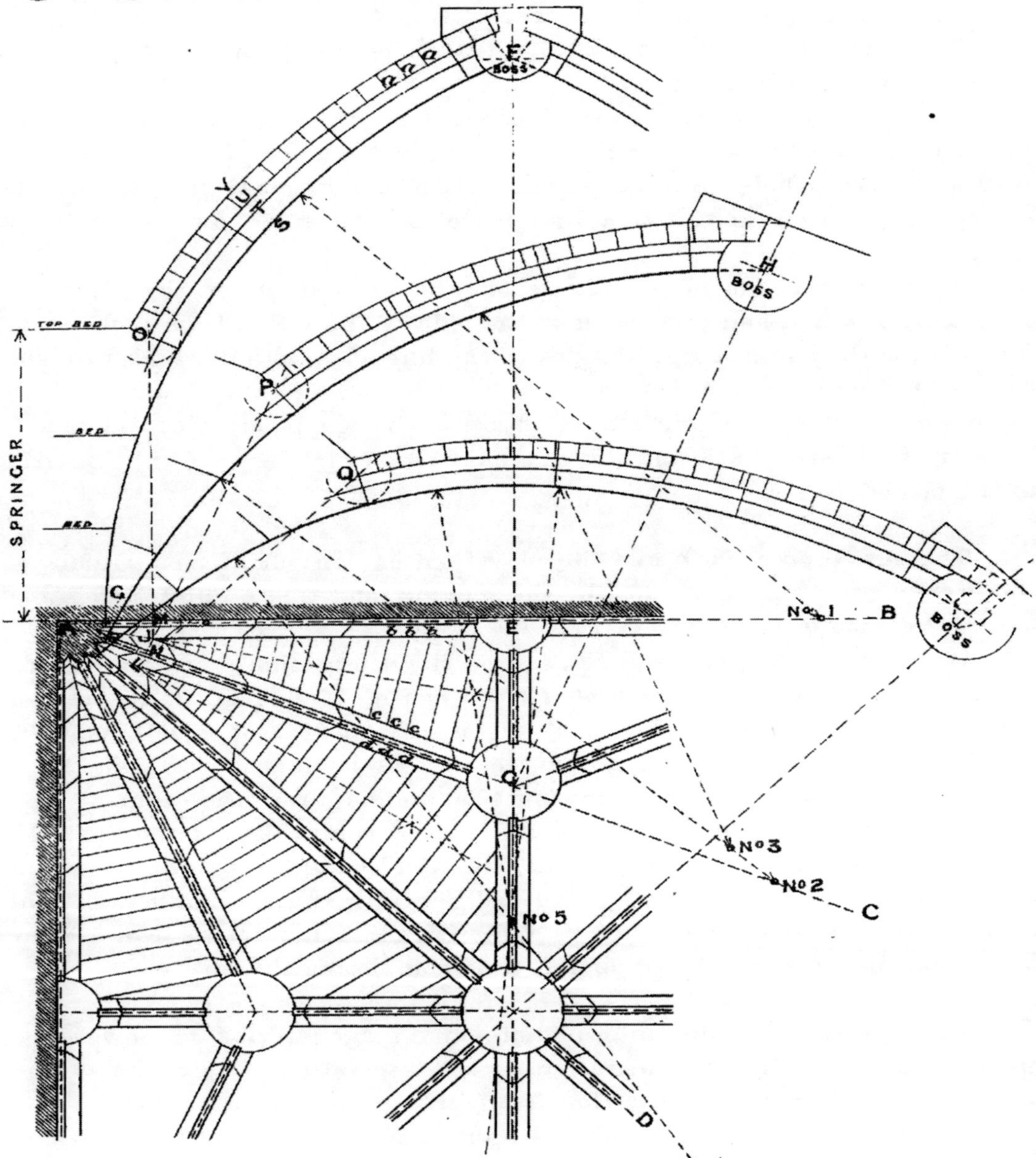

FIG. 2

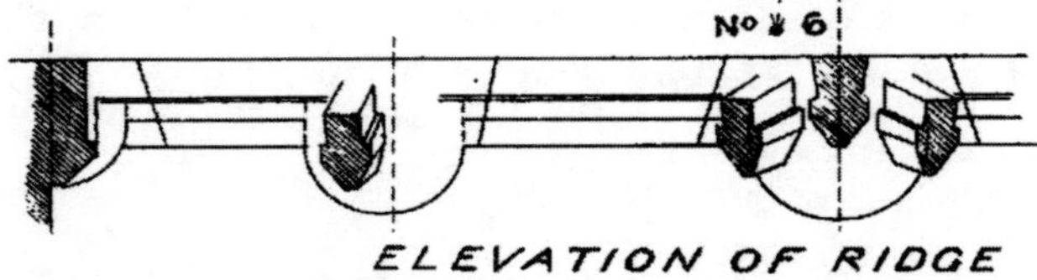

ELEVATION OF RIDGE

wall ribs are only a little more than half the width of the others, in order that the nosings should be of one size.

To complete the portion of the plan, the filling in, to the vaulted surface, must now be set out.

Narrow bands of stone, or chalk, of various widths, but generally parallel, are mostly used. In the spandrel pieces on the plan, between the wall and intermediate ribs, and intermediate and diagonal ribs, the joints are set out at right angles to a line bisecting the angle formed by these ribs.

Space out these bands, on the rebate line of wall rib, on the elevation Fig. 2, as at *a a a*, and project on to the side of the wall rib on plan, as at *b b b*; draw the joints at right angles to the line of bisection, which produce to side of the intermediate rib as *c c c*. Square the joints across this rib as shewn at *d d d*; the points thus obtained give the position of the bands, between the intermediate and the diagonal rib, which are drawn similarly to the preceding.

The next process is to find the elevation, or contour of ribs, which in the present example is governed by the wall rib, and this regulates to some extent the form of vaulting.

Begin by drawing the wall rib, taking the centre line *A B* on plan as a base or springing line, then at *E*, the centre of side of vault, erect a perpendicular as a centre line, and set up the height of vault as at *F*. Point No. 1 is the centre from which the wall rib is struck, with this point as a centre, and the distance to nosing *G* as radius, draw the segment line *S* for the nose of rib on the soffit, cutting the centre line at the apex *F*, which may be also called a datum line, this line being the height to which all the ribs are drawn. Next gauge on the width of the members of rib, from the line of soffit *S*, as *T U V*, and with the same centre No. 1 draw segmental lines through these points, thus completing the wall rib.

The elevation of the intermediate and diagonal ribs is now to be obtained, and the first consideration is the separation of the ribs at one level. This separation of the ribs is of primary importance both in the working and the setting out, and has been fully explained in the previous section, page 91.

For the elevation of the intermediate rib, commence on the centre line of rib *A C* on the plan, and at *G* erect a perpendicular to *A C* as the centre line; on this set up the height *G H*, equal to *E F*, on the elevation of the wall rib.

FIG. 1

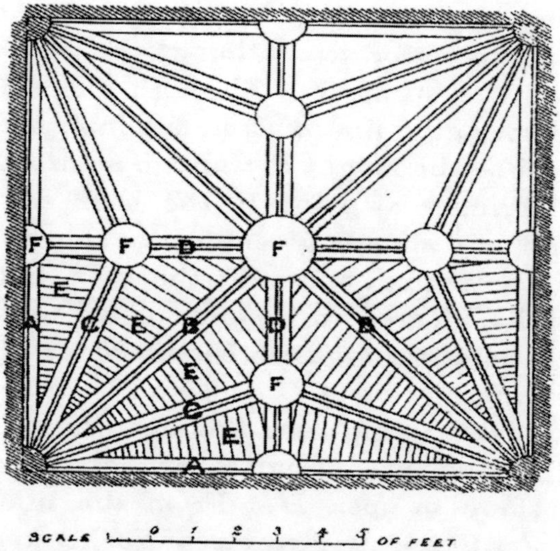

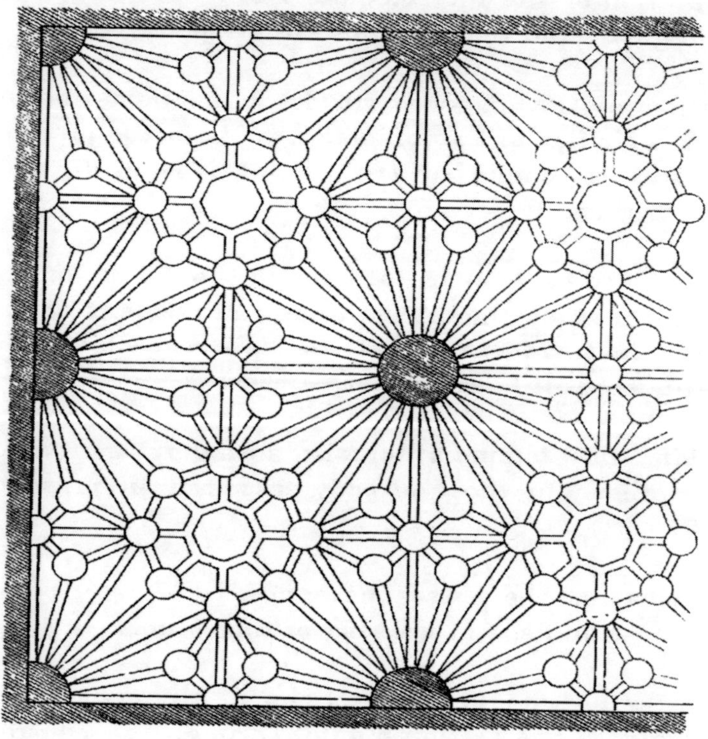

FIG. 8

Next find the point in the elevation of the wall rib, where the rib clears itself and separates from the springer. At *J* erect a perpendicular to the springing line *A B*, cutting the upper edge of the rib at *O*, in elevation, which is the point of separation of the rib, or where it is fully developed, and clears the springer. Through the same point *J* erect a perpendicular to the springing line *A C* on the intermediate rib, and set off the height *N P*, equal to the height of wall rib at *M O*. The intermediate rib thus clears the springer at point *P*, the back edge of rib at vaulting surface. Two points are already given in the curve of the intermediate rib, namely, at *R* the springing, and at *H* the apex, but a third is required. Now at point *P* describe an arc, with radius equal to the depth of the rib as at *O*, containing a point through which the curve of rib must be drawn. Commence on the springing line *A C*, and find by trial a centre, and draw the curve from *R* to touch or approach the arc, whose centre is *P*. Find a centre No. 2, and draw the curve from *R* towards the arc, and with centre No. 3 continue the curve to apex *H*. From the line of soffit gauge the width of members of rib, and with centres Nos. 2 and 3 draw the curves, forming the elevation of the intermediate rib. Care must be taken that the curves are regular, and that cripples are avoided.

The elevation of the diagonal rib is to be next obtained, and the method adopted is similar to the foregoing, or as in the preceding example, page 92. Centres are found by trial, as at Nos. 4, 5, and 6, and the curves drawn from them.

The next thing to be done is to arrange the joints of the springers, and the ribs, and these may be drawn to any convenient size. The joints of the ribs, above the springers, radiate to their respective centres, and the joints of the springers will have horizontal beds.

The moulds and templets for the springers are made, and the stones worked similarly to those already described in preceding example, pages 94, 96, 97.

The ridge ribs and the bosses have now to be described, for the purpose of making the moulds, and working of the stones.

Fig. 4.—Is the bed mould and sections of the central boss stone, *A* being the bed mould, *B* the section mould, through the centre of the boss, and curved ribs, and *C* is part section mould, through the centre of boss,

PLATE. XL.

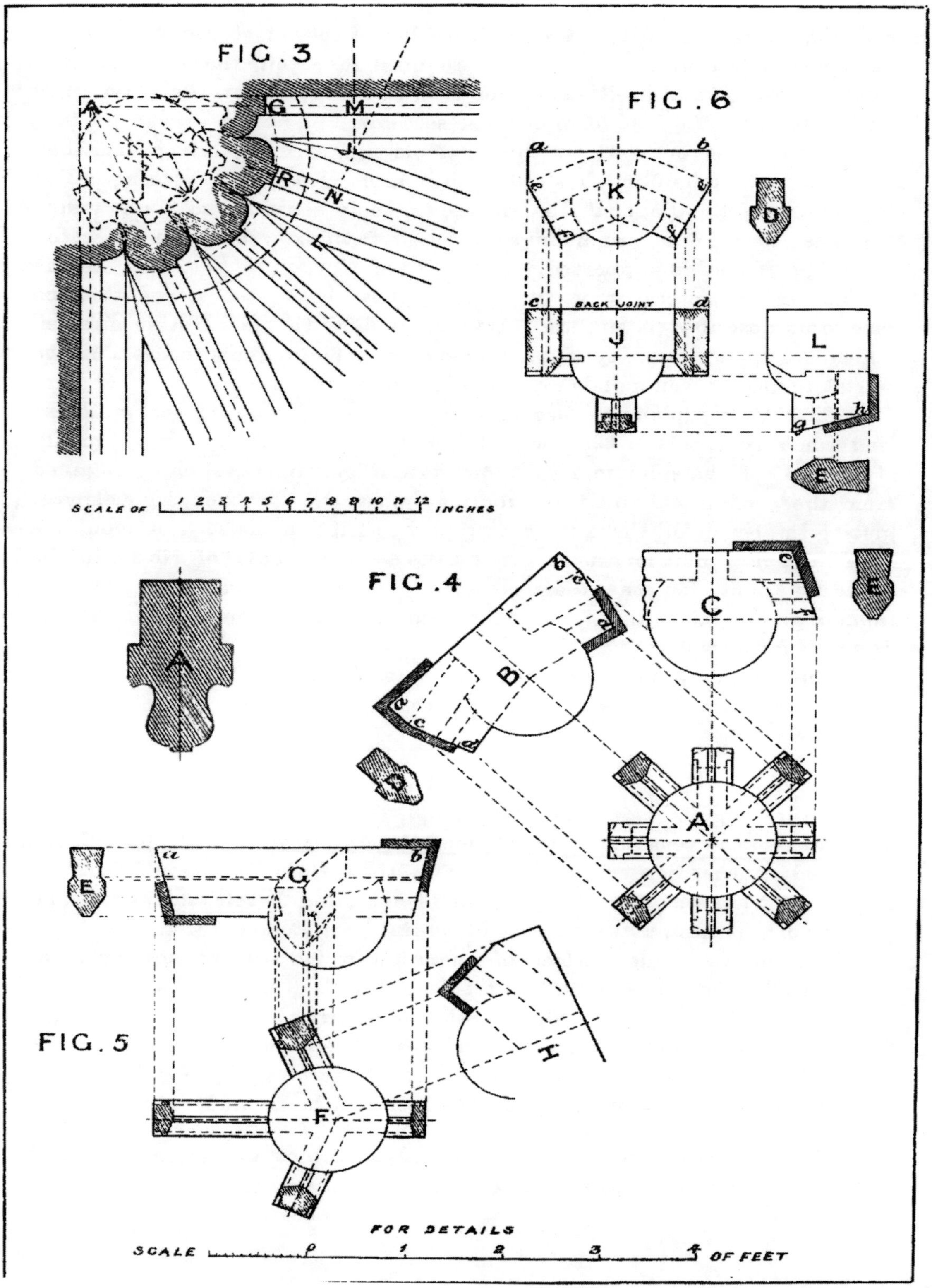
FIG. 3
A
G
M
J
R
N
L
SCALE OF 1 2 3 4 5 6 7 8 9 10 11 12 INCHES
FIG. 6
a
b
K
D
BACK JOINT
c
d
J
L
h
g
E
FIG. 4
A
B
C
D
E
FIG. 5
E
a
b
G
F
H
FOR DETAILS
SCALE 0 1 2 3 4 OF FEET

and ridge ribs. It will be seen that neither of these last two moulds can be applied direct on the stone, but are used to obtain the bevels of the joints, curvature and position of the ribs, and contour for the carving, as well as to shew the true form at those sections.

The stumps, or arms, in this example are perhaps longer than they need be, but are here emphasised to shew more clearly the working. The four joints of the diagonal ribs radiate to their centres, and form a key, the other four joints are arranged so as to form skew backs, upon which the ridge stones are supported.

There are several ways of working these boss stones, and the one now to be described is similar to that adopted by the old Gothic masons, which has also simplicity to recommend it. There must necessarily be waste of stone as well as labour, whatever method is chosen.

First form a plane surface of operation, as *a b* on the section *B*, so that when fixed, this bed is horizontal, and on this scribe in the bed mould *A*. Work off the splay joints *e f* to receive ridge, the bevel being obtained from the section *C*, and the radiating joints *c d*, for the diagonal ribs, getting the bevel for these from section *B*, scribe in the section mould of rib *E*, to splay joint for the ridge, and the section mould of rib *D*, to the radiating joint for the diagonal ribs. Now work the stumps and mouldings in against the boss, using templets made from section moulds *B* and *C* for guidance.

The boss may be shaped out and carved before fixing, or left rough from the point, and carved after fixing, the latter method being generally adopted.

Fig. 5.—Is the bed mould and sections of intermediate boss stone, and part of the ridge, *F* being the bed mould, *G* the section mould, through the centre of the boss and ridge rib, and *H* part section mould through the boss and intermediate ribs. Neither of these last two moulds can be applied, but are used for the purpose of obtaining bevels, curvature, and position of ribs, &c., as in the case of central boss stone (Fig. 4.)

First form a plane surface of operation, which will be horizontal, as *a b*, on the section *G*, and on this scribe in the bed mould *F*, then rough the stone out to shape and work off the joints, the bevels being obtained from the section moulds *G* and *H*, scribe in the section moulds *E*, for the ridge rib, and *D* for the intermediate ribs. Next work the ribs in against boss, and complete the mouldings; the boss may be treated as in Fig. 4.

Fig. 6.—Shews the bed mould, and also sections of key to ridge and wall ribs, *J* being the bed mould, *K* and *L* the section moulds.

First form a plane surface of operation, which is horizontal as *a b* on the section *K*, and on this scribe in the bed mould *J*, work off the vertical back joint *c d*, and scribe in the section mould *K*, and work the splay joints *e f* through for wall ribs. Next work the splay joint *g h*, by aid of bevel taken from the section *L*, and scribe in the section mould of ribs, cut ribs in against boss, and complete the mouldings. The boss may be treated as in Fig. 4.

In Fig. 3, at section *A*, the mouldings to ribs are shewn, but in the other figures these mouldings are represented by a chamfer, on account of the smallness of the scale to which they are drawn.

On the plan of the springing (Fig. 3), the letters are identical with those at the springing on the smaller scale (Fig. 2), in order that the reference to them may be more clear.

Fig. 7.—Shews a sketch of part of the vault.

Fig. 8.—The extent to which vaulting of a complicated nature may be carried out is shewn in the plan here given of part of the vaulting at the Members' private entrance, House of Commons.

The student may be reminded that the examples here given of groined vaulting deal only with a small portion of this intricate subject, but it is hoped that the general principles have been sufficiently illustrated, so as to enable him to deal with other cases as they come before him.

GROINED VAULTING

FIG. 7

SKETCH OF PART OF VAULT

Plates XLII., XLIII., XLIV., XLV., XLVI.— TRACERY WINDOWS.

Tracery Windows are of the most extensive variety, both in design and form, and require no little consideration and study on the part of the student. The correct carrying out of the designs for such works affords valuable evidence of the mason's skill.

Without going into the principles governing the composition and design of tracery, it may be remarked that, with few exceptions, geometrical tracery is based upon the combination of the equilateral triangle with the polygon and circle; and the examples here given will mostly illustrate this particular style.

In setting out tracery windows generally, commence by drawing the vertical centre line of window, then the springing line at right angles to the same, and set off the span, or opening, and draw segment line of the arch. Divide the span for small openings, and draw in the mullions. This may also be obtained from the plan if first drawn. Now draw in the construction lines for centres of tracery to the required design, care being taken that the curves must properly intersect with each other, or be drawn tangental, as the case may be. The mouldings which form the mullion, on taking a curved shape in the tracery, are termed monials.

Gauge on from the centre lines of tracery last drawn the width of monial, giving the lines of nosings, fillets, splays, &c., and complete the window by drawing the foliations, eyes, and cusps.

The joints of all tracery windows should be drawn in to radiating lines from the centres, by which the principal curves of monials are drawn; this is not always possible, but the rule should be borne in mind.

For the purpose of making the moulds, one half the window only is necessary to be set out.

Fig. 1.—Shews the constructional lines of completed window (Fig. 2). The equilateral triangle *A B C*, divided into four similar figures *d d d*,

TRACERY WINDOWS

FIG. 2

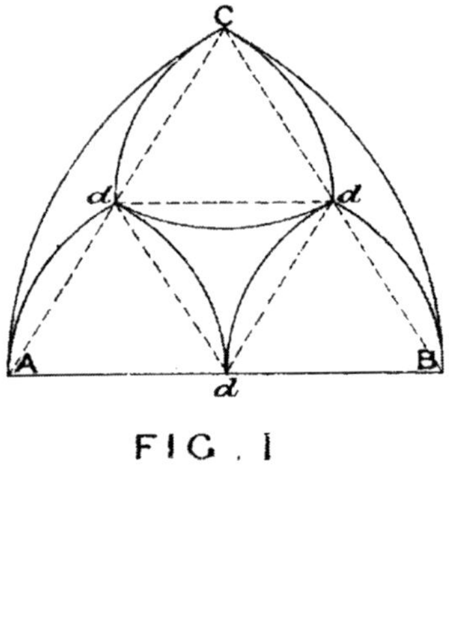

FIG. 1

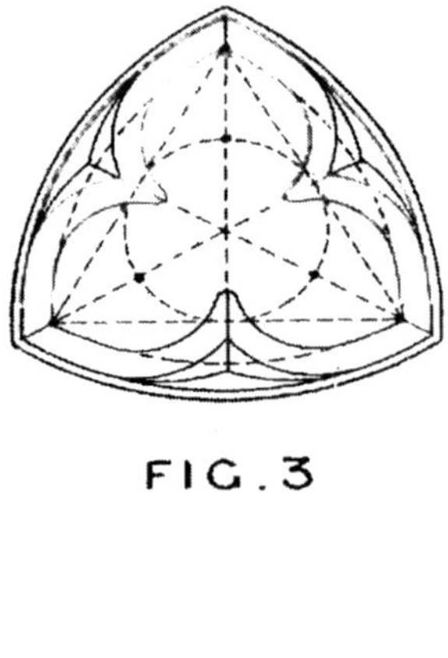

FIG. 3

TRACERY WINDOWS

FIG. 5

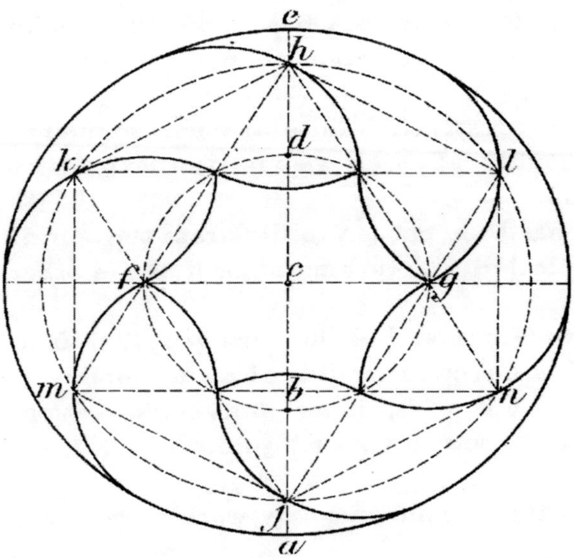

FIG. 4

gives the centres for the tracery. This is again exemplified in Fig. 3, which shews the trefoil, the centres of which are evident, and need no description.

Fig. 4.—Shews the constructional lines of circular window (Fig. 5).

To construct the figure, divide the diameter into four equal parts, as at *b c d e*, and with *c* as centre and *b* or *d* as radius, describe a circle, and inscribe a regular hexagon, intersecting with the opposite diameter at *f g*. The points of intersection will give one half of the centres of tracery.

On the diameter at *f g*, as a common base, construct the two equilateral triangles *f g h* and *f g j*, and with *c* as centre, and *h* or *j* the apex, as radius, describe a circle, and inscribe the hexagon *h j k l m n*, or produce the equilateral triangles, cutting the circles in these points. These give the other half of the centres, for completing the main lines of tracery.

Fig. 5.—Is the completed window, with foliations, eyes, and cusps, and label moulding.

It may be observed, that four face moulds, with a slight modification in two of them, will work all the tracery in this window.

Fig. 6.—Shews the elevation and part plan of window, the right-hand half in elevation, shewing constructional lines, and the left hand the completed half of window.

This will be understood without further instruction than is afforded by the illustration.

Fig. 7.—Shews the elevation and part plan of window, the right-hand half in elevation shewing constructional lines, and the left-hand the completed half of window.

The geometrical constructive lines are not so marked or apparent in this window, yet it has a purely geometrical expression, the trefoil and circle predominating.

This example has been chosen to illustrate the working of one of the stones, which is typical of the working of each of the others.

Fig. 8.—Shews face mould of the springer *A*, transferred from elevation (Fig. 7). *B B* are section moulds of main monials, *C* is section mould of mullion, or bottom bed, of springer, and *D* is section mould of small monial ; this applies to the two branch joints.

To work the springer, commence by working a plane, as a surface of

TRACERY WINDOWS

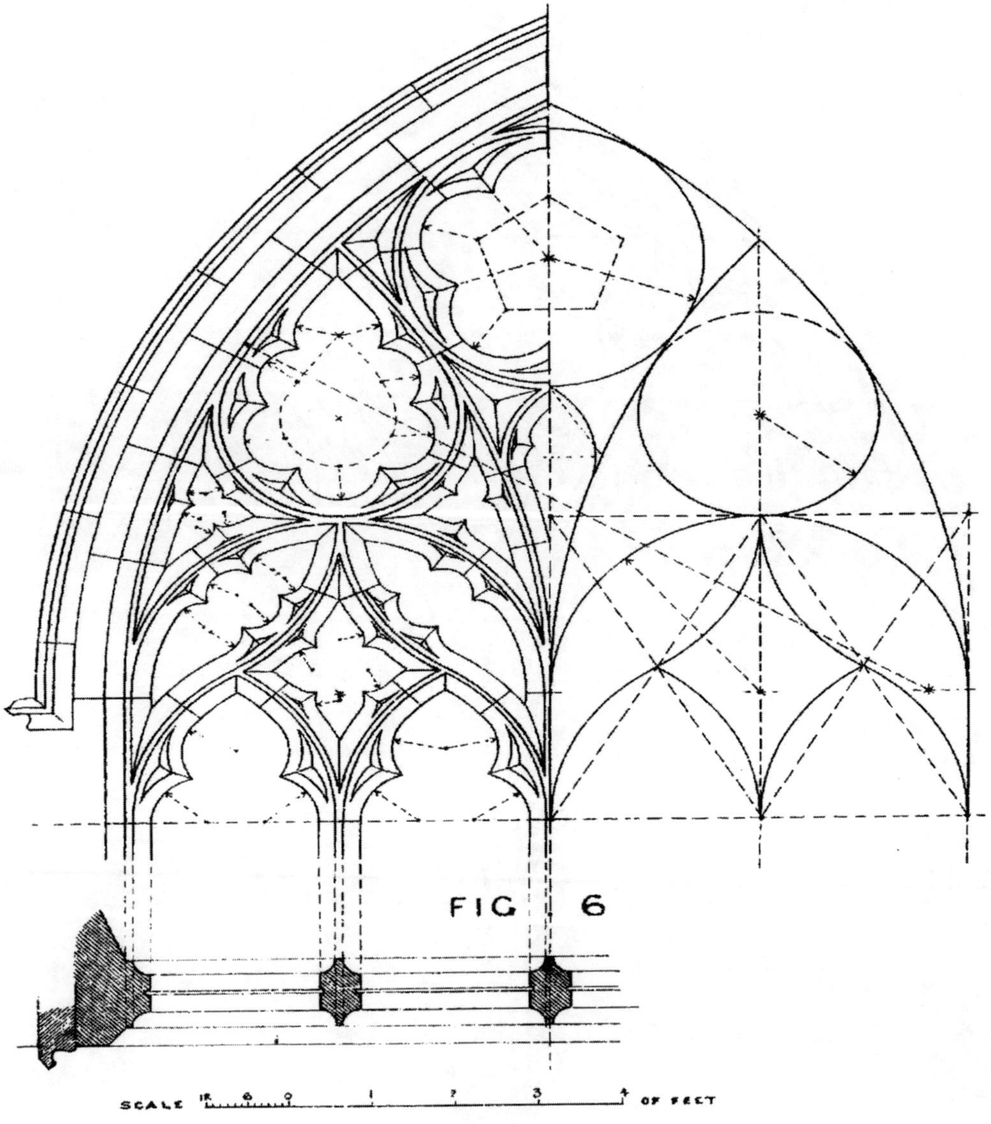

FIG. 6

TRACERY WINDOWS

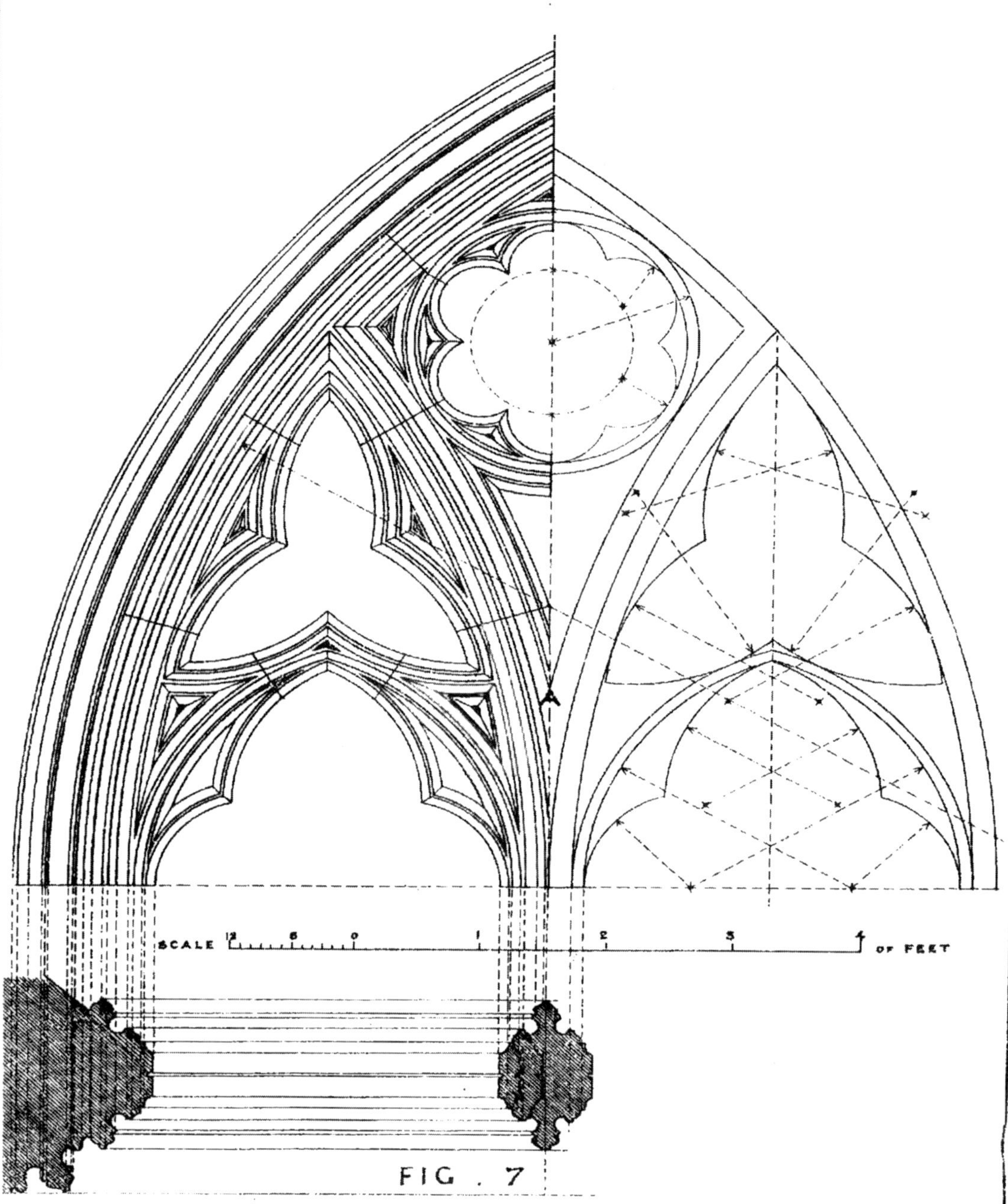

FIG. 7

operation, and on this scribe in the face mould *A*, marking-in the nosings *a a b* by the aid of a templet, the nosings being the only portion of the plane not cut away. Next point the stone roughly to shape of the face mould, and then take it to a parallel thickness, equal to the thickness of the section mould *B* or *C*. Now work the joints through square from the face, and scribe in joint moulds *B D* and *C* on their respective joints. Then work through the nosing *a a* and *b*, and boutel mouldings, and fillets, and sink down the whole of the remainder of face to lower nosing *c c c*, scribe in on each side of nosing the skeleton face mould (Fig. 9), and work the soffits through to shape. Sinkings are now made for the several mouldings, the eyes of cusps are pierced, and the stone finished to its correct shape, templets and reverses being used in guidance.

Fig. 9.—The using of the skeleton mould, here illustrated, saves the working through of the soffits, from the outside, or first surface of operation.

The section moulds for monials, in several cases, will require a little widening out, as at *D*, and these may be projected from the face mould. The reason for this is, that the joints are not always on a true sectional line.

Fig. 10.—Shews sketches of various examples of cusps, which require no explanation.

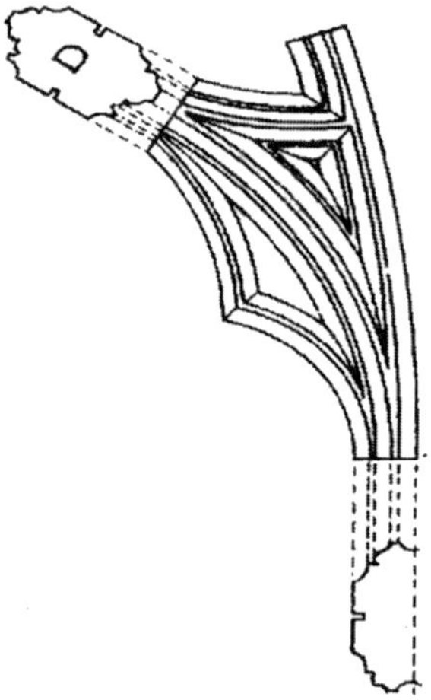

FIG. 9

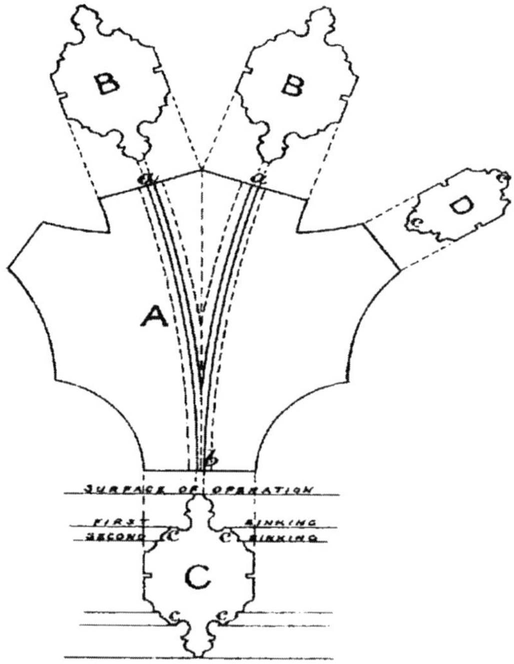

FIG. 8

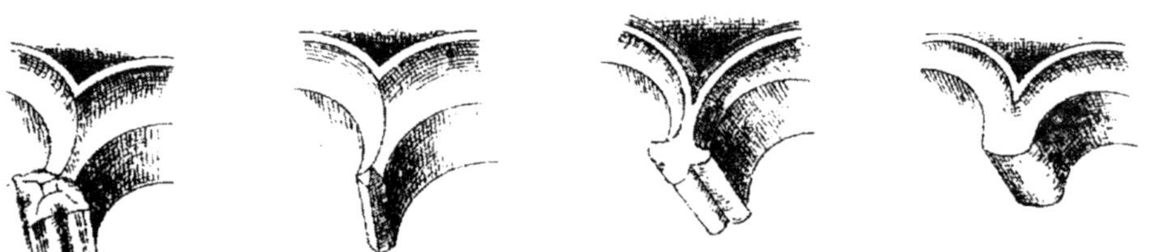

FIG. 10

SKETCH OF CUSPS

PLATES XLVII., XLVIII., XLIX., L.—GOTHIC MOULDINGS.

The profiles of mouldings here given are indications of the various styles or periods, and are of great interest to the student of Masonry, and also because they attest the working skill of the mason.

The characteristics generally of each period and the dates are briefly as follows :—

Norman, 1066 *to* 1189.

The mouldings consist chiefly of chamfers, round, and quarter round members, with shallow hollows, the edge roll or bead being the principal member. These are frequently entirely covered with ornament, such as the chevron or zigzag, the billet, the lozenge, the double cone, the star, the pellet, and others, producing great richness of effect.

Early English, 1189 *to* 1300.

In this period the mouldings are bold and deeply undercut, and generally arranged on rectangular planes; they are composed chiefly of the bowtell and keel members, with a combination of fillets and deep hollows of irregular curves, resulting in a beautiful effect of light and shade. The curves of these mouldings are easy and graceful, and are usually drawn by hand, the compasses being little used.

The principal ornament of these mouldings is the dog-tooth, which is greatly varied, and belongs exclusively to this style.

Decorated, 1300 *to* 1377.

The mouldings in this style are bold and well-proportioned, and arranged on rectangular as well as diagonal planes. The rounds and hollows are not so deeply cut as in the preceding style, the hollows being segments of circles, the deeper hollows being confined to the inner angles; the roll moulding, the quarter round, and wave moulding are also very much used in combination of the groups.

The ornament is chiefly the ball flower, of which there are several varieties, and the four-leaved or diaper flower; these are nearly as characteristic of the Decorated style as the tooth ornament is of the Early English.

Perpendicular, 1377 *to* 1547.

This style is characterized by mouldings which have large and shallow members, and generally a large hollow in the centre of each group, and arranged on diagonal planes. Another feature of this style is the constant use of beads of three-quarters of a circle and also flat wave mouldings; to this may be added the absence of fine detail.

The common ornaments are the Tudor flower, rose, and fleur-de-lys cresting, an example of the last-named being given on Plate 50.

GOTHIC MOULDINGS.

PROFILES OF GOTHIC MOULDINGS.

Norman Period, 1066 *to* 1189.

1 to 5. Cushion caps of various forms, principally from Peterborough Cathedral.

6 to 14. Bases, various.

15. Base from nave, Worksop Priory.

16. Arch mould from transept, Peterborough.

17. Arch and label mould from nave, Tutbury.

18. ,, ,, ,, Southwell.

19. ,, mould from transept, Peterborough.

20. ,, and label from mould nave, Worksop Priory.

21. ,, ,, ,, Wenlock Priory.

22. ,, ,, ,, transept, Peterborough.

23. ,, ,, with various enrichments.

24 to 29. Strings, various.

30. The sunk star ornament.

31. ,, billet ,,

32. ,, square billet ,,

33. ,, lozenge ,,

34. ,, double cone ,,

35. ,, chevron or zigzag.

36. ,, beakhead.

1A, 2A. Ornament in caps, Worksop Priory.

GOTHIC MOULDINGS

PLATE. XLVII.

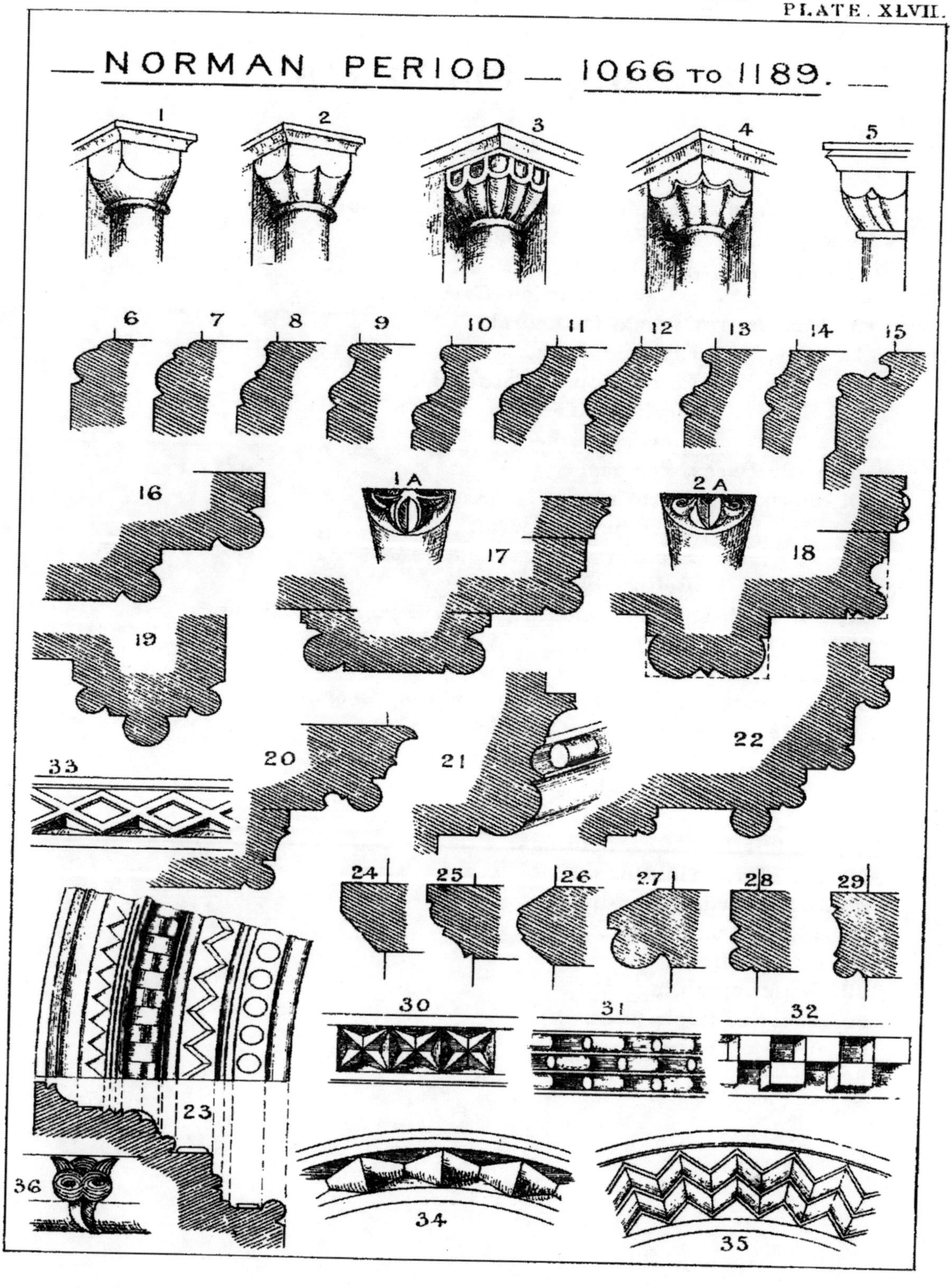

GOTHIC MOULDINGS.

Early English Period, 1189 to 1300.

1, 2, 3. Caps from Westminster Abbey, Triforium.
4 and 6. ,, ,, Bolton Abbey.
5, 7, 8. ,, ,, various.
9. ,, ,, from Carlisle Cathedral.
10. Base from Carlisle Cathedral.
11. ,, Ely ,,
12. ,, Peterborough Cathedral.
13. ,, Cowling, Kent.
14. ,, Lincoln Cathedral.
15 to 19. Bases, various.
20. Base from Warmington, N. Hants.
21. ,, Durham Cathedral.
22. ,, Lincoln ,, Arcade.
23. ,, Bolton Abbey.
24, 25. Arch and label moulds, Warmington, N. Hants.
26. ,, ,, Carlisle Cathedral.
27. Jamb mould.
28. Arch and label moulds, Warmington, Doorway.
29. Arch mould, Lincoln Cathedral, Arcade.
30. ,, Langham Church, S. Transept.
31. ,, Beaulieu, Hants.
32. ,,
33, 34, 35. Bowtell mouldings.
36, 37. Keel mouldings.
38 to 44. String mouldings, various.
45, 46. Rib mouldings.
47, 48. Mullion.
49. Scroll moulding.
50. Roll and triple fillet.
51. Dog-tooth ornament.
52. Crocket ,,

— EARLY — ENGLISH — PERIOD — 1189 TO 1300 —

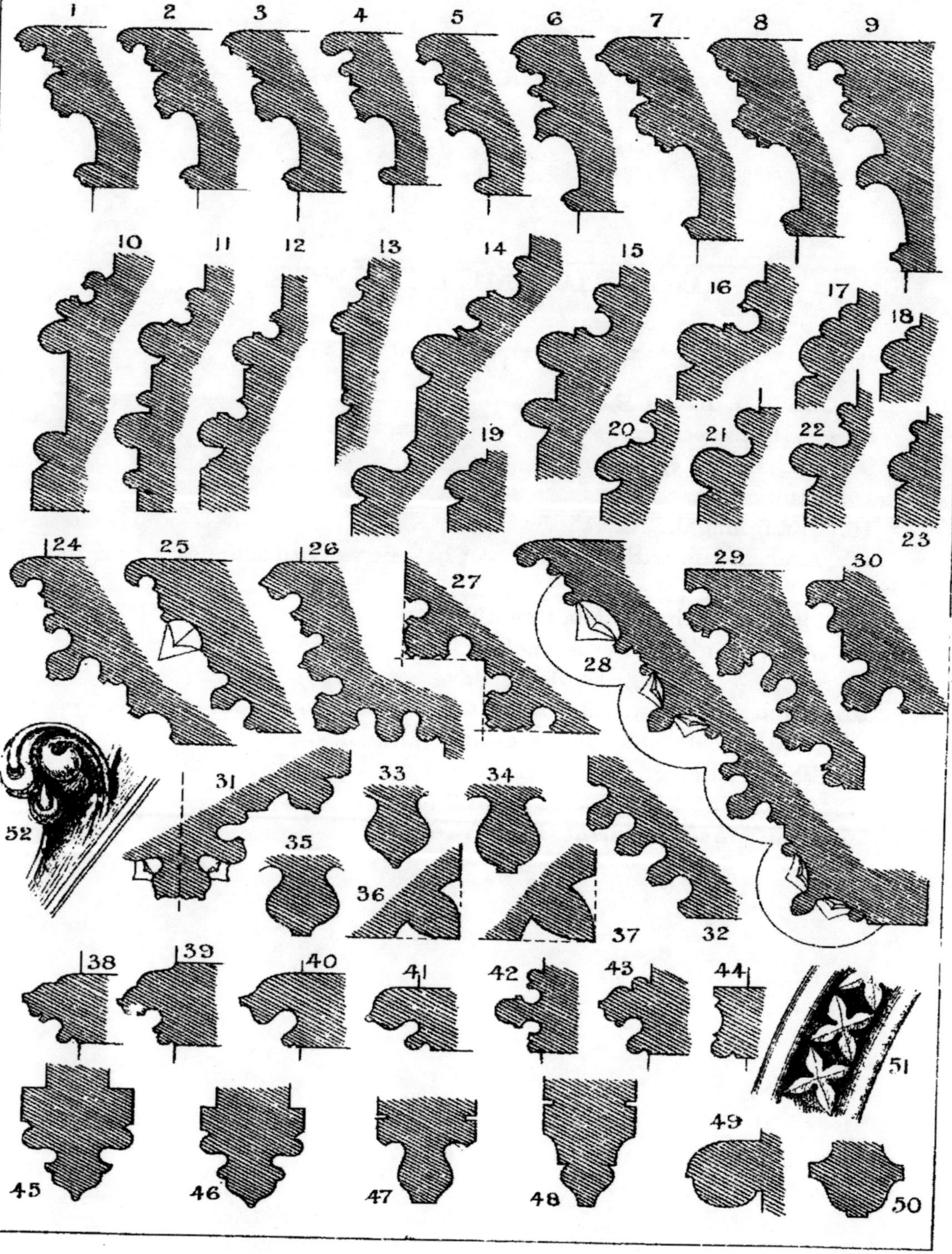

GOTHIC MOULDINGS.

Decorated Period, 1300 *to* 1377.

1. Cap from Irthlingborough.
2 to 8. Caps, various.
9 to 14. Bases, various.
15. Mullion.
16. Jamb mould.
17. Arch mould with ornament of ball flower and four-leaved or diaper flower.
18, 19, 20. Arch and label moulds.
21. Arch mould from Lichfield, Choir.
22. ,, ,, ,, Stafford, Nave.
23. Jamb ,, ,, Holbeach Church, Lincolnshire.
24 to 30. String and label moulds, various.
31. Triple filleted roll.
32 to 35. Varieties of wave mouldings.
36. Ball-flower ornament, three varieties.

DECORATED PERIOD — 1300 TO 1377

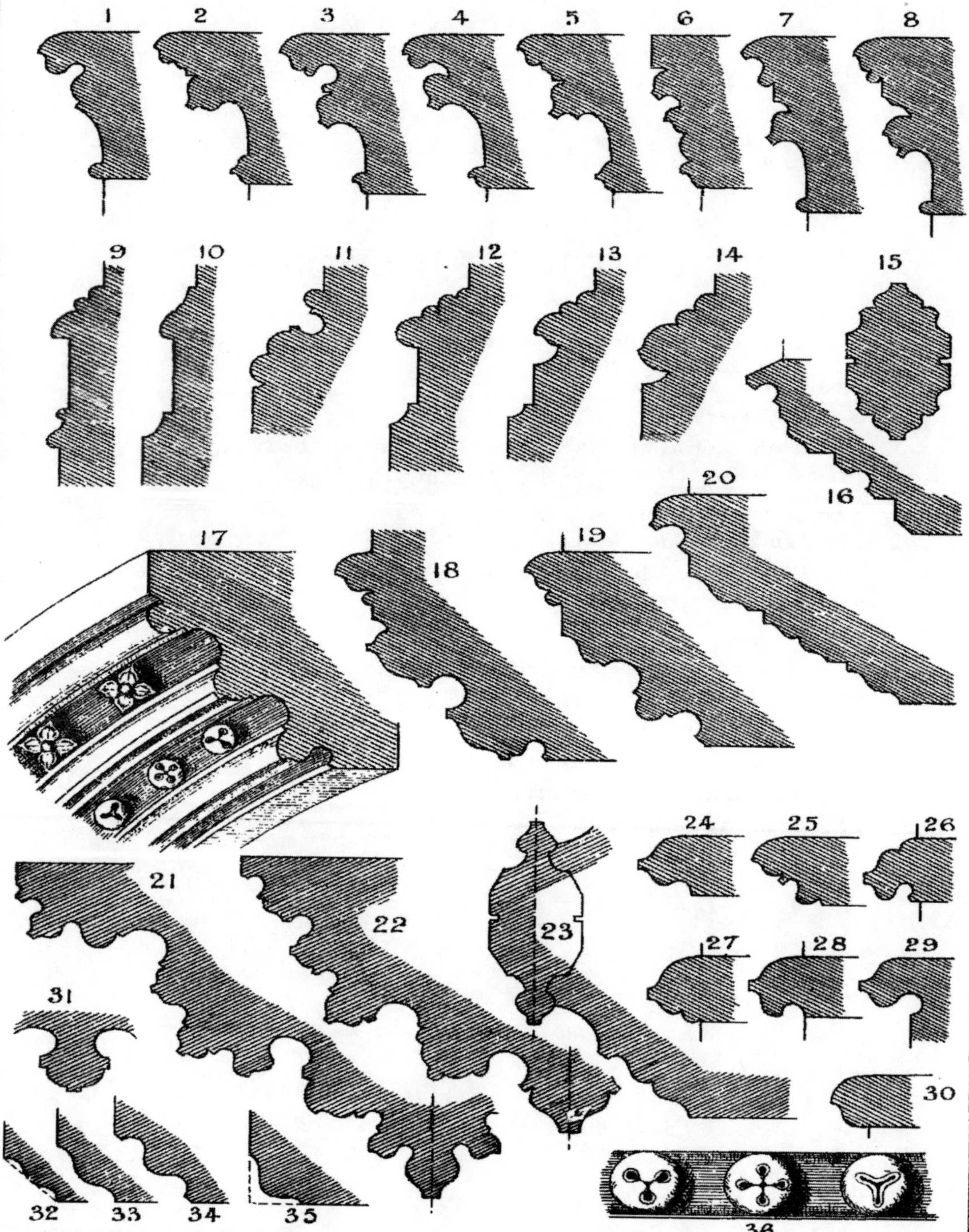

GOTHIC MOULDINGS.

Perpendicular Period, 1377 *to* 1547.

1 to 7. Caps, various.
8 to 15. Bases, ,,
16. Arch mould and label from Chester Cathedral.
17. ,, ,, Newark, Nave.
18. ,, ,,
19. Jamb mould.
20. Pier ,, from St. Stephen's Cloisters, Westminster.
21. Wave moulding.
22. ,, ,,
23. Mullion, St. Stephen's Cloisters.
24. Rib moulding ,, ,,
25. Buttress moulding.
26 to 33. Strings and labels, various.
34. Sill mould, Christchurch.
35. Cresting ornament.

PLATE. L.

PERPENDICULAR PERIOD 1377 TO 1547

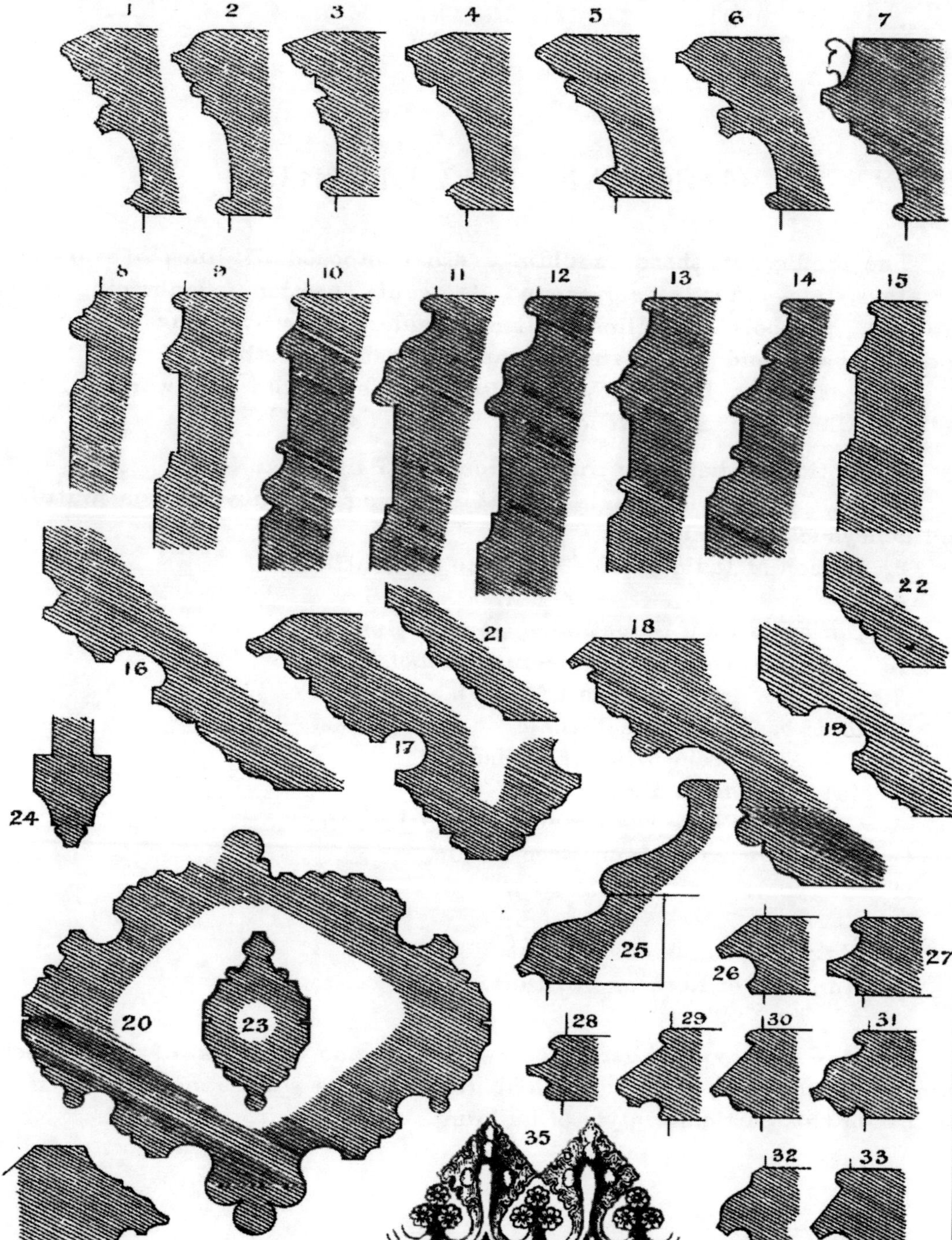

GRECIAN MOULDINGS.

The profiles of these mouldings are composed of lines of varying curvature, and mostly correspond to conic sections, embracing the hyperbola, parabola, and ellipse. It is considered, however, that they were drawn by hand, and not obtained by any mechanical method.

The examples here shown are taken chiefly from the works of Sir William Chambers and Inwood.

1. Section of the Doric cornice from the Parthenon.
2. Plan of external angle of ditto, looking up, showing the mutules and honeysuckle enrichment.
3. Section of Ionic cornice from the Erectheium.
4. ,, ,, ,, ,,
5. Doric cap from Samothrace (Hyperbola).
6. ,, from the Theseum (Parabola).
7. ,, from Selinus (Ellipse).
8. Ionic base from the Temple on the Ilyssus.
9. ,, from Minerva Polias.
10. ,, from Prienne.
11. Corinthian base from Monument of Lysicrates.
12. Capital of Antæ from Erectheium.
13. ,, ,,
14. ,, ,,
15. Egg and tongue enrichment.
16. Annulets or neckings to Doric caps.

Note.—It may be here observed that the columns of the Greek Doric have no base, but are planted direct on the square step which is a feature of this particular style of building.

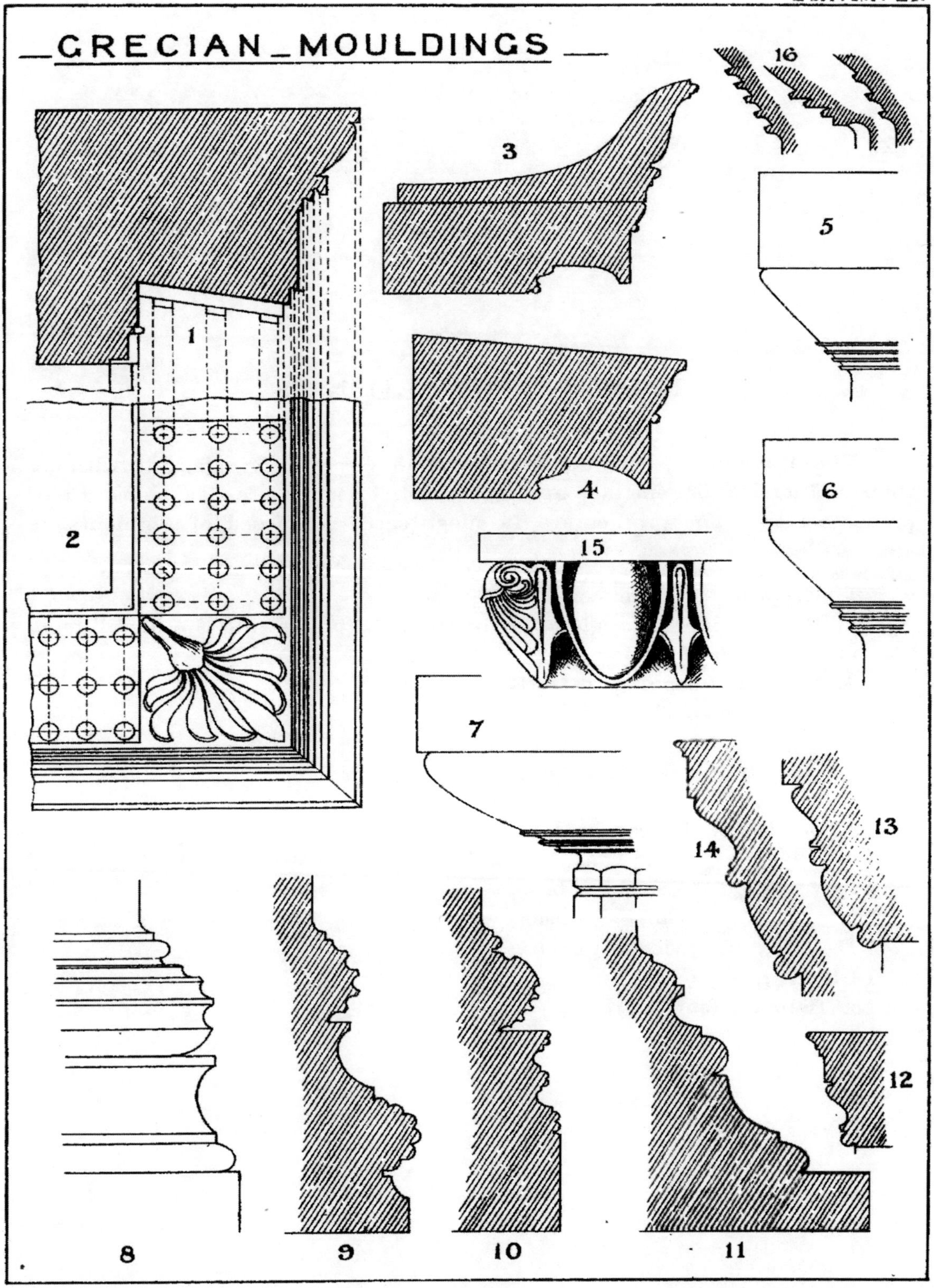
GRECIAN MOULDINGS
1
2
3
4
5
6
7
8
9
10
11
12
13
14
15
16

ROMAN MOULDINGS.

These mouldings are all derived from Greek originals, but without their refinement of outline, and in artistic beauty are far below their predecessors. The profiles are in most cases composed of segments of circles.

1. Elevation of Doric cornice.
2. Plan of external angle of ditto, looking up, showing the modillions.
3. Elevation of Doric cap.
4. Section of capping to Doric pedestal.
5. Section of Architrave.
6. ,, ,,
7. Section of pedestal capping.
8. ,, ,,
9. Section of Tuscan base.
10. ,, Doric base.
11. ,, Corinthian base.
12. ,, Composite base.
13. ,, pedestal plinth.
14. ,, ,,
15. Baluster (enriched).
16. ,,
17. ,,

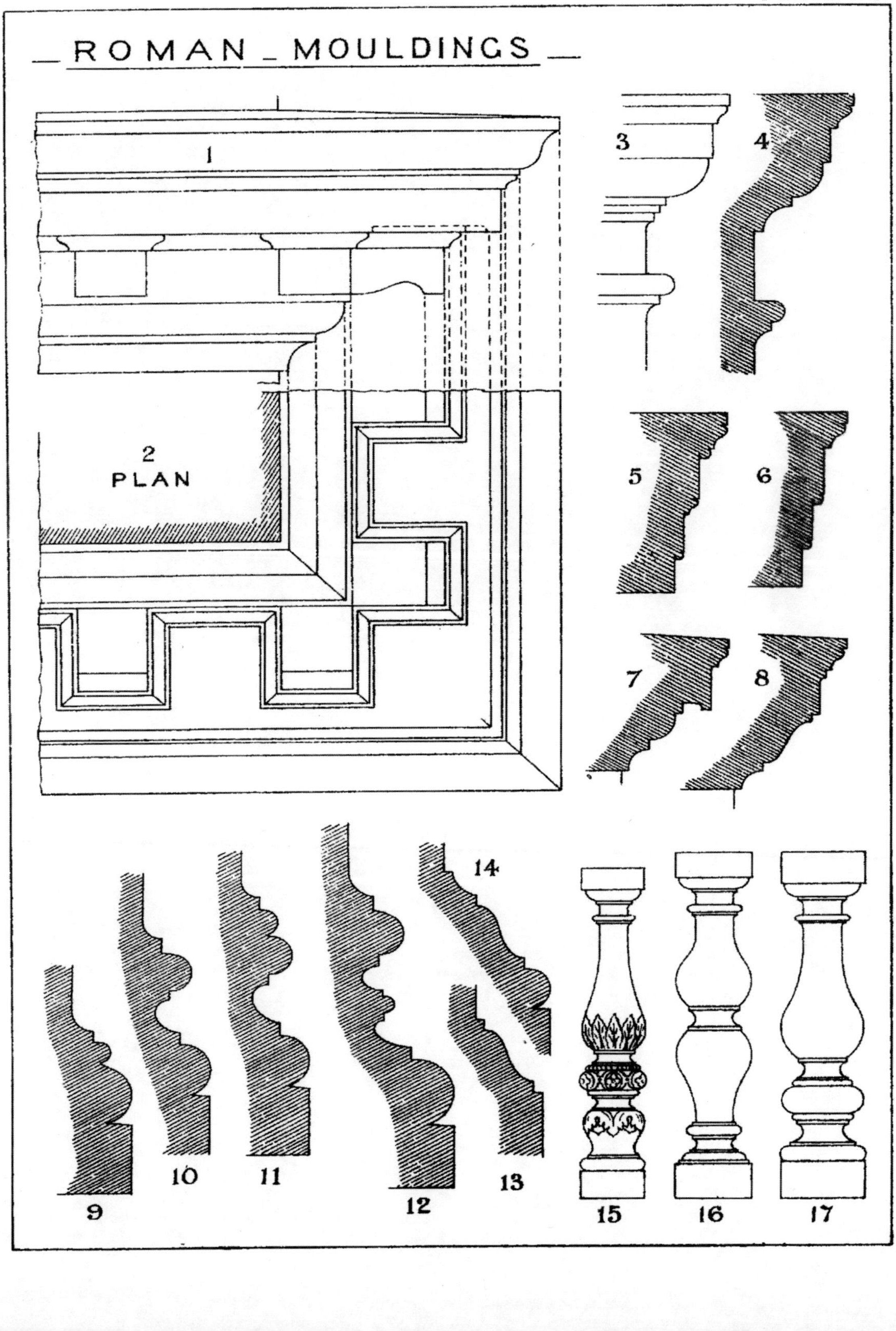
ROMAN MOULDINGS
1
2
PLAN
3
4
5
6
7
8
9
10
11
12
13
14
15
16
17

MASONRY ESTIMATING AND QUANTITY SURVEYING.

K

MASONRY ESTIMATING AND QUANTITY SURVEYING.

Estimating.—In regard to measuring and estimating the values of masonry, it will be necessary to state, by way of preliminary, a few particulars which are essential to good and sound estimating.

The advantage to the mason in estimating for his own trade is, that he knows the various processes the stone has to go through, together with the different labours. In order to do this in the proper way, he should be well versed in the science of construction as applied to buildings, and competent to read any drawing; and it will be better still if he be also qualified to prepare any detail drawing in connection with the work, as by this means he will be able to discover any particulars that relate to the practical working of the stone, which otherwise might escape his notice. Again, the more thorough the mason is as a draughtsman, the more thorough he is as an estimator.

The first step in connection with estimating, after the drawings have been consulted, is to carefully read and digest the specification, and to ascertain if there is any hidden work which is not shown on the drawings—in other words, where to expect and where to look for all stonework not clearly shown or described. The mason should also know how the stonework butts against the different materials, the various notchings, rebates, &c., against girders, brick, wood, &c.; and in general he should satisfy himself that he understands from the requirements of the drawings and specifications exactly how the stonework should be cut and set in the wall.

Next, but not least, is the mathematical qualification necessary for the mason, which in general is simply arithmetical, although there are times when his knowledge of practical geometry, as well as plane trigonometry, will help him to advantage. Lastly, a neat and methodical way of "taking off quantity" should be cultivated, and also to figure the various items correctly from such data as may be obtained from the shop records of labour, which consist of a series of ascertained values of actual work done. When there is any intricate or new work to which the shop records have no reference, the mason's practical experience and judgment will enable him to determine the values, and thus the approximate cost may be obtained.

It should also be remembered that, to be successful in estimating, it is necessary above all to have order and method, and in the cultivation of these gifts the mason is in the right way of becoming master of the principles of his craft, in this particular branch.

Quantity Surveying.—There is perhaps a greater diversity of opinion as to the proper system to be adopted in estimating for stonework than is to be found in any other branch of the building trade. This arises from the fact that masonry generally is in itself very complex, and that no two buildings are alike in style, material, or finish. These differences of systems, however, are being gradually narrowed down by custom and usage, and one might almost say that the only difference—certainly the greatest—is the description of the labour on stonework.

At one time half-sawing was taken on all the six sides of the cube, and any labour expended on these sides or faces was added; but now, what is called the "London system" of measuring being generally adopted, half-sawing is ignored except for the back of the stone built into the wall, it being assumed that all other labours include the price of sawing.

According to Leaning,* another method is to take out the stone including labour, and to divide it into a few main items, each composed of stone upon which the labour is similar, and giving sketches to the more ornate parts, as "stone and labour in chamfered jambs"; "ditto in moulded ditto"; "ditto in chamfered plinths, and strings"; "ditto in arcading," &c.

Yet another method, instead of wading through the quantities, is to work out an average block of each kind of work upon the other and more correct system, and reduce the cost thus found to a set of prices "per cubic foot." This is a somewhat haphazard way of estimating, and not to be recommended. It may save time and facilitate progress, but it is equally undeniable that it is as uncertain in results as careless in process.

The method, therefore, adopted here is to measure net the cubical block of stone, and take all the labours upon it separately; this is known as the "London system."

* "Quantity Surveying for the use of Surveyors, Architects, Engineers, and Builders."

In taking off quantities, it is essential to take them in the following order, viz., length, breadth, and depth (height). This plan will invariably prevent confusion, and it also admits of after-identifications of dimensions if necessary.

In measuring cube stone per foot cube, the stone is measured the net size of a rectangular block, which just encloses the finished stone. When any fraction of an inch occurs, call it another inch, as for instance 1 ft. $4\frac{3}{4}$ in. by $11\frac{1}{2}$ in. by $9\frac{1}{2}$ in. should be called 1 ft. 5 in. by 1 ft. 0 in. by 10 in.

Add to the price of the stone the labour of setting, hoisting, and scaffolding per foot cube; and so describe.

State in all cases how stonework is finished, whether tooled, chiselled, rubbed, dragged, combed, &c.

If stone is hoisted to a height of 40 ft. it is kept separate, and so stated, and also in heights of 20 ft. above same, as 40 ft. to 60 ft., 60 ft. to 80 ft., etc.

This course is sometimes modified, as when a well-defined line occurs a little under or over the limit; the height, however, should be stated.

All stonework up to 3 in. in thickness is taken by the foot super, and all labours on same described.

If any of the stones are above 6 ft. in length, take the cubical contents and call it scantling.

Beds and Joints per foot super are described as "one face measured for two."

It is usual to take a bed and a joint to each stone, which will be equal to half-bed or joint on four out of the six surfaces of the block—that is, the top, bottom, and two sides. Sometimes beds and joints and preparatory faces are omitted, and the stone described as including all plain beds and joints, and preparatory faces. When this course is adopted every other labour is measured as it finishes.

If the drawings do not indicate the joints, as in cornices, strings, plinths, capping, &c., take a joint to every 3 ft. in length.

An average of beds and joints to each cubic foot of stone is in Modern Classic $1\frac{1}{2}$ ft. super; Gothic, 2 ft. super.

The labour to back of stone is generally described as half-sawn or drafted and measured by the foot super.

Sunk Beds and Joints per foot super, described as "all measured," are taken to all beds and joints, when sunk below the general surface.

Circular Beds and Joints per foot super, described as "all measured," are taken to all beds and joints, when sunk below the general surface, as in arch stones, and may be either concave or convex. The extrados and intrados of an ordinary arch are an illustration.

Circular Sunk Joint per foot super, described as "all measured." These are joints sunk below the circular face, as in the reveals and rebates of arches; when stopped, state so and keep it separate.

Plain Face or Plain Work per foot super. When dressed to an even finished surface, either tooled, rubbed, or dragged as may be required; this includes also preparatory faces, as to tracery windows, &c.

Sunk Face per foot super, taken to all faces below the general surface, as in panels, weatherings, &c. When the sinking cannot be worked straight through the stone it is called "Sunk face stopped."

Sunk face not exceeding 3 in. wide is measured per foot run and the width stated.

Rough Sunk Face per foot super is taken to the general surface of all mouldings over 3 in. below the general surface.

Circular Face per foot super, and describe as "all measured," is taken to surfaces that are convex, as in shafts of columns, &c.; state if stopped, and keep separate.

Circular Face Sunk per foot super, and describe as "all measured," to all surfaces that are concave, such as soffits of arches, &c.; state if stopped, and keep separate.

Circular Circular Face per foot super, and describe as "all measured," to all surfaces that are circular on plan and elevation, such as convex surfaces of domes, spheres, &c.; state if stopped, and keep separate.

Circular Circular Face Sunk per foot super, and describe as "all measured," to the concave surfaces of domes or niche heads; state if stopped, and keep separate.

Moulded Work per foot super, and describe as "all measured"; taken to the profiles of all mouldings in strings, cornices, caps, and bases, &c. Girth the mouldings to get at the superficial area.

Mouldings not exceeding 6 in. in girth, measure per foot run and state girth. Mitres in mouldings to be numbered; these are sometimes taken (for pricing) as equal 1 ft. run of the moulding to which they belong.

Where mitres occur in mouldings, measure to the extreme length of the nosing for running length.

Mouldings not exceeding 9 in. in length, take as short lengths and keep separate.

Stopped Ends, numbered, stating girth of moulding.

Ashlar is sometimes measured per foot super; state average thickness and how the face is finished, whether rubbed, tooled, chiselled, or dragged; if bond stones state their size, the proportion of bond stones to the area of wall face, also that the ashlar includes all labours to beds and joints. When backed up by brickwork, state it, and keep brickwork separate and describe as extra only in backing to stone ashlar.

The other method is to measure the stone by foot cube, and all labours separately per foot super, as before described.

Bosting, per foot super, where over 6 in. girth. This is the preparatory or rough dressing in outline for carving.

Carving. The value of this so much depends upon the ornate quality of the work, that it is usual to obtain an estimate from the carver.

Measure spandrel steps (when two are cut out of one block) the extreme width from the nose of the tread to the acute end of the angle by half the riser, taking from top of tread (front of nosing) to the acute end of angle downward.

When the stooling is left on the end for pinning into the wall, the steps must be measured solid.

Measure winders the extreme length, including the wall hold, by the mean width and by the whole height.

The labour to spandrel steps may be taken as plain work to tread and soffit, sunk moulded work to riser and quoin per foot super, rebates (front and back) at per foot run, mitres numbered.

When the soffits are moulded the girth must be taken, and described as sunk moulded work.

The soffit of winders to be taken as circular sunk face.

Landings per foot super; measure the length and the width, adding the bearing on the walls; state the thickness, and whether tooled or rubbed on one or both sides; measure the cutting and pinning into walls by the foot run; if above 30 ft. super in one stone state such, and keep separate, being more valuable.

Window Sills per foot run; measure the lengths, giving the width and thickness; state if quarry-worked, tooled, rubbed, or sunk, and if throated.

Coping per foot run; collect the lengths; state the thickness and width, and whether tooled or rubbed, if parallel, feather-edged or saddle back, and if throated; also if bedded in mortar or cement.

Curbs per foot run; measure the lengths, state the size and how worked; number all mortises for iron railing and standards, giving the size and depth.

Dentils to cornices, numbered, with the sizes and spaces between each; state whether fixed in a level or raking line; number the enriched pendants to angle dentils, giving the sizes, with sketch.

Balusters moulded, numbered, give size, description, and sketch; state if turned or worked square; number the mortises, with sizes and depths.

Consoles, numbered, give proper description of the moulded fronts, caps, &c.; state the enrichments, give the size and sketch.

Capitals to pilasters and columns (carved), to be numbered; give the sizes with full description of the moulded and enriched parts, and sketch.

Rebate, or moulding not exceeding 6 in. girth, per foot run.

Throat per foot run.

Joggles, state what kind, per foot run.

Chamfer, not exceeding 3 in. wide, per foot run.

Groove for flashings, per foot run.

Groove for lead lights, and pointing in cement on both sides, per foot run.

Holes and perforations, numbered, stating size and thickness of stones.

Mortises and Dowels, numbered, and state if copper, gun-metal, lead, iron or pebble dowels, and if run in cement, or sulphur, &c.

Cramps, numbered; state if in copper, gun-metal, slate, or iron; give size and weight.

Chimney-pieces. Usually a provisional sum is allowed, otherwise they are numbered, stating size of opening, width of jambs and shelf, and how finished, if flat or boxed, and whether stone or marble.

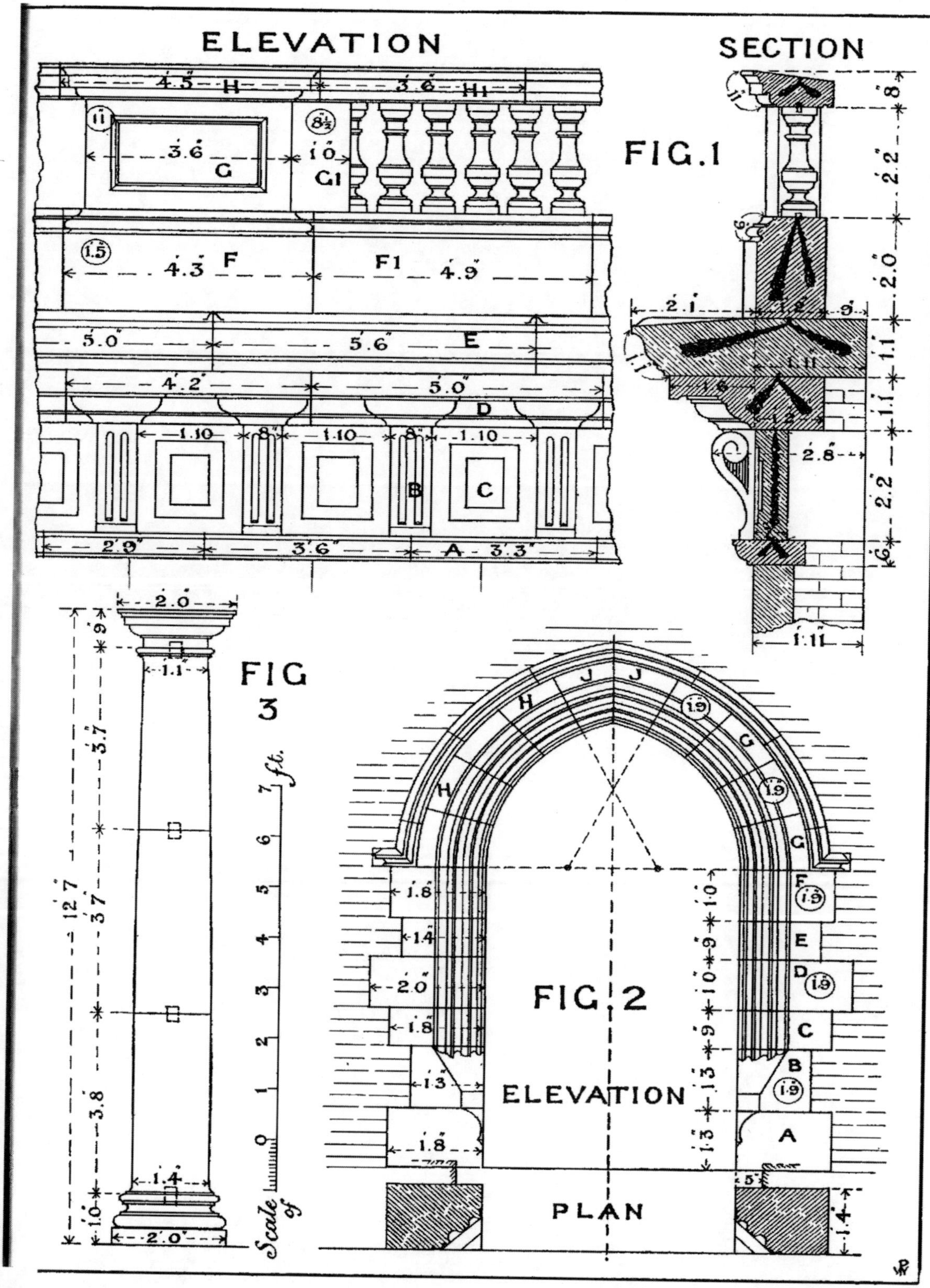
ELEVATION
SECTION
FIG.1
FIG 3
Scale of ft.
FIG. 2
ELEVATION
PLAN

EXAMPLES OF TAKING OFF QUANTITIES.

Abbreviations.

These should only be used (where well understood by frequent use) in dimensions and abstracts, and not in bills.

B.	Bed
B. & J.	Bed and joint
C.	Cube
Cir.	Circular
Cir. B. & J.	Circular bed and joint
Cir. F.	Circular face
Cir. F. S.	Circular face sunk
Ddt.	Deduct
Dia.	Diameter
Lab.	Labour
Mo. F.	Moulded face
P. F.	Plain face
P. F. S.	Plain face sunk
R.	Run
R. S. F.	Rough sunk face
S.	Superficial
S. F.	Sunk face
S. B. & J.	Sunk bed and joint.

MAIN CORNICE AND BALUSTRADE.—Fig. 1.

	Dimensions	Quantity		Description	
	9 6 1 3 6	6 0	Cube.	Portland stone.	**A** *String.* 3 3 3 6 2 9 9 6
	9 6 1 3	12 0	Super.	Bed.	
	9 6 6	4 9	S.	Half-sawing.	*Back.*
3/	1 3 6	1 10	S.	Joint.	
3/	6	1 6	Run.	V. joggles and cement grout.	
	9 6 4	3 2	S.	Plain face and ddt. bed.	
	9 6 8	6 4	S.	Moulded face.	
4/	8 2 8 2 2	15 5	C.	Portland stone.	**B** *Consoles.*
4/	2 8 8	7 1	S.	Bed.	
4/	2 8 2 2	23 1	S.	Joint.	
4/	1 9	7 0	R.	V. joggles and cement grout.	
4/	8 2 2	5 9	S.	Half-sawing.	*Back.*
4/	8 2 5	6 5	S.	Cir. face.	*Front.*
8/	2 0 1	16 0	R.	Flutings, 1 in. by $\frac{3}{4}$ in. deep, stopped top and bottom.	

Times	Dimensions	Squaring		Unit	Description	Notes
8/	10 2 2	14	5	S.	Scroll and fluting and ddt. half joint.	*Side.*
3/	1 10 7 2 2	7	0	C.	Portland stone.	**C** *Panels.*
3/	1 10 7	3	2	S.	Bed.	
3/	7 2 2	3	9	S.	Joint.	
3/	1 9	5	3	R.	V. joggles and cement grout.	
3/	1 10 2 2	12	0	S.	Half-sawing.	*Back.*
3/	1 2 1 6	5	3	S.	Sunk face, ¾ in. deep.	*Panel.*
3/	8 1 0	2	0	S.	Sunk face, ¾ in. deep.	*Centre panel.*
	9 2 2 8 1 1	26	6	C.	Portland stone.	**D** *Cornice bed mould.* 5 0 4 2 9 2
	9 2 2 8	24	5	S.	Bed.	
2/	2 8 1 1	5	9	S.	Joint.	
2/	1 6	3	0	R.	V. joggles and cement grout.	
	9 2 1 1	10	0	S.	Half-sawing.	*Back.*
	9 2 6	4	7	S.	Plain face.	*Front.*
3/	1 0 1 4	4	0	S.	Rough sunk face.	*Moulding.*
4/	1 4 9	4	0	S.	Rough sunk face.	*Moulding.*
4/	1 6 11	5	6	S.	Moulded face in short lengths.	

3/	1 9 11	4 10	S.	Moulded face in short lengths.	
8/	7 11	4 3	S.	Moulded face in short lengths.	
No. 16.				Mitres.	8 *extl.* 8 *intl.*
3/	10 6	1 3	S.	Plain face sunk.	*Soffit.*
	9 2 3	9 2	R.	Throating.	
	10 6 4 0 1 1	45 6	C.	Portland stone.	E *Top bed cornice.* 5 6 5 0 10 6
	10 6 4 0	42 0	S.	Bed.	
2/	4 0 1 1	8 8	S.	Joint.	
2/	3 0	6 0	R.	V. joggles, pebbles and cement grout.	
	10 6 1 1	11 4	S.	Half-sawing.	*Back.*
	6 3 2 1	13 0	S.	Plain face sunk, stopped ends.	*Weathering.*
	4 3 1 10	7 9	S.	Plain face sunk, stopped ends.	*Weathering.*
	3 11	3 11	R.	Saddle joint.	2 1 1 10 3 11
	10 6 1 1	11 4	S.	Moulded face.	*Moulding.*
	4 3 1 5 2 0	12 0	C.	Portland stone.	F *Plinth under die.*
	4 3 1 5	6 0	S.	Bed.	
	1 5 2 0	2 10	S.	Joint.	

	3 0	3 0	R.	V. joggles and cement grout.	
	4 3 3 6	14 10	S.	Plain face.	*Back* 2 0 *Front* 1 6 3 6
	4 3 9	3 2	S.	Moulded face.	*Front.*
2/	3 9	5	S.	Moulded face, in short lengths.	*Returns.*
No. 4.				Mitres.	2 *extl.*, 2 *intl.*
	4 9 1 2 2 0	11 1	C.	Portland stone.	**F 1** *Plinth or blocking.*
	4 9 1 2	5 6	S.	Half bed.	
	1 2 2 0	2 4	S.	Joint.	
	3 0	3 0	R.	V. joggles and cement grout.	
	4 9 1 0	4 9	S.	Plain face.	*Top.*
	4 9 3 6	16 8	S.	Plain face.	*Front and back.*
	4 9 9	3 7	S.	Moulded face.	*Moulding.*
	3 6 11 2 2	6 11	C.	Portland stone.	**G** *Die.*
	3 6 11	3 2	S.	Bed.	
	11 2 2	2 0	S.	Joint.	
	2 6	2 6	R.	V. joggles and cement grout.	
	3 6 4 4	15 2	S.	Plain face.	

2/	3 2 2	1 1	S.	Plain face and ddt. half joint.	*Margin.*
	2 3 1 2	2 7	S.	Plain face sunk.	*Panel.*
	4 0	4 0	R.	Ovolo moulding, 2 in. girth.	*Panel.*
No. 4.				Mitres.	*2 extl., 2 intl.*
	1 4 9 2 2	2 2	C.	Portland stone	**G 1** *Half baluster and die.*
	1 4 9	1 0	S.	Bed.	
	0 9 2 2	1 7	S.	Joint.	
	2 6	2 6	R.	V. joggles and cement grout.	
	2 8 2 2	5 9	S.	Plain face.	*Front* 1 4 *and back* 1 4 2 8
	9 2 2	1 7	S.	Plain face.	*Preliminary face.*
	2 2	2 2		Moulded circular face, stopped to half baluster.	
No. 5/	7 7 2 2	3 8	C.	Portland stone, turning and labour to moulded balusters.	
No. 10.				3 in. by 1 in. by 1 in. slate dowels, mortises and cement grout.	
	3 6 1 5 8	3 3	C.	Portland stone.	**H 1** *Capping.*
	3 6 1 5	5 0	S.	Plain face sunk.	*Weathering.*
	3 6 11	3 3	S.	Plain face.	*B. bed.*
	1 5 8	11	S.	Joint.	

	1 3	1 3	R.	V. joggles and cement grout.	
	3 6 11	3 3	S.	Moulded face.	*Front.*
	3 6	3 6	R.	Throating.	
	4 5 1 8 8	4 11	C.	Portland stone.	**H** *Capping to die.*
	4 5 1 3	5 6	S.	Half bed.	*Bottom.*
	1 8 8	1 1	S.	Joint.	
	1 3	1 3	R.	V. joggles and cement grout.	
	4 5 1 5	6 3	S.	Plain face sunk.	*Weathering.*
	4 5 3	4 5	R.	Plain face and ddt. joint.	*Weathering.*
	4 5 6	2 3	S.	Plain face.	*Back.*
	4 5 11	4 1	S.	Moulded face.	*Front.*
2/	3 11	6	S.	Moulded face, in short lengths.	*Return.*
	4 5	4 5	R.	Throating.	
No. 4.				Mitres.	2 *extl.* 2 *intl.*

ABSTRACT OF THE FOREGOING.

Cube. Portland Stone.	Super. Half-Sawing.	Super. Beds.	Super. Joints.	Super. Plain Face.	Super. Plain Face Sunk.	Super. Moulded Face.	Super. Circular Face.	Run. Throat.	Run. V. Joggles and Cement Grout.
6 0	4 9	12 0	1 10	3 2	4 7	6 4	6 5	9 2	1 6
15 5	5 9	7 1	23 1	14 10	1 3	11 4		3 6	7 0
7 0	12 0	3 2	3 9	4 9	7 9	3 2		4 5	5 3
26 6	10 0	24 5	5 9	16 8	2 7	3 7		17 1	3 0
45 6	11 4	42 0	8 8	15 2	5 0	3 3			6 0
12 0	43 10	6 0	2 10	1 1	6 3	4 1	Super. Moulded Circular Face Stopped to Half Baluster.	Run. Flutings, 1 in. by ¾ in.	3 0
11 1		3 2	2 4	5 9	13 0	31 9			3 0
6 11		1 0	2 0	1 7	5 3				2 6
2 2		98 10	1 7	3 3	2 0		2 2	16 0	2 6
3 8			11	2 3	47 8				1 3
3 3			1 1	68 6					1 3
4 11			53 10						36 3
144 5									
	Super. Ddt. Joint.	Super. Half Bed.	Super. Ddt. Half Joint.	Super. Ddt. Bed.	Super. Rough Sunk Face.	Super. Moulded Face in Short Lengths.	Super. Scroll and Flutings.	Run. Saddle Joint.	Mitres.
	1 1	5 6	14 5	3 2	4 0	5 6	14 5	3 11	No. 16
		5 6	1 1		4 0	4 10			4
		2)11 0	2)15 6		8 0	4 3	Run. Ovolo Moulding, 2 in. Girth.	Run. Plain Face, 3 in. wide.	4
		5	7 9			5			4
					No. 5. Balusters.	6			28
						15 6	4 0	4 5	

No. 10.—3 in. by 1 in. by 1 in. Slate Dowels, Mortises, and Cement Grout.

THE ABSTRACT PUT INTO BILL FORM AND PRICED.

Ft.	in.			@		£.	s.	d.
144	5	Cube	Portland stone, including waste, hoisting from 40 ft. to 60 ft. above street level, scaffolding, and setting	3*s*.	6*d*.	25	5	6
43	10	Super.	Half-sawing		4*d*.		14	8
101	2	,,	Beds, as one face measured for two		10*d*.	4	4	4
45	0	,,	Joints, as one face measured for two	1*s*.	0*d*.	2	5	0
68	6	,,	Plain face	1*s*.	2*d*.	3	19	11
47	8	,,	Plain face sunk	1*s*.	6*d*.	3	11	6
8	0	,,	Rough sunk face		6*d*.		4	0
31	9	,,	Moulded face, all measured	2*s*.	6*d*.	3	19	5
15	6	,,	Do. do. in short lengths	3*s*.	0*d*.	2	6	6
2	2	,,	Moulded circular face stopped to half baluster	6*s*.	6*d*.		14	1
6	5	,,	Circular face, all measured	1*s*.	6*d*.		9	8
14	5	,,	Scroll and flutings to consoles	3*s*.	3*d*.	2	6	10
4	0	Run	Ovolo moulding, 2 in. girth in panel		9*d*.		3	0
17	1	,,	Throating, 2 in. girth		3*d*.		4	3
16	0	,,	Flutings, 1 in. by $\frac{3}{4}$ in. deep		4*d*.		5	4
3	11	,,	Saddle joint, 4 in. girth		9*d*.		3	0
4	5	,,	Plain face, 3 in. wide		4*d*.		1	6
36	3	,,	V. joggles and cement grout		9*d*.	1	7	2
No.	5		Labours to balusters	3*s*.	0*d*.		15	0
No.	28		Mitres to mouldings, 10 in. girth, average	2*s*.	6*d*.	3	10	0
No.	10		3 in. by 1 in. by 1 in. slate dowels, mortises, and cement grout		6*d*.		5	0
						£56	15	8

DOORWAY.—Fig. 2.

Times	Dimensions	Squared	Description	
2/	1 8 1 4 1 3	5 7	Cube. Red Mansfield stone.	**A** *Plinth.*
2/	1 8 1 4	4 6	Super. Bed.	*Top and botton*
2/	1 8 1 3	4 2	Half joint.	*Back.*
2/	1 4 1 3	3 4	Half joint.	*Ends.*
2/	1 8 1 3	4 2	Plain face.	*Front.*
2/	1 4 1 3	3 4	Plain face.	*Side.*
No. 1.			Stop 10 in. girth.	
2/	1 3 1 9 1 3	5 4	Cube. Red Mansfield stone.	**B** *Jamb.*
2/	1 9 1 3	4 4	Super. Bed.	*Top and botton*
2/	1 9 1 3	4 4	Half joint.	*Ends.*
2/	10 1 3	2 1	Sunk joint.	*Reveal.*
2/	10 1 3	2 1	Half-sawing.	*Back.*
2/	1 3 1 4	3 4	Plain face.	*Side.*
2/	1 3 1 3	3 1	Plain face.	*Front.*
2/	11 1 0	1 10	Sunk face in short lengths.	*Splay.*

2/	5 4	4		Plain face.	
No. 1.				Stopping moulding on to splay 18 in. girth.	

NOTE.—The jambs may be averaged, as, for instance, C is 1 ft. 8 in. long and E is 1 ft. 4 in., the average being 1 ft. 6 in.

4/	1 6 1 4 9	6 0	Cube.	Red Mansfield stone.	*Jambs.* C *and* E
4/	1 6 1 4	8 0	Super.	Bed.	
4/	1 4 9	4 0		Half joint.	*Against brickwork.*
4/	1 6 9	4 6		Half joint.	*Back.*
4/	1 2 9	3 6		Plain face.	*Front and side.*
4/	9 1 6	4 6		Moulded face in short lengths.	
4/	1 10 1 9 1 0	12 10	Cube.	Red Mansfield stone.	*Jambs.* D *and* F
4/	1 10 1 9	12 10	Super.	Bed.	
4/	1 9 1 0	7 0		Half joint.	*Against brickwork.*
4/	10 1 0	3 4		Sunk joint.	*Reveal.*
4/	2 3 1 0	9 0		Plain face.	*Front and side.*
4/	1 6 1 0	6 0		Moulded face.	
4/	1 4 1 4 1 2	8 3	Cube.	Red Mansfield stone.	G *Arch stones.*

Times	Dimensions	Squared	Unit	Description	Note
4/	1 4 1 3	6 8	Super.	Sunk joint, V. joggles and cement grout.	
4/	1 4 1 3	6 8		Joint.	
4/	1 4 1 2	6 3		Circular sunk joint.	*Extrados.*
4/	1 4 1 2	6 3		Half joint.	*Back.*
4/	6 1 2	2 4		Plain face.	*Front.*
4/	6 10	1 8		Circular face sunk.	*Soffit.*
4/	1 6 1 2	7 0		Moulded face circular.	
4/	1 4 1 9 1 2	10 11	Cube.	Red Mansfield stone.	**H** *Arch stones.*
4/	1 9 1 3	8 9	Super.	Sunk joint, V. joggles and cement grout.	
4/	1 9 1 3	8 9		Joint.	
4/	1 9 1 2	8 2		Circular sunk joint.	*Extrados.*
4/	1 2 10	3 11		Circular sunk joint.	*Reveal.*
4/	9 1 2	3 6		Plain face.	*Back.*
4/	6 1 2	2 4		Plain face.	*Front.*
4/	6 10	1 8		Circular face sunk.	*Soffit.*
4/	1 2 1 6	7 0		Moulded face circular.	
2/	1 4 1 4 1 2	4 2	Cube.	Red Mansfield stone.	**J** *Keys.*

2/	1 4 1 3	3 4	Super.	Joint.	*Preparatory joint.*
2/	1 4 1 3	3 4		Sunk joint, V. joggles and cement grout.	
2/	1 4 1 3	3 4		Joint.	
2/	1 4 1 2	3 2		Circular sunk joint.	*Extrados.*
2/	1 4 1 2	3 2		Half joint.	*Back.*
2/	6 1 2	1 2		Plain face.	*Front.*
2/	6 10	10		Circular face sunk.	*Soffit.*
2/	1 6 1 2	3 6		Moulded face circular.	
6/	2 0 9 6	4 6	Cube.	Red Mansfield stone.	*Label.*
6/	9 6	2 3	Super.	Sunk joint.	*Radiating.*
6/	9 6	2 3		Joint.	
6/	2 0 6	6 0		Circular sunk joint.	*Extrados.*
6/	1 10 6	5 6		Circular sunk joint.	*Intrados.*
6/	1 10 7	6 5		Moulded face circular.	
2/	1 2 10 9	1 6	Cube.	Red Mansfield stone.	*Kneelers.*
2/	9 4	6	Super.	Sunk joint.	*Radiating.*
2/	11 6	11		Sunk joint.	*Extrados.*

Times	Dimensions	Squaring		Description	Remarks
2/	11 6	11		Sunk joint.	*Intrados.*
2/	8 6	8		Half bed.	
2/	10 7	1 0		Moulded face circular.	
2/	6 7	7		Moulded face.	
No. 4. No. 2.			Mitres. Stopped ends.		*2 intl. 2 extl.*

COLUMN.—Fig. 3.

Times	Dimensions	Squaring		Description	Remarks
	2 0 2 0 1 0	4 0	Cube.	Portland stone.	*Base.*
	2 0 2 0	4 0	Super.	Bed.	*Top and bottom.*
4/	2 0 6	4 0		Plain face sunk.	*Square plinth.*
	6 3 11	5 9		Moulded face circular continuous.	
4/ ½	1 0 1 0	2 0		Sunk face stopped.	*Top of square plinth.*

Note.—This item may also be described as Portland stone, turning and labour to circular base, with square plinth.

Dimensions	Squaring		Description	Remarks
1 6 1 6 3 8	8 3	Cube.	Portland stone.	*Bottom stone.*
3 8 6 0	22 0	Super.	Half-sawing.	4/ 1 6 6 0
1 6 1 6	2 3		Bed.	
4 2 3 6	14 7		Circular face sunk to swelled and diminished shaft.	
4 9	4 9	Run.	Hollow and fillet 2 in. girth.	

Times	Dimensions	Quantity	Unit	Description	Side notes
	1 4 1 4 3 7	6 4	Cube.	Portland stone.	*Middle stone.*
	5 4 3 7	19 1	Super.	Half-sawing.	4/ 1 4 5 4
	1 4 1 4	1 9		Bed.	
	4 0 3 7	14 4		Circular face sunk to swelled and diminished shaft.	
	1 3 1 3 3 7	5 7	Cube.	Portland stone.	*Top stone.*
	5 0 3 7	18 0	Super.	Half-sawing.	4/ 1 3 5 0
	1 3 1 3	1 7		Bed.	
	4 0 3 5	13 8		Circular face sunk to swelled and diminished shaft.	
	4 0		Run.	Astragal nosing, 2 in. girth.	

NOTE.—The three stones in column may be taken as turning and labour to shaft of column.

Times	Dimensions	Quantity	Unit	Description	Side notes
	2 0 2 0 9	3 0	Cube.	Portland stone.	*Cap.*
	2 0 2 0	4 0	Super.	Plain face.	*Top.*
	2 0 2 0	4 0		Half bed.	
4/	2 0	8 0	Run.	Moulding in short lengths, 4 in. girth.	*Abacus.*
	4 6	4 6		Moulding circular continuous 6 in. girth.	
4/½	11 11	1 8		Sunk face, stopped.	*Soffit of cap.*
No. 4.				Mitres, 4 in. girth.	
No. 4.				Slate dowels 2 in. by 2 in. by 4 in., mortises and cement.	

The last two examples of "taking off" (Figs. 2 and 3) are not abstracted or billed, but simply given to illustrate the method adopted, and although each job will vary in character, the system as shown will always be the same. When once the mason has thoroughly mastered this, however complex the work may be, he will be able to apply his knowledge and obtain a correct result.

In the foregoing section an endeavour has been made to explain in some degree the clerical work with which the mason, in estimating, should also make himself familiar.

Abbreviations have not been used except in Fig. 1, in which a column has been set apart for cube, super, and run. Although it is sometimes done in this way, it is more often shown as in Figs. 2 and 3, the dimensions in themselves showing whether they are cube, super, or run.

The mason is a methodical man, who has been instructed, from his apprenticeship in the first instance, how to hold the chisel and to use the mallet with the greatest possible effect, so that every stroke tells, with the result that in carrying out work the most complicated piece or section of masonry is completed within a given time readily estimated beforehand, and with a nice exactitude that leaves nothing more to be required. The mason stamps his banker mark upon the block, and it then takes its seat in the crutch of a groin or crown of a dome with perfect composure.

BUILDING STONES.

BUILDING STONES.

THE importance of choosing a good building stone for durability is well known, but unfortunately too little attention is generally given to the selection of the stone in order to obtain a perfect structure. Yet, however careful the selection may be, it should be borne in mind that there are no stones of any kind, whether they are the hardest and most intractable of the syenites or granite, or the softest lime or sandstone, that are not perishable in a greater or lesser degree in the course of time.

The physical forces and agencies, within and without, which produce this effect are apparently invisible, although always present, each working in its own way, with the same result, that the stones begin to disintegrate and gradually fall away into dust.

A high authority has observed that "in modern Europe, and particularly in Great Britain, there is scarcely a public building of recent date which will be in existence a thousand years hence. Many of the most splendid works of modern architecture are hastening to decay in what may be justly called the infancy of their existence, if compared with the dates of public buildings that remain in Italy, in Greece, in Egypt, and the East" (Gwilt's "Encyclopædia").

Should this be true, it is a serious outlook, and it is therefore obvious that the mason should have a full and accurate knowledge of the general structure of rocks, as well as of the situations where the best materials may be obtained, the composition of the stone he uses, and the destructive agencies that it will have to face, so as to direct his choice in the selection of particular stones, and enable him to estimate the advantages to be gained from their proper application for building purposes.

He should also know whether the material is good or poor, whether it is perfectly adapted for the particular work he has in hand, how it should be handled to produce the best results and fulfil the conditions of economy, utility and good workmanship.

It should not be forgotten that a bad selection of stone cannot be rectified when once used in a building, and is a lasting testimony to want of care and experience, and that a good selection remains a permanent record for posterity.

In order to identify a good stone, the mason must use his powers of observation. Examine carefully a building which has stood the wear of time, and which is subjected to a similar atmosphere to that of the proposed new building; note its general appearance and its condition as to soundness; should tool marks be visible, they can generally be accepted as a good sign.

Next find out where the stone was quarried, examine carefully the various beds in the quarry, and from what stratum the stone has been obtained; note the weathering of exposed surfaces in the older portion of the quarry, and learn which part is liable to decay first, and the conditions under which it does so.

Take every precaution to ensure getting the stone from a sound and compact bed, and one that is easily wrought and convertible.

It should, however, be recollected that most building stones last longest in the particular locality in which they are found; and that the same quality of stone which stands well externally in the neighbourhood of the quarry, ofttimes goes rapidly to decay when fixed in another part of the country.

Chemical tests and analyses, to determine the quality of a building stone for durability, are admitted by practical men to be somewhat unreliable. The processes which are successful in the laboratory of the chemist are generally of little value when brought into practical use; for chemical analysis will only give the constituents, and microscopical analysis the physical construction of a stone; and neither has as yet been proved to have any direct relation to its weathering quality.

And although stones have been subjected to severe tests in the laboratory—such as being dissolved in various acids, saturated with salts, ground into semi-transparent discs, disintegrated, pulverized, baked and boiled, and treated in various other fashions—yet none of these processes have as yet furnished sufficient data by which a correct judgment or estimate can be formed as to the weathering properties of any stone.

This is perhaps a sweeping assertion to make, but a striking illustration of its truth has been furnished in no less important a case than the new Houses of Parliament at Westminster, erected (1839 to 1860) to replace the buildings destroyed by fire in 1837, a sufficient time having now elapsed to enable one to form a judgment from actual experience as to the weathering qualities of the stone used. And one may say that, since the Houses of Parliament were erected, little (if any) advance has been made in chemical investigation of the properties of building stones.

Before building operations upon the new Houses were commenced, a Royal Commission was appointed in 1838, comprising eminent chemists, geologists, and others, who were instructed to visit the principal quarries in England and Scotland, and to report and advise as to the most suitable stone to be adopted for the projected new building. "Bolsover," a magnesian limestone, was selected by the Commissioners, and finally approved after being subjected to chemical and other tests. The building having been commenced and a large amount of that stone used, it was found that there was not a sufficient quantity to be obtained in the required time, and the Bolsover stone was therefore abandoned. A similar stone was, however, selected of the same class, named "Anston." This after being chemically tested was considered rather better than the first selection, and was used until the final completion of the building.

The stones selected proved, however, to be quite unsuitable for the purpose, being ill-adapted to withstand the deleterious influence of the surrounding atmosphere, and the result is that this splendid building is fast going to decay; thousands of pounds have already been spent on restorations and "preservative" solutions, but these efforts have failed to arrest the rapid decomposition that is taking place. It is a serious matter to contemplate what will be the condition of the building after it has stood a few more score of years.

Great things were expected of this Royal Commission, its appointment being the first step with a scientific purpose which the Government of the country had ever taken in respect of practical building; the result, however, as regards the selection of a suitable stone has (as we have seen) been disappointing to a degree. There can be little doubt that had three or four experienced and intelligent masons been added to the Commission, a far better stone would have been recommended; for it was well known at the time to observant masons that magnesian limestones of a similar structure to that selected were liable to rapid decay in the atmosphere of cities and towns, charged as it is with moisture, smoke, and deleterious gases.

In the foregoing remarks there is no wish to depreciate or disparage the true value of tests by chemical analysis, but rather the contrary. These, however, should be confined to ascertaining the constituent or component parts of the stone; its cementing material; the absorption of water, which gives a fair indication of the power of a stone to resist rain and frost; the subjecting of the stone to a freezing temperature and ascertaining the weight lost from the sample; the microscopic test, which is useful in determining the homogeneity of its structure, and others.

With regard to the crushing strength of stone, this is always in excess of requirements, and is to be considered as unimportant.

It should, however, be stated that there is no detail in connection with stone that the mason should not be familiar with. By this means he will be able to remedy defects in existing work, suggest improvements, and build to greater advantage for the future.

The following characteristics are therefore important to be remembered and weighed in the choice of a building stone :—

Weathering properties.
Seasoning.
Appearance.
Porosity and absorption.
Natural bed.
Facility for working.
Compactness and weight.
Agents of destruction.

Weathering.—The weathering power of a stone is dependent upon its physical structure, its composition, and the nature of the atmosphere in which it is placed. The most destructive agent that the stone has to contend against is rain, or a moist atmosphere.

The air of towns is charged in a greater or lesser degree with carbonic acid, and in manufacturing towns it also contains quantities of hydrochloric and sulphuric acids. These acids are dissolved by the rain, which penetrates the stone more or less according to its physical structure, and combines with the constituents of the stone, causing it to ultimately crumble away.

A stone which may be sufficiently durable when laid beneath water, as in piers of bridges, docks, quay walls, &c., may not be so when kept alternately wet and dry by the rise and fall of the tide, or when wholly exposed to the action of the atmosphere. A somewhat porous sandstone, for instance, may do well when kept constantly under water; but the same stone when exposed to the weather, more particularly in a climate subject to frost, might disintegrate and crumble away.

Stones which are formed of particles of sand cemented together by different substances, the cementing matter being sometimes silicious, at others calcareous, and at others, again, formed of oxide of iron—each of these weathers in a different way. In the first case, the stone would not materially suffer from the chemical action of atmospheric influences upon it; while in the second, rainwater containing carbonic acid would tend to dissolve the calcareous matter, and deprive the sand of its cement; and in the third, the action of atmospheric influences would tend to render the material unsightly by staining it with iron rust.

Buildings having their face exposed to the prevailing (south-west) winds and rain are generally those in which signs of decay to any extent first appear; also the parts that are in the shade, such as the bed mould of cornices, underside of strings, sills, &c. These seldom get the wet dried out of them, and consequently decay first.

Seasoning.—Stones are often valued because they are easily wrought when first taken from the quarry, and subsequently become harder when exposed to the atmosphere; and this quality arises from the chemical change which takes place on the evaporation of the water (termed "quarry sap") contained in the stone when forming part of the natural rock.

The old masons—and "there were giants in those days"—were very particular about the seasoning of the rough stone blocks before using, and each block as it came from the quarry was placed under cover from the rain, and instead of being laid flat on the ground, was tilted up or inclined upon one of its corners to enable the quarry sap to drain out. Its position also allowed a free access of air to play round the block, which facilitated its drying. This process was carefully watched, and if any latent defect appeared during the drying the block was rejected.

The operation of seasoning the stone took several months before any work could be commenced upon or with it, and it is admitted that this method would add to the cost; but, on the other hand, it is believed that the money would be well spent if this precaution should prevent the wasting of such stones by atmospheric influences, which (especially in cities and large towns) soon act on the surface of a newly-quarried stone.

Again, stone that is quarried one day and built into the wall the next is in a "green" state, and is not in condition. It is at its weakest; its pores are open, and ready to absorb not only moisture but deleterious agents which tend to its destruction.

It is well known to every mason that work on a stone that has lain by for some time is very different from what is obtained on one fresh from the quarry, the former being the hardest and toughest, a fact which of itself is regarded as sufficient evidence to warrant the course recommended—namely, to thoroughly season the stone before using.

Appearance.—The stone which holds its colour best will, as a rule, be the most desirable to use, and this feature is also a good guide as to its durability. The value of a good colour or combination of colours is well known, and a judicious placing of each colour where its particular qualities will best serve the design produces a pleasing effect in a building. The colours to choose from are very numerous, and in all gradations, and a discreet choice of these will give a general effectiveness of appearance when the structure in which they are utilised has been completed.

Porosity and absorption.—All stones are porous more or less, and those which readily absorb moisture should not be used for the external exposed portion of public buildings, as when frosts occur the freezing of the water on the wet surface continually peels off the latter, and eventually destroys the ornamental and carved work upon it.

This, however, is not a universal rule, as although a stone may be very porous and absorbent, it may also be extremely durable ; its durability depending upon the cementing substance which holds the grains together being strong enough to resist the physical forces acting upon the stone, such as the rain, frost, and wind.

The wind in some instances acts deleteriously, as when it drives the rain with more or less force into the pores of the stone, and again when it carries away loose particles which have been dislodged by other means ; but, on the whole, the effect of the action of the wind is to enhance the durability of the stone by drying out the moisture and thus assisting its lasting powers.

Natural bed.—All worked stones, with few exceptions, should be fixed on their natural bed—that is, as near as possible to the position they held before being quarried—for set in this manner they are most durable.

In arches, the bed or (what is the same in effect) the laminæ of the stone should be at right angles to the thrust, or as near as may be parallel to the radiating joints of the arch stones. For cornices, the stones are better edge-bedded, except the quoin blocks, which should be specially-selected stones and laid on their natural bed.

The laminæ of the stone are in some cases so obvious, that the natural bed is easily determined; in other instances, a good deal of practical experience is required to determine the way of the bed. In the oolitic series, such as Bath and Portland, small shells are sometimes visible, and faint streaks of earthy matter; these should always be parallel to the bed, and are seen better when the stone is wetted, but it requires an observant eye to detect them. In the absence of these marks, the mason is often guided by the free working of the stone.

Facility for working.—This is an important factor as regards cost, some stones being so hard, and therefore so difficult to cut and dress, that it hardly pays to quarry them for building purposes. Where ornamental work—such as fine mouldings or carvings—is required, a compact stone of even grain should be selected, free from flaws, shakes, vents, clay holes, &c., so that it may be converted with readiness into the various shapes required.

Compactness and weight.—As a rule, the more consolidated the grains or particles composing the stone, the longer will it resist detrimental atmospheric conditions; for this reason Craigleith is one of the best building stones.

The weight of a stone has to be at times considered, and should be such as to suit the work to be carried out. In quay walls, piers of bridges, buttresses, &c., it is advisable to use heavy stones, as their weight adds to their stability; while for the filling-in of panels in vaulting, and similar work, lighter stones are preferable.

Agents which destroy stones.—These are (as before explained) chemical agents, consisting of acids, &c., in the atmosphere, and physical agents, such as rain, frost, wind, dust, &c.

Other enemies are worms or molluscs, which may just be noticed here. The *Pholas dactylus* is a boring mollusc found in the sea, which attacks limestones and sandstones, however hard, with great vigour. It bores holes close together, of various sizes and depths, which so weaken the stonework that it is ultimately destroyed. The *Saxicava* is another small boring mollusc, which bores holes six inches deep in hard limestones. The only way to resist their attacks is to case the work with granite, which successfully withstands them.

A portion of Plymouth Breakwater, constructed of limestone blocks, in consequence of the attack of these *pholades* had to be replaced with granite.*

* Stevenson on Harbours.

CLASSIFICATION OF STONES.

According to geologists, all rocks from which building stones are obtained may be primarily divided into two great classes—viz., aqueous rocks, formed by the agency of water; and igneous rocks, formed by the action of subterranean heat. There is also a sub-class—viz., metamorphic rocks, including either of the above classes—which, originally stratified, or aqueous, have since been changed in their texture by great heat or pressure.

Aqueous rocks constitute by far the greater proportion of the rocks of the earth's crust, and comprise most of the limestones and sandstones in common use for building purposes.

These aqueous rocks are also termed stratified or sedimentary rocks, owing to the nature of their formation; that is, their particles were once held in solution in water, and gradually sank to the bottom of the sea or a lake, and in process of time became solidified, afterwards making their appearance on the surface of the earth by reason of upheavals and disruptions thereof.

Igneous rocks form a much smaller portion of the earth's crust than the aqueous rocks, and are of volcanic origin; they appear to be formed by fusions due to intense heat, generated by chemical action in the bowels of the earth. Hence the stones in this class are as a rule extremely hard; they comprise the granites, traps, and syenites, some of which are quite unworkable.

GRANITES, TRAPS, AND SYENITES.

Granite is the rock most commonly met with in this class. Its component parts consist of quartz, felspar, and mica. The first of these is practically indestructible, and when largely present renders the stone extremely hard.

The quartz is in the form of clear, colourless, or grey crystals, and is easily recognised, being not unlike fragments of glass, and is pure silica. It surrounds the other ingredients like a wrapper, the felspar and mica being embedded in it.

The felspar is in compact, opaque grains or crystals of a white or flesh colour, and is the predominant constituent and usually the first to show signs of decay. The mica is in small, white, silvery scales, easily removable with the point of a knife, and capable when large enough of being bent.

Granite usually contains more of felspar than of quartz, and more of quartz than of mica; and the colour of the granite is influenced to some extent by that of the principal ingredient.

The best quality of granite is considered to be that in which the grains or particles are fine, uniform in size, and lustrous, and equally distributed throughout the whole mass, its durability depending upon the quantity of its quartz, and upon the nature of its felspar, whether containing potash or soda; potash felspar being more liable to decay than soda felspar.

Syenite granite is tougher and more compact than the ordinary granite, but is less commonly found, and owing to its colour and intractable qualities in working is not often used. In syenitic granite the mica is replaced by hornblende, which is in black or dark green grains; it is easily distinguished from mica by the scales not separating so freely; these also are brittle instead of elastic, and sometimes have a fibrous appearance.

Granite is one of the most valuable of building stones, owing to its great strength, hardness, and compact texture, which renders it able to resist in a high degree the action of wind and rain, and other physical agencies surrounding it. A great amount of labour, however, is required to cut and bring it to a high finish, hence it is only used in building for special purposes, and in good monumental work. It is found in various gradations of colour, and great variety of texture and composition, and takes a high and permanent polish.

Porphyry, owing to its granular structure and extreme hardness, is little used for building or ornamental purposes, and is almost, if not quite, unworkable. It is incapable of being raised in large blocks, and is principally used for road metalling, for which its hardness and toughness render it specially suitable.

The ancients are believed to have been in possession of some secret of preparing bronze tools, which were capable of acting upon this intractable material, and carving in it with facility their colossal statues, obelisks, &c., which remain to this day monuments of their skill in the use of the chisel. And it is very humiliating to think that, with all our modern scientific knowledge and extended manipulation of metals, we cannot produce steel or other tools sufficiently hardened to successfully attack and work this beautiful material.

Trap rocks comprise basalts and greenstones, which occur in dykes, sheets, or other eruptive masses of volcanic origin, and are sometimes stratified and sometimes columnar. These rocks are of a dense and compact texture, extremely hard and tough, and are seldom used in building. The colour is too sombre, being of a dark green inclined to black, but the stone is much used for kerbs, paving, road metalling, &c. Basalt, which occurs in columnar form, is seen at the Giant's Causeway, Ireland, and Fingal's Cave, Staffa. It is composed of several minerals—felspar, augite, magnetic iron, &c.; these, however, can rarely be detected by the eye alone.

Greenstones show larger crystals, are heavier than granite, but not so durable, owing to their containing more of the bases of iron, lime, &c., and much less silica.

SANDSTONES.

Sandstones are sedimentary rocks, which have been deposited by the action of water. They consist generally of grains of sand (silex) cemented together by different substances—such as carbonate of lime, carbonate of magnesia, silica, alumina, oxide of iron—or a combination of those substances.

In a good building stone very little lime should be present as a cementing material, it being the first to give way under atmospheric influences. The cementing property of the stone, to be of an enduring nature, should therefore be silicious. The general characteristics of a good sandstone are that the grains should be compact and homogeneous, and on crushing a bit of the stone the grains should be lustrous, as those with a dull lustre are generally found in a stone that weathers indifferently. Sandstones with large angular grains are termed gritstones, and the most compact of these are used for grindstones and similar purposes. Sandstones often exhibit distinct beds of stratification along which they have a tendency to split. A good example of this is seen in paving slabs in which the planes of cleavage are strongly defined.

The Carboniferous system is fertile in excellent sandstones, especially in Yorkshire, Lancashire and Derbyshire, where they are worked both in the coal measures and the underlying millstone grit.

LIMESTONES.

Limestones are also sedimentary rocks that have been deposited by the action of water; they are composed largely of carbonate of lime, cemented together by the same substance, or by some mixture of carbonate of lime with silica or alumina. They belong to what is termed the calcareous series of rocks, which also include the chalks (the purest form of limestone) and marbles which are crystalline and take a high polish. Limestones usually contain fossil remains, both animal and vegetable.

Portland and Bath stone are the best known of the group which are used for structural purposes, and belong to the oolitic series. Oolite (Gr. *oon*, an egg; *lithos*, stone) is composed of small round grains, which in appearance resembles the roe of a fish, and on that account is sometimes termed Roestone. When the grains are flat and as large as peas it gets the name of Pisolite, or pea grit.

Siliciferous limestones, which also belong to the oolitic series, are Chilmark and Tisbury stones. These have excellent weathering qualities, owing to the siliciferous nature of the cementing material which binds the particles of the stone.

Magnesian limestones contain carbonate of lime, carbonate of magnesia, and a small quantity of silica and alumina, and are termed dolomites. They are more or less crystalline in their nature, the crystals being small and compact.

Kentish Rag is a hard silicious limestone. It occurs in association with a soft calcareous sandstone locally known as "hassock."

Subjoined (pp. 170—192) is a list of some of the principal quarries, chiefly in Great Britain, where stone for building purposes is obtained. In many cases great difficulty has been experienced in getting reliable information for purposes of this work, some of the merchants and quarry owners not having the courtesy even to reply to polite enquiries.

A great number of the stones to be referred to have, however, come under the observation of the author. But it should be noted that the descriptions of the various stones here enumerated are chiefly those of the quarry owners or merchants.

The relative value of labour, as compared with Portland stone, has been given where known, computing Portland at 1·0; thus plain work 0·9 would be 10 per cent. under Portland, while 1·1 would be 10 per cent. above.

LIST OF SANDSTONES.*

Alderley, Cheshire.—A fine-grained stone. Colour, reddish-brown. Weight, 132 lbs. per cubic foot. "The stone is of great durability, going very hard with exposure; has been extensively used for church work by some of our leading architects." "The grey stone is of uniform colour, of about the same texture as the red, but practically without any grain."

Prices on truck at Alderley Station for best selected stone in large blocks for sawing is 1*s.* 1*d.* per foot cube.

Railway rate to London, 12*s.* per ton of 14 feet cube.

J. E. Mills, Alderley Red and Grey Stone Quarries, Alderley Edge, Cheshire.

Alton, Staffordshire.—There are three qualities, viz., reddish-brown, white, and mottled. The red stone consists of fine quartz grains, showing distinct bedding. The white is coarser in grain. The ordinary stone is more or less mottled. Weight: Red, 130 lbs. per cubic foot dry, and 138½ lbs. wet; white, 132 lbs. per cubic foot dry, and 140 lbs. wet.

Been used at Alton Towers, Hoarcross Church, Yoxall, Staffs; Rolleston Church, Burton-on-Trent; Longford Church, Derby; Meryvale Church, near Atherstone, and numerous other places.

Price per cube foot on rail at Alton Station: Best white, 1*s.*; seconds, 10*d.*; best red, 1*s.*; seconds ditto, 10*d.*; mottled, 9*d.*

Mr. John Fielding, Alton, Staffs, or Messrs. J. Hodson & Son, Nottingham.

Appleton, Yorks (Shepley, near Huddersfield).—Greenmoor Rock. A very strong, fine-textured stone. Colour, greenish-grey. Weight, 152 lbs. per cubic foot. Specially adapted and is largely used for steps and landings where there is much wear.

Price, 1*s.* 6*d.* per cube foot on rail at quarry. The railway rate to London is 10*s.* 10*d.* per ton, say, 10*d.* per foot cube.

W. Hampson & Co., Ltd., Appleton Quarries, Shepley, near Huddersfield.

London agents: Messrs. S. Trickett & Sons, No. 3 Wharf, King's Cross, N.; W. and J. R. Freeman, 57, Millbank Street, Westminster.

Blue Pennant, Craig-yr-Hesg Quarries, Pontypridd.—A compact, fine-grained stone. Colour, deep blue. Weight, 168 lbs. per cubic foot. Crushing strain (Kirkaldy), 1617·4 tons per square foot. Its chief

* Particulars and prices, with descriptive matter, are given here as furnished by quarry owners and merchants. It need hardly be pointed out that inquiry should be made and quotations sought when building operations are in prospect on a particular occasion.

constituents are, silica 83·15, alumina 8·10, oxide of iron 4·54. Specific gravity, 2·68. Absorption of water after 24 hours' immersion, 0·28. The stone is chiefly used for rubble masonry, facework for engineering purposes, paving, kerbs, channels, sills, quoins, &c.

Blocks can be obtained any reasonable size up to 10 tons. Labour, 2·2

Price, 1*s.* 3*d.* per cubic foot for random blocks. Steps, landings, headstones, 4*s.* per cubic foot on rail at quarry.

Railway rate to London, 9*d.* per foot cube.

Mackay and Davis, Railway Contractors, St. Mary Street, Cardiff.

Bolton Wood, Bradford, Yorks.—A very fine-grained stone, close texture, and very durable, bedding not observable. Colour, light greenish-brown. Weight, 146 lbs. per cubic foot dry, and 148 lbs. ditto wet.

Been used at Leeds, Bradford, and Middlesboro' Town Halls; Leeds and Bradford Post Offices, Midland Railway Station extension, Derby; and a number of other places too numerous to mention.

It is a stone specially adapted for monumental work, as it carries a good sharp arris, and a fine finished surface.

Price on rail at quarry in random blocks, 1*s.* 10*d.* per foot cube; if to dimensions, 2*s.* ditto. Railway rate to London about 11*s.* per ton. Labour, 2·0.

Messrs. Dyson and Tetley, Bradford, Yorks.

Bramley Fall, Horsforth, near Leeds.—A coarse-grained stone of the millstone grit. Colour, whitish-grey. Weight, 140 lbs. per cubic foot. Crushing strain, 400 to 500 tons to the square foot. It contains 95 per cent. of silica. A first-class weather stone, becoming harder the more it is exposed. It is extensively used for heavy engineering purposes, such as docks, sea walls, bridges, engine beds, and general building and railway work; has been used at the Millwall Docks, Tilbury Docks, Abbey Mills Pumping Station, Victoria Railway Bridge over the Thames, and at the new docks at Hull, Boston, and Lynn.

Price on rail at quarry, 11*d.* to 1*s.* per cube foot; in London, 1*s.* 9*d.* to 1*s.* 10*d.* per cube foot for blocks of ordinary dimensions.

Large stones may be obtained up to 10 tons in weight. Labour 0·9.

Messrs. B. Whitaker & Sons, Horsforth, near Leeds, Yorks.

Brunton and Wideopen Quarries, Northumberland.—Brunton stone: Colour, light brown. Weight, 142 lbs. per cubic foot. This stone has been used at the principal buildings in Newcastle and the neighbourhood.

Prices on rail at quarry, not exceeding 10 feet cube, 1*s.* 2*d.* per cube foot; not exceeding 20 ft., 1*s.* 3*d.*; not exceeding 30 ft., 1*s.* 6*d.* Put on board London steamer in the Tyne, 6*s.* per ton extra.

Wideopen stone: Colour, brownish-yellow. Weight, 140 lbs. per cubic foot. Used for fire stone only. Price from 3*s.* per cube foot on rail.

Mr. Robert Robson, No. 12, Lisle Street, Newcastle-on-Tyne.

Cefn, Ruabon.—A coarse-grained gritty sandstone, bedding discernible. Colour, light yellowish-brown. Weight, 142 lbs. per cubic foot. An entirely reliable weather stone. Largely used in the vicinity, and at Liverpool, Bangor, Windsor, London, Plymouth, &c.

Was also used at Valle Crucis Abbey, Llangollen Bridge, and Rhug Hall, Corwen. Labour, 1·2.

Price at quarry, 1*s.* 3*d.* and 1*s.* 4*d.* per foot cube.

Messrs. Dennis & Co., Cefn, near Ruabon, Wales.

Church Quarries, Sheriff Hill, Gateshead-on-Tyne.—Top bed, a beautiful grey stone; bottom bed, a brown stone of fine grit. Weight, 15 feet cube to the ton.

This stone is being used in some of the principal buildings in Newcastle and district.

Prices from 1*s.* 6*d.* to 3*s.* per cube foot on rail at quarries. The railway rate to London is about 16*s.* per ton.

Messrs. J. and W. Lowry, 1, Corporation Street, Newcastle-on-Tyne.

Corsehill, Annan, Dumfries.—A fine-grained micaceous stone of even texture. Colour, a rich red. Weight, 141 lbs. per cubic foot. Its chief constituents are, silica 95·25, carbonate of lime 1·40, carbonate of magnesia 1·23. Specific gravity, 3·262. It crushes with 372 to 643 tons (Kirkaldy).

An excellent weather stone, and suitable for all architectural purposes as well as for sculpture; it retains its colour as well or better than any other red stone.

It has been used very largely in London for the last twenty years; among other places, at the Hand-in-Hand Insurance Office, Blackfriars; Offices, Rood Lane; St. Paul's Railway Station; Great Eastern Railway Station Hotel, Liverpool Street; Cadogan Square Mansions, Chelsea; and also extensively used in buildings all over the country.

Price at depôt in London is about 2*s.* 3*d.* per cubic foot (random blocks). Labour, 1·3.

J. Murray & Sons, Corsehill Quarries, Annan, Dumfries.

London agents: Messrs. Saml. Trickett & Sons, No. 3 Wharf, King's Cross, N.

Corncockle, Lockerbie, Dumfriesshire.—Colour, light terra-cotta red. Weight, 134 lbs. per cubic foot. Crushing strength (mean), 383·8 tons per square foot. Its chief constituents are, silica 92·04, alumina 3·97. An excellent fine-grained stone, free from lamination and good to dress. It has been extensively used in Glasgow, Edinburgh, Perth, Dundee, and most of the principal towns in Scotland; as also in Newcastle, Leeds, Sunderland, Manchester, London, and other centres in England. Labour, 1·2.

Price on rail at the quarry is 10*d.* to 1*s.* per cubic foot.

Railway rate to London is 15*s.* 6*d.* per ton.

Messrs. Benson, 1, Bellevue Street, Edinburgh.

Craigleith, Edinburgh.—Colour, whitish-grey. Weight, 146 lbs. per cubic foot. Crushes with 820 to 900 tons per square foot. Its chief constituents are silicon oxide 98·3, carbonate of lime 1·1. A compact fine-grained stone of close texture, bedding slightly discernable. A good durable weather stone. The quarry produces a "Liver" rock and a "Bed" rock. The public and private buildings of the New Town, Edinburgh, were almost entirely built with this famous stone.

"In 1823 a stone (a 'scuntion') was excavated in this quarry 136 ft. long by 20 ft. broad, and its weight was computed at 1,500 tons."

It has been extensively used in public buildings in London, such as banks, museums, post offices, law courts, &c. The old Blackfriars Bridge was chiefly built of it, but is now pulled down.

It is also much used for staircases, pavings, &c., for which purpose it is well adapted, as it does not wear slippery.

The labour on the stone is great owing to its extreme hardness. Labour, 3·0.

Prices in quantities of not less than four tons in trucks at Camden Station, London, N.W., in blocks scappled to make as nearly as possible the sizes required:—

Blocks not exceeding 5 ft. cube, per foot cube	4/3
5 ft. and under 10 ft. ,, ,,	4/9
10 ft. ,, ,, 15 ft. ,, ,,	5/3
15 ft. ,, ,, 20 ft. ,, ,,	5/9
20 ft. ,, ,, 25 ft. ,, ,,	6/3
25 ft. ,, ,, 30 ft. ,, ,,	6/9

Cost of sawing, about 2*s.* 6*d.* per foot super.

Mr. John Best, Warriston House, Edinburgh.

London agents: Messrs. J. and A. Crew, Cumberland Market, London, N.W., who keep a large stock of blocks on their wharves.

Darley Dale, Stancliffe, near Matlock.—A close-grained micaceous grit, compact and very hard. Colour, light brown. Weight, 148 lbs. per cubic foot. Its chief constituents are, silica 96·40, iron and alumina 8·30. A splendid weather stone, extensively used in London, Crystal Palace, Sydenham, Birmingham, Liverpool, Manchester, Nottingham, Derby, and various churches and chapels throughout the country. St. George's Hall, Liverpool, is perhaps the finest example of a building in which the stone has been employed. Labour, 1·3.

Prices on rail at quarry from 1*s.* 6*d.* to 1*s.* 9*d.* per cube foot. Railway rate to London, about 9*s.* per ton.

The Stancliffe Estates Co., Stancliffe, Darley Dale, near Matlock; and Messrs. Drabble, same address.

Denwick, Northumberland.—A very fine-grained stone, bedding not obvious. Colour, brownish-grey. Weight, 142 lbs. per cubic foot dry, and 148 lbs. ditto wet. The stone carries a sharp arris, and is well adapted for carving and sculptors' work. All the principal carvings at Alnwick Castle are executed in it. Has been very largely used in Newcastle, Sunderland, Shields, Carlisle, Durham, &c. In London it has been used in the new Post Office, &c.

Price for random blocks up to 30 feet cube, free on rail at Alnwick Station, is 1*s.* per cube foot.

Messrs. Green and Douglas, Amble, Northumberland.

Dukes' Quarries, Whatstandwell, near Matlock.—A coarse-grained angular quartz stone. Colour, brownish-grey. Weight, 141 lbs. per cubic foot. Used extensively where great strength and durability is required for railway bridges, docks, warehouses, engine beds, &c., all over England.

Prices, blocks up to 30 feet cube on truck at quarry, 1*s.* per foot cube; blocks, 30 ft. to 40 ft., 1*s.* 3*d.*; blocks, 40 ft. and up to 150 ft., 1*s.* 6*d.* per foot cube. Ordinary sized blocks delivered in London at St. Pancras Station, 1*s.* 8*d.* per foot cube.

Quarries have been worked for upwards of 100 years.

Mr. Anthony Sims, Dukes' Quarries, Whatstandwell, Matlock, Derby.

Forest of Dean, near Lydney, Gloucester.—A compact-grained hard sandstone of superior quality and texture. It comprises several distinct varieties of stone suitable for building purposes, engineering and monumental works of all kinds, and is obtained from various quarries in close proximity to each other. Blocks of any size can be procured of a uniform colour, blue, grey, and red. Weight, 149 lbs. per cubic foot (15 ft. to the ton). Used very extensively all over the country on cathedrals, churches, chapels, hotels, docks, public buildings, &c. Labour, 1·8.

Prices on rail at quarry, best blue blocks, 2*s.* per foot cube; best grey, 1*s.* 6*d.*; second quality, 1*s.* 3*d.*; red stone, 2*s.* 6*d.*

Railway rate to London, about 9*d.* per foot cube.

Sawn landings, steps, sills, &c., also supplied.

Forest of Dean Stone Firms, Ltd., stone merchants, 44, High Street, Bristol.

Gatton or **Godstone**, Surrey.—A very fine-grained, chalky-looking sandstone. Colour, light greenish-grey. Weight, 102 lbs. per cubic foot. Used at Hampton Court; Windsor Castle; Henry the Seventh's Chapel, Westminster Abbey, the lower part; arcade arches, Stone Church, Kent; and several churches and modern buildings in the neighbourhood. It is most essential that this stone should be fixed in buildings upon its natural bed. It has also been much used as a fire stone, as it resists the action of heat in a similar manner to the ordinary firebrick.

Thick bedded stones are not obtainable.

Prices, 1*s.* 4*d.* to 1*s.* 6*d.* per cube foot at quarry, Gatton, Surrey.

No recent information.

Gazeby, near Shipley, Yorkshire.—Colour, light grey. Weight, 179 lbs. per cubic foot. This is a fine close-grained sandstone. It has great strength, and is very hard and durable. The principal staircases of the British Museum are constructed of it.

Price, for random block on truck at the quarry, 1*s.* 8*d.* per foot cube, or at London depôt, 2*s.* 8*d.*

For further information apply to Messrs. Samuel Trickett & Sons, No. 3 Wharf, King's Cross, London, N.

Grinshill, Shropshire (Bridge and Cureton Quarry).—A fine-grained stone, bright and clean, of proved durability. Colour, creamy white. Weight, 122·5 lbs. per cubic foot. Crushing load (mean), 209·3 tons per square foot. Its chief constituents are, silica 95·5, alumina 1·2.

Used at Moreton Corbet Castle, 13th century; ancient bridges over the Severn; oldest buildings in the town of Shrewsbury, including St. Chad's Church; lofty monument to Lord Hill, &c. Labour, 1·0.

Price on rail at the quarry station, random block 1*s.* 2*d.* per foot cube. On rail at London, 1*s.* 11*d.*

Messrs. Geo. Hancock & Son, Bridge and Cureton Quarry Co., Grinshill, Shropshire.

Guiseley, Leeds.—A coarse grit sandstone. Colour, greyish-brown. Weight, 142 lbs. per cubic foot. Used in Bradford Town Hall up to base course; new Goods Station, Midland Railway, Bradford; West Riding, Yorks, Asylum; and numerous other public and private buildings.

Beds from 2 ft. to 4 ft. thick.

Price on railway at Guiseley Station, 1*s.* per cube foot. Railway rate to London about 11*d.*

Agents: Messrs. Samuel Trickett & Sons, No. 3 Wharf, King's Cross, London, N.

Hollington, Staffordshire—Fine-grained sandstones, bedding observable. There are two kinds, the white and the red. Weight, about 132 lbs. per cubic foot.

This stone has been extensively used in modern works, among which are the Exchange, Sheffield; the Theatre, Grammar School, and Post Office, Longton; Baths, Free Library, and Assembly Rooms, Newcastle; St. Ann's Church, Nottingham; Holy Trinity Church, Burton-on-Trent, and numerous other churches and buildings in the Midlands.

Blocks can be obtained of almost any size.

Price on rail at Rocester Station: Red stone, 10*d.* per cube foot; white stone, fine quality, 1*s.* 6*d.*; best seconds, 1*s.*

Railway rate to London, 9*s.* 2*d.* per ton of 15 cubic feet.

Messrs. Hodkinson and Stevenson, Hollington Quarries, near Uttoxeter, Staffordshire.

Howley Park, Yorkshire (near Morley Station).—A fine close-grained stone. Colour, a light ferruginous brown. Weight, 143 lbs. per cubic foot. This is a good durable stone, standing the weather well. Very suitable for sawn landings, staircases and monumental work. Used at Colosseum, Leeds, and various buildings in the vicinity. Labour 1·0.

Price, 1*s.* 10*d.* per foot cube on rail at quarry (random blocks), and 11*d.* per foot cube carriage to London in not less than 5 tons, that is 2*s.* 9*d.* at London depôt.

Messrs. G. Armitage & Sons, Robin Hood, near Wakefield, Yorks.

Idle, Abbey Quarry, Bradford, Yorks.—A light yellow fine-grained stone. Weight, 146 lbs. per cubic foot. Crushes with 514 tons. Resistance in thrusting stress (Kirkaldy), 7·996 lbs. per square inch. Examples, public buildings in Leeds, York, Bradford, Manchester, &c. Labour, 1·5.

Prices, random blocks, on rail at quarry, 2*s.* per foot cube; in London, 2*s.* 11*d.* per foot cube; also supplied in sawn slabs, steps and landings.

These quarries are owned and worked by Messrs. Geo. Vint Bros., Idle, Bradford.

Kenilworth, Warwick.—A fine-grained sandstone. Colour, dull purplish-red. Weight, 138 lbs. per cubic foot. Used at the Castle, the Church, Midland Bank, Kenilworth; Erdington Monastery, &c.

Prices, block stone, 1*s.* 1*d.* on rail at quarry.

Beds, 8 in. to 3 ft. 6 in. thick.

Recent information not obtainable.

Knaresborough, Yorks (Lingerfield' Quarries).—A fine, compact, strong, grit stone. Colour, light grey. Weight, 142 lbs. per cubic foot. Used at the York County Hospital, Knaresborough Church, Victoria Docks, London; railway works on the North-Eastern line, and numerous other buildings.

The stone can be obtained any size.

Price, 8*d.* per foot cube at the quarry; 10½*d.* per foot cube delivered to Knaresborough Station. Labour, 1·2.

Mr. E. Waite, Rose Cottage, Lingerfield, Knaresborough.

Longwood-Edge, near Huddersfield, Yorks.—Colour, warm light greyish-brown. Weight, 153 lbs. per cubic foot.

Price, at quarry, 8*d.* per cube foot; best ashlar white, 10*d.* per cube foot.

Recent information not obtainable.

Mansfield (Red), Nottinghamshire.—A fine-grained stone of uniform texture. Brick-red colour. Weight, 143 lbs. per cubic foot. Mean crushing load, 591·9 tons per square foot. Its chief constituents are silica 49·4, carbonate lime 25·5, carbonate magnesia 16·1. Extensively used all over the country in public and private buildings; it has the reputation of being a weathering stone of the first quality for general building work. Stones of the darkest colour are considered the best.

Blocks of first-class quality, 7 ft. thick, and up to 15 tons in weight, can be obtained. Labour, 1·6.

Prices, selected blocks, 1*s.* 6*d.* to 2*s.* per foot cube, on truck at quarry, according to thickness, or sawn to dimensions, 3*s.* to 4*s.* per foot cube. Railway rate to London, about 9*s.* per ton.

Messrs. Lindley, Mansfield, Notts. Also of Mr. William Sills, same address.

Mansfield (White), Nottinghamshire.—A weathering stone of the first quality. Colour, yellowish-white. Weight, 140 lbs. per cubic foot. Mean crushing load, 461·7 tons per square foot. Its chief constituents are, silica 51·40, carbonate of lime 26·50, carbonate of magnesia 18·0. This stone is in great favour with architects generally, and is used most extensively all over the country.

Can be readily obtained any length or width for steps or landings, and where columns are required up to 5 ft. or more in depth of bed. Labour, 1·4.

Prices, 1*s.* 4*d.* to 2*s.*, according to size, on truck at quarry, or sawn to dimensions, 3*s.* to 4*s.* per foot cube. Railway rate to London about 9*s.* per ton.

Messrs. Lindley, Mansfield, Notts.

Mansfield (Yellow).—*See* "LIMESTONES."

Matlock Bridge, Derbyshire. — Colour, warm brownish-grey. Weight, 148 lbs. per cubic foot. Used at new Law Courts, Nottingham; Grammar School, Derby; new Borough Asylum, Nottingham, and numerous public buildings in London, &c.

Price, per cubic foot, best selected building stone, quarry scappled, in blocks of ordinary dimensions, 1*s.* 6*d.*; second quality, 1*s.* 3*d.*, loaded on rail at Matlock Bridge Station. A cheaper stone, suitable for bases, girder beds, &c., at 1*s.* per foot cube. Railway rate to St. Pancras, London, 8*d.* per foot cube.

The Stancliffe Estate Co., Ltd., Stancliffe, near Matlock.

Minera, Denbighshire (quarries near Wrexham).—A very fine close-grained sandstone, bedding indistinct. Colour, brownish-grey. Weight, 142 lbs. per cubic foot. This stone has been very largely used, notably at the National Safe Deposit Company's building, near Mansion House, London, E.C., where it was selected for its fire-resisting qualities, after several samples had been subjected to a severe test.

Price, per cubic foot at quarries, in random sizes, on truck, 1*s.* 2*d.*, or at London depôts, 2*s.* 2*d.*

Agents: Messrs. S. Trickett & Sons, No. 3 Wharf, King's Cross, N.

Morley Moor, Derbyshire.—Colour, warm brownish-grey. Weight, 130½ lbs. per cubic foot. Extensively used on numerous buildings in the locality and Bank at Derby, Berniston House, &c.

Price, per cubic foot for random blocks, loaded on rail at Coxbench Station, Midland Railway, 1*s.* 1*d.*; if to dimensions, 1*s.* 2*d.* Rate to London, in trucks of 4 tons, 9*s.* 9*d.* per ton.

Messrs. Samuel Seal & Sons, Wakefield.

Newbiggin, Carlisle, Cumberland. — A fine-grained sandstone, bedding obvious. Colour, light brownish-red. Weight, 121 lbs. per cubic foot wet, 130½ lbs. dry. Its chief constituents are, silicon oxide 84·20, ferric and aluminium oxides 7·37, calcium carbonate 6·70. Crushes with 481·7 (Kirkaldy). Extensively used in vicinity. Labour, 1·7.

Price, 1*s.* per foot cube (random blocks), on rail at Cumwhinton Station.

Beds up to 2 ft. in thickness.

No recent information.

Pateley Bridge, York (Middle-tongue Quarries).—No. 1 Bed is an even-grained sandstone, suitable for bridges, engine beds, girder beds, or other strong rough work.

Price, on rail at quarry, 1*s.* per foot cube.

No. 2 Bed consists of 5 ft. of hard York flatstone, suitable for steps and landings.

Price, on rail at quarry, 1*s.* 8*d.* per foot cube.

No. 3 Bed, fine-grained, hard, block stone, equal to "Bolton Wood."

Price, on rail at quarry, 1*s.* 8*d.* per foot cube.

No. 4 Bed, same as No. 2.

No. 5 Bed, 14 ft. without distinct bed, suitable for bases and other work requiring great strength and durability. "Kirkaldy's" test, 500 tons to the square foot.

No. 6 Bed, 11 ft. thick. Best fine block, light brown in colour, suitable for building purposes and fine masonry, at 1*s.* 8*d.* per foot cube, random block.

Railway rate to London is about 10*d.* per foot cube.

Ackroyd Jennings, Pateley Bridge, near Leeds, Yorks.

Pemberton, Lancashire (quarry near Wigan.)—A fine-grained sandstone, bedding obscure. Colour, a light bluish-grey. Weight, 150 lbs. per cubic foot. Used extensively in the vicinity on churches, schools, railway works.

Blocks can be obtained of almost any dimensions.

No recent information.

Penkridge, Stafford.—A fine-grained micaceous stone. Colour, rich red, and mingled red with grey. Weight, 135 lbs. per cubic foot. This stone hardens with age, has stood the test of weather in every locality for the last fifty years, is free working, and carries a capital arris.

Used at Lichfield Cathedral (West front), church at Walsall, church at Cardiff, Hawkyard Priory, Rugeley; old churches and buildings throughout the country.

Price, 1*s.* per foot cube on rail at quarry, Penkridge. Railway rate to London, 10*s.* 3½*d.* per ton.

Mr. F. Sprenger, Penkridge, Staffordshire.

Pennant.—*See* "Blue Pennant."

Potter Newton, Yorkshire, near Leeds.—A fine-grained stone, free working. Colour, a light yellow. Weight, about 15 cubic feet to the ton. Suitable for sawn landings, steps, sills, coping, &c.

Price, for ordinary sizes on rail, 1*s.* 6*d.* per cubic foot; delivered in London, 2*s.* 4*d.* Stones over 6 ft. long and difficult sizes, extra. Labour, 1·1.

Exors. of Wm. Denton, Potter Newton, Leeds.

Prudham, Northumberland, Fourstones.—Moderately fine-grained sandstone. Colour, warm light brown. Weight, 144 lbs. per cubic foot. Used at General Post Office and Central Station, Newcastle; Army and Navy Hotel, Victoria Street, and Winchester House, Broad Street, London, and various other public and private buildings.

Blocks can be obtained up to 100 feet cube.

Prices, according to sizes, from 1*s.* 1*d.* to 2*s.* 3*d.* per foot cube. Railway rate to London, 15*s.* per ton.

Mr. Wm. Benson, Prudham Quarries, Fourstones.

Quarella, Glamorgan, Bridgend.—A fine-grained sandstone, even texture, highly crystalline, bedding obscure. Colour, light greenish-grey. Weight, 136 lbs. per cubic foot. Its chief constituents are, silicon oxide 91·50, aluminium oxide 3·40. Crushes with 438 to 546 tons (Kirkaldy). Extensively used in old castles and modern buildings, and Llandaff Cathedral; Royal Colonial Institute, St. Luke's Church, London, &c.

The quarries and works are situated near the station at Bridgend, and alongside the main line of the G.W.R.

Price, 1*s.* 6*d.* per foot cube on rail at Bridgend. Railway rate to London, about 8*d.* per foot cube.

Owners, Forest of Dean Stone Firms, Ltd., Stone Merchants, 44, High Street, Bristol.

Red Mansfield.—*See* "Mansfield (Red)."

Robin Hood, Yorkshire.—A light blue fine-grained stone, much valued on account of its even texture and colour, and also its free working. Weight, 145½ lbs. per cubic foot dry, and 151½ lbs. wet. Crushes with 570 to 575 tons. Much used for monumental work, landings, steps, copings, sills, &c.; it is also sawn into thin slabs for box chimney-pieces, linings, &c. Labour 1·2.

Price, 1*s.* 10*d.* per foot cube on rail at quarry in random blocks, and 11*d.* per foot cube railway rate to London in not less than 5 tons, that is 2*s.* 9*d.* at London depôt.

Messrs. Geo. Armitage & Sons, Robin Hood, near Wakefield, Yorks.

Scotgate Ash, Yorkshire (quarries Pateley Bridge).—A fine-grained, compact stone of even texture. Colour, light brown. Weight 145 lbs. per cubic foot. Crushing strain over 700 tons per square foot.

It is chiefly used for landings, steps, sills, coping, sinks, kerbs, headstones, &c. The large landing in the staircase of the London and County Bank, Lombard Street, is constructed of it; it has also been used for the East London Tabernacle, Burdett Road. Labour 2·2.

Prices: Blocks, 1*s.* 8*d.* per foot cube; landings, self-faced under 20 feet super., at 2*s.* per foot cube; monumental stone, 2*s.* 6*d.* per foot cube at Pateley Bridge.

Railway rate to London, 10*s.* 10*d.* per ton of 14 cubic feet.

Scotgate Ash Stone Co., Pateley Bridge, *viâ* Leeds, Yorks.

Silex, Yorks (quarry at Hipperholme, near Halifax).—An even-tinted, light-coloured stone, and on account of its great durability, hardness, and non-slippery nature is especially adapted for steps, landings, pavings, &c.

Its crushing strain, 2·200 tons per foot (Kirkaldy). Absorption, 1·02 per cent. Chemical analysis, silica 97·83, alumina or oxide of iron 1·17, lime 1·00.

Prices not stated.

Joseph Brooke & Son, Hipperholme, Halifax, Yorks.

Spinkwell and Cliffwood, Yorks.—A fine-grained, very hard and durable stone. Colour, greenish-grey. Weight, 146 lbs. per cubic foot. Used at Manchester Town Hall, Bradford Town Hall, steps Bank of England, and numerous other buildings.

Price, put on rail at Bradford: Ashlar, in random sizes, 1*s.* 10*d.* per foot cube; if to dimensions, 2*s.* ditto; random slab sawn one side, 2*s.* 6*d.* per foot cube; if sawn two sides, 3*s.* 6*d.* ditto; random blocks in rough, 1*s.* 8*d.* ditto. Railway rate to London, 10*s.* 10*d.* per ton for 5 tons and upwards. Labour 2·3.

Dyson and Tetley, Bradford.

Stainton, Durham, near Barnard Castle.—A moderately fine-grained stone. Colour, light brown. Weight, 144 lbs. per cubic foot. Used extensively on buildings in the neighbourhood; round keep of Barnard Castle; Joint Stock Bank and Market House, ditto, &c. Beds up to 4 ft. thick.

Price, on rail at quarry, 1*s.* 6*d.* per foot cube. Railway rate to London, 12*s.* per ton.

Mr. John Thompson, Barnard Castle.

Sussex Sandstones.—This is a general term for these stones, which are of the same composition and class. The varieties are very numerous. They chiefly consist of grains of quartz (silica) in contact, with no apparent matrix or cementing material; they also vary in texture, while some are coarse others are fine, and mostly all are free working, although some are considerably harder than others. These stones are found in different parts of the county, but those chiefly used, are found in the neighbourhood of Three Bridges and East Grinstead. As a rule, they are good weather stones, as may be seen in the old churches and buildings in the vicinity, and they are much used in modern churches and mansions at the present time with apparent good results.

These stones are termed by the masons "kettle and brick," from the facility with which these two articles enable them to work the stone.

A few quarries are here enumerated.

Honeywell (Forest Row).—A very fine-grained stone. Colour, greenish-grey, with brown streaks, bedding distinct. Weight, 120 lbs. per cubic foot dry, and 133 lbs. ditto wet. Used at the Constitutional Club, Bank, and North End Church, East Grinstead.

Blocks can be obtained 5 ft. thick.

Price, best white block, 1*s.* 2*d.* per foot cube at quarry.

Paddock Hurst.—A very fine-grained stone. Colour, warm yellowish-grey. Used at the new Parish Church, Hove.

Sir Weetman Pearson (owner).

Scaynes Hill (Three Bridges).—A moderately fine-grained stone. Colour, warm yellowish stone. Used at Lancing College Church and Collegiate Buildings.

Prices not obtainable.

Trustees of Lancing College (owners).

Selsfield (East Grinstead).—A fine-grained stone. Colour, cream. Weight, 115 lbs. per cubic foot dry, and 130 lbs. ditto wet. Used extensively in the neighbourhood. Additions to Graveleye Manor, Wakehurst; Ardingley College; new church, Crawley, &c.

Prices on rail at Rowfant Station, L.B. & S.C. Ry., 1*s.* per foot cube.

Talacre and Gwesbyr, Flintshire.—A fine-grained beddy sandstone. Colour, greenish-grey. Weight, 150 lbs. per cubic foot. Used at Denbigh and Rhuddlan Castles; Bodelwddan Church; modern mansion of Talacre, and many old buildings in the locality. Labour 1·1.

Price, delivered in London, from 2*s.* 4*d.* to 2*s.* 7*d.* per foot cube.

Recent information not obtainable.

Wilderness, Gloucestershire.—A fine, hard red stone of great strength and beauty of colour. Weight, 141 lbs. per cubic foot. Its crushing test is 480 tons per foot super. of bed. The beds vary in thickness from 1 ft. to 6 ft., and blocks up to 8 tons weight can be cut up to 6 ft. thick.

Used at Barnwood Asylum, near Gloucester; new Speech House, Harrow School; new hotels at Birmingham and Newport, Mon.; and various other buildings at St. Albans, Reading, Cheltenham, Gloucester, Bristol, &c. It is also an excellent stone for monumental work.

Price, 2*s.* to 2*s.* 6*d.* per foot cube on rail at Longhope Station. Railway rate to Paddington, 7*s.* 6*d.* per ton.

The quarries are situated at Mitcheldean in the Forest of Dean.

Sole owners, Forest of Dean Stone Firms, Ltd., 44, High Street, Bristol.

Woodhouse, Yorks, Holmfirth.—A moderately fine-grained sandstone, bedding not apparent. Colour, bluish-grey. Weight, 150 lbs. per cubic foot. Used at the Town Hall, Infirmary, Police-courts, and Grammar Schools at Dewsbury; Yorkshire Penny Bank, Sheffield, and various other buildings in the vicinity.

No recent information.

Wrose Hill, Yorks, Shipley.—A fine-grained sandstone, carbon spots in matrix. Colour, brownish-grey. Weight, 148 lbs. per cubic foot. Used extensively in the vicinity, at the Yorkshire College, new Infirmary, Bradford new station, &c. The stone is especially adapted for paving, landings, steps, copings, sills, &c., which are sent out tooled or rubbed.

Prices: Building block, 1*s.* 6*d.* per foot cube; monumental block, 1*s.* 9*d.* per foot cube.

No recent information.

LIST OF LIMESTONES.*

Ancaster, Lincolnshire, near Grantham.—An oolitic, shelly, crystalline stone of good weathering qualities, cream colour. Weight, brown weather bed, 156 lbs. per cubic foot; freestone, 140 lbs. per cubic foot. Crushing load, brown bed, 552·6 tons per square foot; freestone, 184 tons per square foot. Its chief constituents are, carbonate of lime 93·59, carbonate of magnesia 2·90. Used in the restoration of old churches in the vicinity; Colleges at Cambridge and Oxford; St. Albans Abbey; Roman Catholic Cathedrals, Norwich and Cambridge; Belvoir Castle; Beverley Abbey; Wollaton Hall; and many important ecclesiastical and domestic buildings in London.

Price, 1*s*. 2*d*. per foot cube on rail at Ancaster Station in random blocks. Railway rate to London, 7*d*. per foot cube.

The stone can be worked to order at the quarries. Labour, 0·8.

Messrs. Lindley, Mansfield, Notts.

Anston, Yorks, near Sheffield.—A fine-grained magnesian, crystalline limestone; dispersed irregularly through the mass are black particles, apparently carbon. Weight 141 lbs. per cubic foot dry, and 149 lbs. ditto wet. This stone was used in building the Houses of Parliament; Geological Museum; New Hall, Lincoln's Inn; Record Office, Fetter Lane; the Ordnance Office, Pall Mall; the flying buttresses, Westminster Abbey; and numerous other buildings.

Beds up to 2 ft. 6 in. in thickness.

Prices: Random blocks, 1*s*. 3*d*. per foot cube; dimension blocks, 1*s*. 4*d*. ditto, on rail Kiveton Park Station, or about 2*s*. 1*d*. ditto in London. Labour, 1·3.

Messrs. Jas. Turner & Son, Kiveton Park Stone Works, Sheffield.

Bath, Somersetshire.—Oolite, 140 lbs. This useful stone is so thoroughly well known that any lengthened description of it would be quite superfluous. As, however, there are various beds or quarries, a few remarks on the particular characteristics of each are appended.

St. Aldhelm, Box Ground.—Light brown colour. A thoroughly reliable weather stone, of medium grain, unaffected by frost or situation; is especially suitable for exposed positions, and for plinths, sills, string-courses, cornices, and copings. The beds run up to 4 ft. in depth, and any reasonable length can readily be obtained.

Bradford.—Sound, mild and free-working. A good weather stone, well suited for outside work in large towns. Blocks up to 3 ft. 6 in. deep and of any ordinary length. Light brown.

* See footnote to p. 170.

Corngrit.—Light stone colour. A very strong stone, carries great weight, costs more for labour than Corsham Down, being much harder; is not a weather stone, and should not be used externally. For inside columns, and for staircases, landings, and steps it is well suited. Also for engine and machinery beds.

Corsham Down.—Light stone colour. A fine-grained, even-textured, free-working stone, sound and strong, and carries a sharp arris. Is suitable for all outside non-projecting work, jambs, mullions, tracery, and heads, and for all inside work. It stands admirably at the seaside, in large cities, and in manufacturing towns. The finest beds are effectively used for pulpits, fonts, reredoses, screens. This stone runs up to 4 ft. deep in bed, and up to 12 ft. and upwards in length.

Combe Down.—Very light brown. A good weather stone, of medium grain, fairly free working; suitable for plinths, projections, and weatherings. Stands well at the seaside. The beds occasionally run up to 4 ft. 6 in. in depth, but only moderate lengths are ordinarily obtained.

Farleigh Down.—Warm creamy tint. A fine, even-textured stone, of a warm tint; should not be used on the ground or for outside projections, but for flush work outside, and for all inside work it may be used with success. It is the cheapest working stone in the market. Beds from 3 ft. to 4 ft. deep are always being quarried, and blocks of moderate length can be supplied at any time.

Monk's Park.—Cream colour. A compact, close-grained, and very strong stone; suitable for same positions as Corsham Down; carries great weight. The recommendations under the head of Corsham Down apply equally to the Monk's Park stone. Depth of bed is similar, and great lengths are even more common than with the Corsham Down.

Stoke Ground.—Light brown. A weather stone, thoroughly sound and reliable; medium grain and uniform texture, suitable for outside positions. Converts with but little waste. Runs up to 6 ft. deep in bed, and very large, from 30 ft. to 40 ft. average per block.

Westwood Ground.—Light brown. Also a weather stone, unusually sound, of uniform texture, somewhat open in grain. This stone is very free-working, and converts with minimum waste. Blocks run up to 6 ft. deep in bed, and are large and shapely. A supply averaging 40 ft. per block can be guaranteed.

The labour on Bath stone may be taken as about half that on Portland.

Price per cubic foot in not less than 4 ton lots; computed weight 16 cube feet to the ton, random blocks:

In railway trucks at quarries, from 1*s*. to 1*s*. 1*d*. per foot cube.
At Paddington Station, London, 1*s*. 7*d*. to 1*s*. 8*d*. ditto.
At Nine Elms Station, London, 1*s*. 8*d*. to 1*s*. 9*d*. ditto.
In barge at Brentford Docks, 1*s*. 6½*d*. to 1*s*. 7½*d*. ditto.
Selected blocks 1*s*. per foot cube extra.

Blocks cut to given sizes, rough from the saw, with sufficient allowance for working, 8*d*. to 10*d*. per foot cube additional.

Plain dressings of moderate dimensions cost about 3*s*. 6*d*. per foot cube, and ordinary Gothic church work from 3*s*. 6*d*. to 4*s*. per foot cube on truck at loading stations, including stone and labour.

The principal quarry owners until recently were :—Messrs. Pictor & Sons; Randell Saunders & Co., Ltd.; Isaac Sumsion; Corsham Bath Stone Co., Ltd.; R. J. Marsh & Co., Ltd.; S. R. Noble; and Stone Brothers, Ltd. All these are now incorporated in "The Bath Stone Firms, Ltd.," to whom all inquiries should be addressed at the Bath Stone Office, Abbey Yard, Bath.

Stone-Preserving Liquids and Cements.—"Fluate."—The Bath Stone Firms, Ltd., have brought the merits of this stone preservative prominently before the public. It is a compound of silica with another mineral, which being applied to limestones and marbles renders them thoroughly impervious alike to acids, gases, and atmospheric influences generally. It is easily applied with a brush, and the cost may be taken at 1½*d*. per foot super of surface treated.

Beer, Devonshire (quarries at Seaton, near Lyme Regis).—Oolite, cream colour, of a somewhat lighter tint than Bath stone. Weight, 138 lbs. per cubic foot. Used extensively in the old churches of Devonshire, and more recently in the restoration works at Exeter Cathedral, Charmouth Church, Honiton, &c. It has also been much used in London, especially for interior work, for which it is well adapted.

Blocks up to 120 feet cube, 5 ft. thick on bed can be supplied.

Price in blocks not exceeding above size, 1*s*. 6*d*. per foot cube, at Nine Elms Depôt, London. Labour, 0·6.

The Beer Freestone and Lime Co., Seaton, Devon.

Bolsover (Moor), Derbyshire, near Chesterfield.—This quarry appears to be closed. The Mansfield Woodhouse is now commonly called "Bolsover," being a similar stone in every respect. *See* "Mansfield Woodhouse."

Campden Hill, Gloucestershire.—A fine oolitic stone with carbonate of lime, partly crystalline. Colour, warm cream, approaching orange. Weight, 140 lbs. per cubic foot. Blocks can be obtained up to 40 ft. cube. Of a very even texture and grain, and has a slight fret, easily worked and is an excellent weather stone. Used extensively in buildings in the locality, and also at Leamington and other places.

Price, 1*s*. per foot cube for random blocks at the quarry.

Mr. Charles Grove, Chipping Campden.

Casterton, Rutland, near Stamford.—A coarse oolite. Colour, brownish cream. Weight, about 130 lbs. per cubic foot. A good weather stone, adapted for external and internal use, very easily worked and nearly imperishable. Used very extensively in the mediæval buildings in the locality and many of the principal buildings, colleges and churches in Cambridge and elsewhere.

Price, best quality, 1*s*. 5*d*. per foot cube on rail at Stamford; railway rate to London is about 7*s*. per ton. Labour, 0·6.

Messrs. Roberts Bros., Wharf Road, Stamford.

Chalk.—A pure carbonate of lime. Weight, from 117 lbs. to 150 lbs. per cubic foot according to its density. Crushing weight, 72 tons per square foot (Rivington). Although not considered a building stone, yet in chalk districts it is extensively used for internal dressings, being easily worked with drags, and cut with a toothed saw, it carries a sharp arris and works with a slight fret. Chalk is used in the panels in groined vaulting, arcade columns, wall facings, and occasionally in the construction of walls. At the large cathedral-like church at Lancing College, Sussex, it is much used, especially in the crypt, where the piers, if not built of chalk, are faced with chalk ashlar, and although sustaining a great weight, they show no indications of fracture by crushing. Chalk is at once disintegrated by frost, so that it is necessary it should be used internally.

Chilmark and Wardour, Wiltshire.—A siliciferous limestone. The colour varies with the different beds, from cream to yellowish-brown. The general excellence of the Chilmark stone would, it is said, have induced the Commissioners to recommend it for the construction of the Houses of Parliament, had not its cost at that time, owing to the want of railway accommodation, been prohibitive. Salisbury Cathedral is constructed of it, and among other buildings where it has been used may be mentioned Chichester and Rochester Cathedrals, Westminster and Romsey Abbeys, Wardour and Longford Castles; numerous churches, schools, banks, offices, warehouses, &c., in London and the home counties. It is an excellent weather stone, has a slight fret, is easily worked, and is well adapted for any kind of buildings.

The Chilmark consists of three beds, viz., the "trough" or hard bed, the labour of which is about equal to Portland; the "pinney" or green bed, working about 40 per cent. less than Portland; and the white oolite bed, the labour on which is about equal to Bath stone. The Wardour consists of two kinds, viz., the "Chantry" and "Garden" beds, which very much resemble the "pinney" or green beds of the Chilmark. All these are cut with a wet saw, and run from 1 ft. to 5 ft. in thickness.

		Weight per cubic foot lbs.	Weight required to crush one cubic foot Tons.
Chilmark,	Trough bed ...	153·8	411·4
,,	Pinney bed ...	135·0	136·5
,,	White Oolite bed ...	135·0	125·5
Wardour,	Chantry bed ...	135·0	139·0
,,	Garden bed ...	135·0	280·9

Price: Random blocks from Chilmark or Wardour quarries, not exceeding 16 feet cube, average 1*s*. 3*d*. per cube foot, on rail at Tisbury or Dinton Stations, L. & S.W. Ry. Large or selected blocks from 2*d*. per cube foot extra, if had separately. Carriage to Nine Elms, 6*s*. per ton of 16 cubic feet, in lots of 4 tons and upwards.

Mr. T. P. Lilley, Gillingham, Dorset.

Clipsham, Rutland.—A coarse shelly oolitic stone, very similar to the Old Barnack stone. Colour, cream. Weight, 135½ lbs. per cubic foot wet, and 144½ lbs. ditto dry. Beds from 9 in. to 2 ft. thick.

Used at Peterborough, Norwich and Ely Cathedrals; Uppingham School; churches at Melton Mowbray, Bishop's Stortford, Stainby, Ridlington, Exton, Wartaby Ashley, and most of the old churches and buildings in the locality.

Blocks can be obtained from 3 ft. to 50 ft. cube.

Price in quarry, 1*s.* per foot cube; on rail at Little Bytham Station, G.N.R., 1*s.* 4*d.* per foot cube; railway rate to King's Cross, 7*s.* 3*d.* per ton of 15 cubic feet.

Matthew Medwell, Clipsham Quarries, Oakham.

Doulting, Somerset (Shepton Mallet).—An oolitic crystalline stone. Colour, a warm cream. Weight, from 130 lbs. to 135 lbs. per cubic foot. This is a good weather stone of uniform tint, homogeneous in structure and very durable. There are two beds, viz., the "Brambleditch," a fine stone, worked at the same cost as Box Ground, Bath, suitable for inside work; and the "Chelynch," a coarser-grained stone suitable for weatherings, strings, sills, &c. The labour on this is about 5 per cent. more than the former.

Used at Wells Cathedral, Glastonbury Abbey, and various churches and buildings in the locality and elsewhere. Labour, 0·9.

Price, on rail at quarry (35 ft. cube average), 1*s.* 2*d.* per foot cube; at Paddington, 1*s.* 10*d.*; Nine Elms, 2*s.* ditto.

The Ham Hill and Doulting Stone Co., Norton, Stoke-under-Ham, Somerset.

Dundry, Somerset (near Bristol).—A silicious oolitic limestone of immense durability and strength. Colour, a warm yellow. Weight, 133 lbs. per cubic foot. Used extensively in the West of England at nearly all the cathedrals and churches, and lately at restoration of Bristol Cathedral, Nempnett Church, Somerset; Dundry Schools; St. John's Church, Cardiff; Llandaff Cathedral; the Mayor's Chapel, Bristol; St. Mary, Redcliffe; Bristol Waterworks Pumping Station, &c.

Blocks any size up to 10 tons, and 4 ft. deep in bed.

Price, 1*s.* per foot cube at quarry rail, 2*s.* per foot cube at Paddington.

The stone is easily worked and cut up with the usual cross-cut saw.

Lewis Told, Dundry, near Bristol.

Ham Hill, Somerset.—Shelly limestone, deep ferruginous brown, 141 lbs. 12 ozs. Used in all the principal buildings in the locality, is an excellent weather stone, and presents a very handsome appearance. It can be got of almost any superficial size. The beds run from 6 in. to 24 in. thick. There are two kinds distinguished as the "Grey" and "Yellow" beds.

Price at quarry, 1*s.* 2½d. per cube foot; or delivered at Paddington Station, Great Western Railway, 1*s.* 10½*d.* per cube foot. Labour, 0·9.

For further particulars apply to the Ham Hill Stone Company, Norton, Stoke-under-Ham, Somerset.

Haydor, Lincolnshire.—Oolitic limestone, 133 lbs. 7 ozs., brownish cream colour, somewhat resembling Ancaster. It has been used largely in Lincoln Cathedral, Boston, Grantham, and Newark Churches, Belvoir Castle, Culverthorpe House, &c. The labour is about 5 per cent. more than Ancaster and one-fifth less than Portland; blocks have been got 14 ft. by 3 ft. by 4 ft. in size.

Price, 11*d.* per cube foot at quarry, 1*s.* 1*d.* in truck at Ancaster Station, 1*s.* 8*d.* at King's Cross.

Hopton Wood, Derbyshire, Middleton by Wirksworth.—A compact, hard, crystalline stone showing encrinital shells; it is a good weather stone, suitable for all purposes, especially for internal work, such as staircases, columns, pilasters, chimney-pieces, &c., and is also well adapted for monumental work. Weight, 158 lbs. per cubic foot. Crushing stress, 810 tons per cubic foot. There are three qualities of stone, viz., the "white" bed, "grey" bed, and "dark" bed. The white bed is used for monumental purposes. The grey bed is used for best finished and polished work. The dark bed is the hardest, and is used for all descriptions of general masonry. Extensively used all over the country, at Chatsworth, Belvoir Castle, Trentham Hall, Baliol and Keble Colleges, Oxford; Southwell Minster, Houses of Parliament, New Law Courts, the Tower of London; new Council Chamber, Guildhall; Imperial Institute, &c. Blocks have sometimes been got as long as 14 ft., and can now be obtained of any reasonable size.

Prices, blocks on rail at quarry, from 2*s.* per foot cube and upwards according to size. Railway rate to London, Camden Station, 8*s.* 4*d.* per ton, and worked stone 16*s.* 9*d.* per ton in 4 ton lots. Labour, 2·3.

Killer Bros., Middleton, near Wirksworth, and Hopton Wood Stone Co., John Simpson (manager), Wirksworth.

Huddlestone, Yorkshire.—Magnesian limestone, 137 lbs. 13 ozs., whitish-cream colour. Used at York Minster, Selby Abbey, Sherborne Church, Westminster Hall, &c. Labour about the same as Portland.

Building stone, 1*s.* 8*d.* per foot cube on rail; monumental stone, 2*s.* ditto. Railway rate to London, 10*s.* 10*d.* per ton.

Messrs. W. H. Newton & Co., Leeds, and Huddlestone Quarries, Sherburn-in-Elmete.

Ketton, Rutlandshire.—Oolitic, dark cream colour, 128 lbs. 5 ozs. Used at Peterborough and Ely Cathedrals; St. Dunstan's Church, London; St. John's College, Cambridge; Wisbech, Lynn, Norwich, Leicester, Bedford, Bury St. Edmund's, Stamford, Northampton, Exton Hall, &c. The blocks run from 1 ft. up to about 50 ft. cube, and up to about 7 ft. in length, and from 1 to 2·9 cube on bed. Labour 0·65.

Price, in random blocks, from 2 ft. cube upwards, 2*s.* 6*d.* per foot on rail at quarry, or 3*s.* per foot at St. Pancras Station, Midland Railway.

Owners, Messrs. R. & W. Nutt, and T. C. Molesworth & Co., Ketton, near Stamford.

Kentish Rag, Kent, Maidstone, Sevenoaks, and neighbourhood.—A compact crystalline limestone, which absorbs very little water and resists the weather well. Colour, bluish-grey. Weight 166 lbs. per cubic foot. Used chiefly for walling and rubble work, generally in churches and ecclesiastical structures, in connection with free-stone dressings. It is somewhat difficult to work on account of its hard nature, but in some churches in the vicinity of Dartford in Kent it has been used for tracery windows, in which the arrises and mitres are quite sharp and the tooling distinct, although it has been done over a century. "Hassock," a kind of sandstone, is generally found attached to the ragstone; this is soft and porous and totally unfit for resisting the weather, and should therefore be knocked off in the working; it is, however, frequently used as lining to walls built of ragstone.

The chief quarries are Iguanadon, Chillington, Allington, all near Maidstone; also at Aylesford and Boughton.

Prices, rough rag, delivered within 4 miles of the Thames, per ton, 8*s*. Ragstone ashlar, scabbled (only), per foot cube, 2*s*. 9*d*. at quarry.

Mansfield (Woodhouse), Nottingham.—A magnesian limestone of compact and crystalline texture, fine grained with carbon spots. Weight, 145½ lbs. per cubic foot. Mean crushing load, 577·4 tons per square foot. Colour, warm yellow. Its chief constituents are, carbonate of lime 51·65, carbonate magnesia 42·60, silica 3·70. This was the selected stone for the Houses of Parliament, but owing to the difficulty in obtaining the size blocks required, it was superseded by Anston stone, although upwards of 25,000 ft. were used for the base moulding above the plinth before it was set aside. This stone is eminently adapted for highly carved work. Used at the Amicable Life Office, Fleet Street; Martyr's Memorial, Oxford, &c.

The price is according to the size, commencing from 2*s*. per foot cube for small blocks on truck at station. Railway rate to London, about 9*s*. per ton. Labour 2·1.

Wm. Sills, Mansfield, Notts, and Messrs. Lindley, Mansfield, Notts.

Painswick, Gloucestershire.—Sold also under the name of Nailsworth stone. A fine-grained oolitic stone of even texture. Colour, whitish-cream. Weight, 145 lbs. per cubic foot. This well-known stone is not greatly used now, probably from the sale of it not being pushed. It is well adapted for staircases, chimney-pieces and internal work generally.

Price, 1*s*. per foot cube on rail at quarry. Carriage to London in full truck loads of 16 ft. to the ton is 8*s*. 3*d*. per ton, or about 1*s*. 8*d*. per foot cube in London. Labour 0·9.

Charles Essex, Avening, near Stroud.

Park Nook, Yorkshire.—A magnesian limestone. Colour, light cream. Weight, 137½ lbs. per cubic foot. Used at Pontefract Old Church, Melton, Campsall and Skelbrooke Church restorations, Yorks, &c. Beds 6 in. to 3 ft. thick.

Price, on rail at Adwich Station, near Doncaster, 1*s*. 2*d*. per cubic foot. At depôt in London, 1*s*. 11*d*. ditto. Labour 0·8.

Portland, Dorset (Isle of Portland).—Oolite, a fine-grained stone of even texture. Colour, whitish-brown. Weight, 135½ lbs. per cubic foot. This well-known stone may be considered the premier building stone in the United Kingdom; it has been so extensively used, that a list of buildings and places would be quite superfluous, and the demand for it is always increasing.

The prices for random blocks, as quarried, averaging 20 ft. cube, delivered to ship or rail at Portland. "Whitbed" (Brown Bed), 1*s.* 6*d.* per foot cube; "Basebed" (White Bed), 1*s.* 7½*d.* ditto. Delivered by rail to Nine Elms, Paddington, Chelsea Basin, or West Kensington Station, London, add 6½*d.* per foot cube extra. Labour 1·0.

Principal quarry owners: Mr. F. J. Barnes (late the Portland Stone Co., Ltd., Steam Saw Mills and Masonry Works); Messrs. Webber and Pangbourne, Easton Steam Saw Mills; and the Bath Stone Firms, Ltd., Isle of Portland, Dorset.

Purbeck, Dorset (Isle of Purbeck).—A shelly, semi-crystalline stone. Colour, whitish-grey. Weight, about 14 cubic feet to a ton.

Prices: In rough block per foot cube, 1*s.* 6*d.* Worked stone, moulded, from 4*s.* to 6*s.* ditto. Hammer-jointed, rock-faced walling, at 2*s.* 6*d.* per super. yard. Chisel-jointed, rock-faced walling, at 3*s.* 6*d.* per super. yard. Chisel-jointed, chisel-faced walling, at 5*s.* 6*d.* per super. yard. Drafted and pitched quoins, 10*d.* per foot rise. Chiselled reveal and pitched jambs, 10*d.* per foot rise. Tooled paving squared, 6½*d.* per foot super. Ditto 6 in. steps at 1*s.* per foot run. The above are quarry prices; add 6*d.* per foot cube for carriage to London.

Messrs. Burt and Burt, Swanage, Dorset.

Purbeck Portland (Seacombe), Dorset.—A fine-grained hard limestone. Colour, whitish-brown. Weight, 151 lbs. per cubic foot. This stone has not been used in large quantities of late years on account of its inaccessibility and means of transit. It is, however, a splendid weather stone, and will no doubt be sought after before the Portland quarries are quite exhausted.

It has been used at the West India Docks; lighthouse at Margate; Clockhouse, Dover Pier; Winchester County Prison; Smith & Co.'s Warehouse, Strand, London; new church on Lord Eldon's estate, Encombe, and numerous churches, mansions, bridges, &c., in the county. It is also in request for steps, landings, &c., for which its hard character well adapts it.

Price, 1*s.* 3*d.* per foot cube at quarry; or about 1*s.* 10*d.* ditto in London. Labour, 1·5.

Messrs. Burt and Burt, Swanage, Dorset.

Roche Abbey, Yorks (Firbeck, near Rotherham).—A fine-grained magnesian limestone. Colour, whitish-grey. Weight, 129 lbs. per cubic foot dry, 141 lbs. ditto wet. Its chief constituents are, calcium carbonate 57·5, magnesium carbonate 39·5. This stone was recommended as a building stone by Sir Christopher Wren.

Used at Roche Abbey, Sandbeck Hall, Selby Hall, Tickhill, Blythe, Bawtry, Doncaster, Osberton and Milton Churches, Buckingham Palace, &c.

Blocks can be obtained up to 64 ft. cube.

Price, in random blocks at quarry, 10*d.* per foot cube. Carriage by traction engine from thence to rail, 4*d.* per foot cube; by rail to London, 8*d.* per foot cube. Labour, 1·0.

James Hodkin, Firbeck, Rotherham.

Smawse, Yorks (Bramham Moor, near Tadcaster).—Magnesian limestone. Colour, light yellowish-brown. Weight, 128 lbs. per cubic foot. All the stone for the repairs and alterations of York Minster, as well as for the restoration of York city walls, has been supplied from this quarry. The stone has also been used at Ripon Minster, Hull old church; St. Mary's Church and Minster, Beverley; church at Bishop Burton; several churches at York and in Lincolnshire, &c.

Blocks can be obtained up to 30 ft. cube.

Price, per foot cube for random blocks, on rail at Tadcaster Station, G.N. Ry., 1*s.* 3*d.* Railway rate to London (King's Cross), 10*s.* 10*d.* per ton for 5 ton lots, and 11*s.* 8*d.* per ton for 4 ton lots. Labour, 1·0.

Samuel Smith, Old Brewery, Tadcaster, Yorks.

Taynton or **Teynton**, Oxfordshire.—A shelly oolitic limestone. Colour, streaky brown. Weight, 134½ lbs. per cubic foot dry, 143 lbs. ditto wet. This stone has been used in the interior of St. Paul's Cathedral; Burford Church; Norman work in the Cathedral, Oxford; Merton College Chapel (13th century); Blenheim; Barrington Park, and in most of the ancient churches and mansions in the neighbourhood.

Blocks range from 5 ft. to 100 ft. cube, but 60 ft. is the usual limit as to size. Labour, 0·9.

Price, 1*s.* 6*d.* per foot cube on rail at Shipton Station, G.W. Ry., or 2*s.* per foot cube at Paddington.

Owners: Charlotte Groves & Sons, Milton-under-Wychwood, near Chipping Norton, Oxon.

Tisbury, Wiltshire (near Salisbury).—A siliciferous limestone of the same series as the Chilmark and Wardour stone, but is not considered as a weather stone so good. It has, however, been used in a number of buildings, churches, &c., in the neighbourhood, and also in London.

Used also in Tisbury Church (13th century), of which the dressings are in good condition, but the ashlar has decayed.

It is a free working stone, and has a slight fret. Labour, 0·9.

The original quarries owned by Lilly, at Tisbury, were closed some years ago.

No recent information.

Totternhoe, Bedfordshire, Dunstable.—A chalky, earthy limestone, containing minute black specks. Colour, light greenish-grey. Weight, 100 lbs. per cubic foot dry, and 118 lbs. ditto wet. Used in restorations to St. Albans Abbey, also at Peterborough Cathedral, Dunstable Priory Church, Woburn Abbey, and many churches in Bedfordshire, Hertfordshire, &c.

Blocks can be obtained from 2 ft. to 20 ft. cube. Labour, 0·55.

Price, 1*s.* 4*d.* per foot cube on trucks at station, or 1*s.* 8*d.* at London stations.

The Totternhoe Stone Co., Ltd., Gower Place, Euston Square, and Messrs. De Berrenger and Gower.

Weldon, Northamptonshire, Corby, Kettering.—A coarse, shelly oolite. Colour, reddish-brown. Weight, 16 cubic feet to the ton. These very old quarries have been recently reopened, and the stone used at the new University Library, Cambridge; restoration of the Chapter House, Lincoln Cathedral; Kettering Parish Church and Board Schools; Royal College of Music. Among the older buildings are Kirby

Hall, Lyveden; Rothwell Market House; Geddington Cross; many of the colleges at Cambridge, and churches in Northants.

The stone is very durable, hardening under exposure, while its close texture and perfect crystallization enable it to resist the action of frost and water. Its crushing weight is 140·3 tons per square foot. It is claimed for it that it can be sawn and worked as cheaply as "Corsham Down" (Bath) stone.

Price at quarry, 1*s.* 2*d.* and 1*s.* 4*d.* per foot cube. Railway rate to London, 5*d.* per foot cube in loads of 4 tons.

Agent: J. Rooke, Weldon Grange, Corby, Kettering.

Windrush, Oxfordshire, Burford.—A shelly oolite, similar to "Taynton" stone. Colour, cream. Weight, 131½ lbs. per cubic foot dry, and 148 lbs. ditto wet. This quarry is a very old one, and large quantities of stone cannot be supplied, owing to its distance from the rail. Used at Blenheim House, Windrush Church, Barrington House, mediæval churches in Oxford, and all the principal buildings in the vicinity.

Blocks can be obtained from 5 ft. to 40 ft. cube. Labour, 0·85.

Price, 8*d.* per foot cube at quarry, or 2*s.* 4*d.* per foot in London.

Mr. Wm. Wright, Windrush, Farringdon.

Caen and **Aubigny** stones are oolitic limestones, which may be mentioned here as they are greatly used in this country, although found in Normandy, France.

Caen stone is of a pale, cream-yellow colour. It is very soft when first quarried, but hardens upon exposure; it is easily worked and carved with the same tools as used for Bath stone. This stone is now only used in this country for internal work, the atmosphere being found unsuitable for it externally. It is well adapted for pulpits, screens, reredoses, fonts, sculpture, carvings, &c., and can be worked to a high finish. Used in Henry VII. Chapel, Westminster Abbey; Houses of Parliament, the Tower, Buckingham Palace, the large club houses in Pall Mall, and many other buildings.

Price per cube foot at depôt, 1*s.* 7*d.* Labour, 0·9.

Agent: Mr. Emile Foucard, 24, Hop Exchange, Borough, S.E.

Aubigny stone is probably of the same nature as Caen stone, namely, oolitic, but much more crystalline in its structure, very fine grained, and hard.

There are two workable beds, one averaging 24 in., the other 15 in., in thickness. The stone is quite unsuitable for external work in this country, as it weathers badly. Labour, 1·2.

Price, delivered to wharf in London, 2*s.* 4*d.* per foot cube.

Agent as for Caen stone.

ALABASTER.

Alabaster is composed of sulphate of lime, in a compact mass of crystalline grains. It is generally white and translucent, with reddish-brown colourings and veins, and when polished has somewhat of a pearly lustre. It is much used for internal decoration and monumental work.

It is found in huge lumps of about 10 or 15 tons, in the Keuper red marls, and resembles great roots of trees. No indication of its position can be ascertained except by searching and removing large quantities of mould.

The blocks are squared up for use with a toothed, cross-cut saw and axe; the small pieces, of which there are a great many, are burnt in the kiln for plaster of Paris.

Analysis: Calcium oxide, 32·60; sulphuric acid, 46·50; water, 20·90.

Alabaster is slightly soluble in water.

The following are the best known English varieties:

Chellaston Hill, Derby.—White, stained brown in veins. Weight, 142 lbs. per cubic foot. Used chiefly for manufacturing plaster of Paris; some blocks make good decorative work.

Fauld, Tutbury, Stafford.—White, stained with brownish-red. Weight, 148 lbs. per cubic foot. Good sound blocks are obtained here. The decorative work in the "marble hall" at Eaton Hall was supplied from Fauld.

Price, about 75*s*. per ton (random blocks) on rail.

Robertsbridge, Sussex.—The alabaster found here is chiefly used for manufacturing plaster of Paris.

Scropton, Warwick.—White, with reddish-brown irregular markings. Weight, 140 lbs. per cubic foot. Used for internal decorative work.

A purely white alabaster comes from Italy: it is a splendid material, semi-translucent, and very choice; small groups of statuary and figures are sculptured with great skill out of it.

A mottled kind resembling granite comes from Carrara; this is often carved into vases, tazzas, pedestals, ornaments, &c.

In Tuscany a white alabaster is found.

In Canada there are extensive quarries of workable alabaster; on the Grand River, and also in the United States, pure white alabaster is found at various places.

MARBLES—FOREIGN.

Marble is a general term given to any hard and compact limestone capable of taking a fine polish. It is found in all great limestone formations, and consists chiefly of pure carbonate of lime in a state of crystallization. The various colours are derived principally from metallic oxides, which give the marble a handsome appearance, much enhanced by polishing.

The Continent supply us with large quantities of marble, plain and decorative, much varied in character, and embracing a vast range of colour.

The chief supplies are obtained from Italy, France and Belgium; lesser supplies are from Switzerland, Spain, Portugal, and also recently from Africa.

The celebrated Carrara quarries in Tuscany, Italy, furnish us with the most important marbles; of these, Sicilian is the most useful. The term "Sicilian" is purely English, and is of doubtful origin: it is, however, a misnomer, as it does not come from Sicily; it is supposed to have obtained its derivation from being in its early days shipped from Leghorn to Sicily, and thence re-shipped to England.

It is known in Italy as Ravaccione, or Bianco Chiaro; in France, Blanc Clair; and in America as Ordinary.

Sicilian marble is of a bluish-white ground, mottled with darker shades of grey; it is used perhaps more than any other kind of marble for works of general utility. It is admirably adapted for monumental purposes, columns, statues, vases, stairs, wall linings, baths, chimney pieces, &c. All the varieties of Carrara marble, when used externally in this country, have perishable qualities; and it has been noticed that after exposure to the weather for thirty or forty years a gradual disintegration of the surface has taken place.

Perhaps the best example of its durability may be seen in the "Marble Arch," at the north entrance to Hyde Park, London.

This building was first erected in 1827 in front of Buckingham Palace and re-erected in its present position 1851. It does not show any great symptoms of decay, but to an experienced eye, disintegration of the surface is visible.

This arch is famed for the sculptured spandrels executed by Flaxman.

Sicilian is extensively used in the Albert Memorial, Hyde Park. The whole of the figures in the podium, the statuary groups on the four angle piers, representing Europe, Asia, Africa, and America, and also the pedestal on which the statue of the Prince Consort sits, are of Sicilian marble. This monument has been erected over thirty years, and generally is in fairly good condition, although portions show signs of decay. It should, however, be stated that no expense was spared in selecting this marble, which was the best for the purpose that could be obtained.

At the Crystal Palace, Sydenham, Sicilian marble is much used in the various statues in the grounds, and in vases, &c.; these have been exposed to the weather for about fifty years, and are generally in a bad state of decay.

In various buildings in London it has been used externally, but with only a fair amount of success.

When used out of doors, the marble with slightly bluish tint and of uniform colour should be selected, this being the hardest and toughest, and better able to withstand atmospheric influences.

Statuary marble is the most beautiful of all marbles, and is from the same Carrara quarries; it is probably the purest limestone in existence, very crystalline in its structure, and of a fine and compact texture. As its name implies, it is almost exclusively used for the higher departments of sculptural art, for which it is so well adapted, such as statues, groups, monuments, and ornamental enrichments where delicate and refined treatment is required.

This marble is considerably varied in character, the best blocks being of a perfectly white colour throughout; these are much sought after, but are only occasionally found quite pure, and then command high prices, as much as £3 per foot cube being paid for them.

Cloudy markings and spots of a bluish-grey colour in the blocks are defects, which must be avoided in sculpture work, hence its costliness.

Bastard Statuary is the name given to blocks having coloured markings; these blocks when hard in texture are of good commercial value, and make up well into chimney-pieces, tablets, &c., and take a high polish.

Vein marble is another of the varieties of Carrara; it is of much whiter ground than the Sicilian, and is marked with dark pencil-tinted veins. It is more or less valuable according to the regularity and fineness of its veinings. It is used chiefly in internal decoration, for stairs, chimney-pieces, wall linings, table tops, &c.

This marble was formerly in much request on account of its appearance, adaptation, and easy working; latterly, however, the demand has somewhat diminished, having been to some extent superseded by the Sicilian marble, which has been previously described.

Bardilla (Bardiglio) is a very chaste and quiet-looking marble, and is one of the Carrara series. It is of a bluish-grey ground, with numerous black veins running through it in all directions. It was at one time much used for chimney-pieces and decorative work generally, but latterly has got out of date, and made way for newer marbles.

Dove marble, as its name indicates, is of a dark bluish-grey colour, with lighter marks or cloudings over its surface; sometimes it has a lighter ground with faint dark marks or veins This marble was chiefly used for chimney-pieces, &c., but is now for a time out of fashion.

This marble also is one of the Carrara series.

Pavonazzo is a new, and now well-known, marble. It is raised near Carrara. It is of a very rich colour, the ground varying from a creamy-white to a yellowish-brown, with veinings of purple, and here and there a greenish tinge, which much enhances its value. It is much used for wall linings, where it is seen to great advantage on account of its markings, and also for chimney-pieces, table tops, &c. It has only been of recent years introduced into this country, but has taken well, and is in much request for decorative purposes.

The above enumeration includes most of the varieties of marble that are found in the extensive quarries at Carrara, but in other parts of Italy are raised coloured marbles of great beauty; the names of a few are here given.

Black and Gold is a very handsome black marble with yellow veins. The veining is very beautiful, running from white through every gradation of yellow to light brown, the pencillings being very delicate. It is not so much in use now as formerly, having gone out of fashion, but it is still used to a considerable extent in good buildings for chimney-pieces, pedestals, table tops, &c.; its dark colour forms an admirable contrast to sculptured figures in statuary, alabaster, or other light-coloured objects of art.

Genoa Green, which takes its name from the town it indicates, is a handsome marble: its ground is dark green in colour, filled with veinings of a lighter green and white; it is used for pilasters, chimney-pieces, and wall surface decoration, for which it is much adapted.

It is frequently sawn up into veneer when a specially good figured block is obtained.

Sienna is quarried near the town of that name. It is of a rich golden-yellow colour, with purple and black veins beautifully interspersed. On account of its scarcity, it is difficult to obtain the deep-coloured blocks, except on payment of a very high price, and it is stated that the best figured blocks are sold by weight.

It is a most beautiful marble for all decorative purposes.

Egyptian Green. This marble has a darkish green ground with spots of grey and occasionally of white. Another variety has a red ground with clear dark green veins and a network of white lines. These marbles are very choice; they are somewhat difficult to work, but look well and take a good polish.

Both marbles are quarried in the neighbourhood of Carrara.

Rhondona, a marble quarried at Mount Rhondona, Tuscany, has a ground of pale pinkish-white, with dark grey veins, and tinges of greyish-purple.

It is a marble of great beauty.

Breccia. This term is applied to brecciated marbles, or those which contain fragments of older rocks, held together by an intermediate material. It is sometimes termed Puddingstones, but this term should only apply to those marbles in which the fragments are rounded instead of being angular.

The Italian Breccias are very beautiful.

Belgian marbles are few in number, and these are generally considered to be of a common and cheap class.

They have been most effectively worked by the Belgians, who, to their credit, have developed a marble trade which has made their country the principal European market for this class of coloured marbles, both in the raw material and the worked-up. Their exportation of chimney-pieces alone must be of enormous magnitude.

St. Anne's marble is the best known and the most useful; it has a greyish-black ground with somewhat lighter shades, and flowered with white patches and veins. It is a sound marble of great utility, looks well, and takes a high polish.

Rouge Royal is a general term for several varieties of these marbles, all of which have fanciful names, such as Rouge Griotte, Rouge Fleurie, Rouge Rose, Rouge Byzantine, &c.; these, however, have much the same colour and character throughout.

The best Rouge is considered to be of a dark brownish-red ground, with grey cloudings, and the veinings well marked, of a clear white.

Selected marble of this description has quite a handsome appearance.

It has come to be generally understood that to specify Rouge Griotte is to specify the best Rouge that can be obtained.

The defects in the Rouge consists of its being generally unsound, and containing clayish shakes, which require some amount of skill and ingenuity on the part of the workman in concealing with stopping.

A large quantity of the above two marbles (St. Anne's and Rouge) are worked up chiefly into chimney-pieces, table tops, fender curbs, &c., and imported into this country at a low price. This particular class of work is much cultivated in Belgium, where labour is cheap.

Blue Belge has a bluish-black ground, with fine white veins; it is a very useful marble, but is not well figured, as the veins run in straight lines, which become somewhat monotonous in appearance when polished; it is the most common of all the Belgian marbles.

Belgium Black is considered the finest black marble to be obtained in the world; no other country produces a marble that will compare with it in uniformity of colour and closeness of texture. It takes a high polish. This marble is, however, difficult to work on account of its hard nature, and is therefore costly to produce.

Of French marbles there are a great number, most of which are very beautiful.

A few of those imported into this country are here given.

Griotte. This marble has a deep red ground, with numerous small spots or eyes scattered over the surface of pure pearly white, which gives it a beautiful appearance. It is difficult to work owing to its formation, which is much laminated, being similar to the leaves in a book, or, rather, the laminations in slate.

It will cut better one way with the chisel than the other, and sand and water are the chief agents in its manipulation.

Languedoc is a bright red marble, streaked with white and grey veins. It is a very handsome marble, the white portion in some cases being semi-transparent.

The result of the sharp contrast in colour between the red and white is very striking, and much enhances its appearance.

It is quarried at Alais (Gard), in the old province of Languedoc.

Rouge Jasper is a marble in which tints of red and yellow appear side by side, with white in sharp contrast, and in irregular patches.

Lamartine. These marbles are known as Brocatelle's, and are found in the neighbourhood of Molinges. They are considered to be very handsome, their contrasts of colour being most pleasing. **Jaune Lamartine** is of a fine yellow ground, and profusely veined with fine pencillings of red and brown; it is the pick of the marbles of Molinges. **Jaune Fleuri** is another variety of the same; it is of similar appearance, but of a much darker yellow, some specimens being of a rich reddish brown, and the veins in it more closely distributed than in Jaune Lamartine.

Brocatelle Violet is another of the series; this has been the longest known and worked. The ground is of a violet tint, and it is veined and figured with white and yellow. It much resembles in appearance Spanish Brocatelle, but cannot quite compare with it in beauty.

Campan. The Campan marbles are so called from the situation of the quarries in the Upper Pyrenees; they are exceedingly beautiful, and present great varieties of colour.

Campan Vert is the best known; it is of two kinds, the clear and the dark. The former has very light shades of green, softly blended with the veins of darker green. The dark variety has a ground of dark green, with numerous flesh-coloured and red spots, interspersed with thin white veins. **Campan Rouge** has a dull red ground, with veins of darker red and bronze-green, mixed with flesh-coloured and greenish-white spots. **Campan Isabelle** has a rose-coloured ground, merging, in some places, into a dark red, with a few white spots and pale green veins.

Brocatelle d'Espagne (Brocatella) is quarried near Tortosa, Catalonia, Spain.

It has a dark red ground, covered with yellowish-grey and clear white spots, with some violet spots and veins; it is composed of crushed shells, and is properly speaking a lumachello. It is a very beautiful and choice marble, but somewhat out of date at the present time.

Emperor's Red is a Portuguese marble, and quarried in the neighbourhood of Lisbon; it is of a mottled yellowish-pink, some large patches of light red occurring occasionally, with veinings of dark red and light brown.

The demand for it, however, is as yet only limited.

Cippollino. This name is given to marbles having a whitish ground traversed with veins of green talc. There are a number of varieties, and to this class belongs the rediscovered Antique Cippollino marble of

Saillon, Switzerland. It is largely used in this country, chiefly for wall linings and internal decoration, for which its colourings render it particularly adapted. A kind found at Pentelicus, in Greece, is called **Statuary Cippollino.**

A fine Cippollino is quarried at Onofrio, in Corsica, and other varieties are found at Basle, in Switzerland.

Numidian. The marbles bearing this name are of great variety, and are obtained near the village of Kleber, about twenty miles north-east of Oran, in the western part of Algiers. These marbles comprise a creamy white **Marmor Bianco**; a flesh-tinted **Rosa**; a fine variety of **Cippollino**; various specimens of **Giallo Antico**; yellow marbles of various tints, and brecciated marbles, including **Breccia Sanguine, Breccia Coronato,** and **Breccia Grande,** the last named of a deep red colour, slightly brecciated, and resembling Rosso Antico.

These breccias are all of great beauty, sound, and even in texture, and take a high polish.

All these marbles are shipped at Oran, Algiers.

Onyx (Mexican), quarried at Pueblos, near Vera Cruz. This marble is a splendid material for the decorative arts: every colour may be found in it—green in all its gradations; white and greys of all tints; red, pink, black, violet, yellow, and even blue, and some portions resemble jade. Its density surpasses all known marbles, and it is considered to be the connecting link between precious stones and marble, being as easily worked as any other marble.

As the polish is equal to that of the finest and most precious stones, such as agate, amethyst, jade and onyx, and will last for many years, so it is adaptable for external as well as internal decoration: this same polish is produced as easily as upon any other fine marble. It can be cut as thin as glass, and is nearly as transparent, and in Mexico it is used in some of the cathedrals and churches for windows, giving that "dim religious light" so much valued. It is obtained in large blocks, but the uncertainty of demand has made it scarce in this country.

Onyx (Algerian). This marble is translucent; its colours are usually amber and white; it is used chiefly for ornaments, small panels, &c.

Onyx (Brazilian). This is a green marble, that is most exquisitely veined with red and yellow, and more than compares in beauty with that produced in Mexico.

The following merchants are the chief importers of foreign marbles into this country:—

Messrs. Arthur Lee, Bros., Canons Marsh, Bristol.

Messrs. Walton, Gooddy and Cripps & Co., 14, Wharf, City Road, London.

Messrs. Anselm Odling & Sons, 132, New North Road, London, N.

Messrs. Farmer & Brindley, Westminster Bridge Road, London, S.E.

Mr. B. Fabricotti, Grosvenor Road, Pimlico, London, S.W., and Carrara, Italy.

The prices hereunder quoted are for marble in block, at the depôt in London, which are subject, of course, to the usual fluctuations. No allowance for waste or profit is made. If blocks of extra dimensions are required, the prices will necessarily range somewhat higher.

Blocks.	Per cubic foot.					Marble slabs, averaging 7 ft. super, polished on face, and edges jointed, in quantities of not less than 100 ft. super, delivered in London, without waste or fixing. Per foot super. ¾ inch.		1 inch.	
	s.	d.		s.	d.	s.	d.	s.	d.
Bardilla	13	0	to	15	0	4	9	5	3
Belgian Black	12	0	,,	14	0	4	6	5	0
Black and Gold	20	0	,,	23	0	5	6	6	3
Brocatello (Spanish)	20	0	,,	25	0	5	6	6	0
Breccia (Sanguine)	22	0	,,	30	0	6	0	7	0
Campan Vert	25	0	,,	28	0	5	9	6	3
Cipollino (Saillon)	16	0	,,	18	0	4	9	5	3
Dove	15	0	,,	18	0	4	6	5	0
Emperor's Red	16	0	,,	18	0	5	0	5	6
Genoa Green	20	0	,,	22	0	5	3	5	9
Griotte (Italian)	46	0	,,	50	0	8	0	9	6
Jaune Lamartine	22	0	,,	24	0	5	3	5	9
Onyx (Mexican)	30	0	,,	60	0	13	0	16	0
Onyx (Algerian)	40	0	,,	50	0	12	0	14	0
Pavonazza (Italian)	39	0	,,	42	0	6	3	7	0
Pavonazza (Numidian)	22	0	,,	30	0	5	9	6	3
Rouge Royal	12	0	,,	16	0	4	6	4	9
Rose Numidian	22	0	,,	30	0	6	3	7	0
Sicilian	10	0	,,	13	0	3	9	4	0
Statuary	30	0	,,	60	0	12	0	13	0
Sienna	30	0	,,	60	0	10	6	12	0
St. Anne's	14	0	,,	16	0	4	0	4	6
Vein	11	0	,,	13	0	3	9	4	0

It should be stated that when marble work is being estimated for, or in prospect, inquiry should be made, and quotations sought, of the various marble merchants herein enumerated, in order to ensure a correct price.

MARBLES—BRITISH.

Of the varieties found in Great Britain, the best known and most beautiful are those of various colours from Devonshire; black and grey from Derbyshire; Purbeck marble from Dorsetshire; Petworth marble from Sussex; and Mona marble from Anglesea.

Ireland produces splendid marbles in all colours; black from Galway, Kilkenny, and other counties; dark grey and sienna from King's County; white from Donegal; Victoria red from County Cork; green from Connemara.

Scotland produces several varieties, but they are chiefly used locally.

The following are a few of the best known quarries:—

Devonshire.

Ashburton, near Torquay.—A dark mottled marble; has a ground of dark warm grey, with fine coral red markings and pinkish-white veins intermixed; also a dark ground with small fossils, and known as "bird's-eye."

Ogwell, near Torquay.—Red clouded, with brown and grey spots and markings. Dark grey, thickly studded with small fossils, corals and shells.

Petitor Marbles, near Torquay.—Fossil Yellow Clouded, having a ground of pale grey, with grey and dark red veins, and slight dashes of yellow; Pink Clouded, having a ground of pale pink, with patches of yellow and grey, and small dark brown markings here and there; Dark Spot, having a ground of warm grey, mottled like granite, with small black specks.

These are known as Babbicombe marbles. Some blocks consist entirely of fossil corals, and are known as Madrepore marble.

Ipplepen, Newton.—Black-clouded, with red and white veins and pink spar. Large quantities of this marble was used for decorative purposes in the new Foreign Offices and India Offices, Whitehall; as columns, pilasters, chimney-pieces, &c. Dove ground, figured with flesh-coloured veins. Purple ground, with red and grey splashings.

The above are supplied by A. W. Blackler & Son, Royal Marble Works, St. Mary Church, Torquay.

Oreston, Plymouth.—Used for Plymouth Breakwater. Attacked by Pholades (see page 165).

A green marble, and a rose-coloured spar, of great beauty, are quarried at Kitley Park.

A marble exhibiting mottled pink and grey, with marks and patches of blood red, is found at Buckfastleigh. Varieties of black and white marble are quarried at Bridestow, South Tawton, and Drewsteighton.

Marbles having a black ground and large veins of semi-transparent white are found at Chudleigh, Staverton, and Berry Pomeroy.

The whole series of these Devon marbles are highly figured, and possess a variety and range of colour that is exceedingly beautiful, quite vying in merit with any foreign variety. In fact, these marbles have been exported to Italy and other parts of the Continent, the East and West Indies, Australia, South Africa, and even to Zanzibar. Among other places in this country where they have been used are the municipal buildings of Birmingham and Leeds, and at the Brompton Oratory, at which latter place are some columns upwards of 2 ft. diameter and 10 ft. high, formed from single blocks of marble.

Blocks.

		s.	d.
Under 3 ft. long	per foot cube	4	9
,, 4 ft. ,,	,,	6	0
,, 6 ft. ,,	,,	7	3

Columns.

		s.	d.
2 in. diameter up to 2 ft. long	per foot run	7	0
3 in. ,, ,, 3 ft. ,,	,,	7	6
4 in. ,, ,, 4 ft. ,,	,,	8	6
3 in. ,, ,, 5 ft. ,,	,,	10	0
6 in. ,, ,, 6 ft. ,,	,,	11	6
8 in. ,, ,, 6 ft. ,,	,,	15	3
10 in. ,, ,, 6 ft. ,,	,,	17	9
12 in. ,, ,, 6 ft. ,,	,,	24	6

Special prices above these dimensions.

Derbyshire.

Ashford, near Rowsley. The marbles quarried here include the finest black marble found in the United Kingdom, and also the kind called rosewood. The latter is a dense brown laminated limestone, with a pattern resembling the grain of rosewood. It is only obtainable in small sizes, and is chiefly employed for small articles, and for inlay work.

Bakewell.—Brown.

Colehill, near Matlock.—Black.

Staverton.—Dove, and red and white.

These marbles have until recently been but little used for decorative purposes, except for chimney-pieces, ornaments, &c. The prevailing colours range from light grey to a dark brown, and are highly figured, containing fossils of all kinds, corals, encrinites (stone lilies), and shells, forming the curious ornamental markings on its surface; hence they have various names, such as bird's eye, dog's tooth, mussel, &c.

Blue John. This is a Derby fluor spar, from Tre-Cliff, near Castleton. It is translucent, exhibiting a ground of clouded white and warm grey, tinged with iridescent amber-colour, with wave-like bands and lines of very dark purple, resembling the colour of writing ink. It has only been obtained in small sizes, rarely exceeding six inches in depth, it is very scarce and much sought after, and consequently expensive.

Dorsetshire.

Purbeck.—This marble shows a number of minute fresh-water winkle shells embedded in a dark bluish-grey limestone, which is very hard and compact and takes a good polish. It is quarried in the Upper Purbeck beds near Swanage, and can be obtained in blocks seven or eight feet long, but rarely more than a foot in thickness.

The Purbeck marble was well known for its quarries during the Middle Ages, when it was in great request for decorating the clustered shafts, tombs, and fonts, and for paving in cathedrals and churches.

All the varieties of this marble contain a proportion of clay in their composition, and because of this, it is not so durable as some of the older marbles of Great Britain, as it is acted upon sooner by damp and atmospheric changes. When used for slender columns, it is worked with the planes of lamination vertical, but the result is a greater tendency to decay; examples of this may be seen in the shafts at the Temple Church, Strand, and in the large columns supporting the clerestorey, Westminster Abbey; and at Salisbury and Lincoln Cathedrals.

At the present time there is not much demand for this marble, being scarcely sufficient to keep more than a few men at work to procure it.

Prices from *4s.* to *8s.* per cubic foot, according to size; the larger blocks being most costly.

Supplied by Messrs. Burt and Burt, Swanage.

Kent.

A marble similar to Purbeck and known as Bethersden, and likewise as Lovelace marble, is obtained near Ashford.

Examples may be seen at Hythe Church and churches in the vicinity, where in some cases the marble has apparently been varnished instead of being polished.

Sussex.

Petworth.—This marble is similar to Purbeck, but shells are a little larger. The episcopal chair of Canterbury is made of this marble; it was also much used in the cathedrals and churches in the south-east of England. There are no traces of marble quarries at Petworth; it is, however, found at Eastbourne, Lewes, and near Horsham.

Serpentine, one of the most beautiful of the ornamental stones of this country, although classed with the marbles, is not considered to be a marble in the general acceptance of the term. It is composed chiefly of hydrous silicate of magnesia, associated with steatite or soap stone, olivine, and other minerals.

Serpentine derives its name from the mottled appearance of its surface, which resembles somewhat the skin of a serpent. It is found in a great variety of colours, from olive green to a rich red, interspersed with white steatite veins, and crystals of green diallage, all of which give it a beautiful appearance. It is easily worked and takes a splendid polish, and is much used for internal decoration, such as columns, pilasters, panels, chimney-pieces, vases, &c. It is not well adapted for outdoor work as it soon loses its polish, although it has been used in several instances externally with a moderate amount of success.

The best, and most used varieties of serpentine, are obtained from the Lizard promontory in Cornwall. The island of Anglesea also supplies very fine specimens, under the name of Mona marble, which much resembles Verd antique.

In Scotland serpentine is found in Aberdeenshire, Banffshire and the Shetland Isles. In Ireland, Connemara furnishes a serpentine in large blocks, which is commonly termed "Irish green."

Some beautiful specimens of these stones may be seen in the Geological Museum, Jermyn Street, London, S.W.

IRISH MARBLES.

Many of these well-known marbles, such as the Connemara Green, from County Galway, and the Victoria Red, from County Cork, are quite equal in beauty to any foreign marbles.

The prices here quoted are free on rail at Kilkenny. Special through rates to London, Liverpool, Bristol, &c., can be obtained on application to the Irish Marble Co. (Richard Colles), Kilkenny.

Sawn Slabs and Scantlings, per foot superficial.

Thickness.	Kilkenny.	Pure Black.	Victoria Red.	Connemara Green.	Dark Grey.	St. Acres.
	s. *d.*	*s.* *d.*	*s.* *d.*	*s.* *d.*	*s.* *d.*	*s.* *d.*
¾ in.	1 1	1 3	1 2	2 6	0 8	1 1
1 in.	1 4	1 7	1 5	2 9	0 10	1 4
1¼ in.	1 8	1 11	1 9	3 6	1 0	1 8
1½ in.	1 10	2 2	2 0	4 0	1 2	1 10
1¾ in.	2 0	2 4	2 2	4 3	1 4	2 0
2 in.	2 3	2 7	2 5	4 6	1 6	2 3
2½ in.	2 9	3 3	3 0	5 0	1 9	2 9
3 in.	3 3	3 9	3 6	5 6	2 0	3 3
4 in.	4 3	5 0	4 6	6 9	2 6	4 3
5 in.	5 3	6 0	5 6	8 0	3 0	5 3
6 in.	6 0	7 0	6 6	9 0	3 6	6 0

If polished, add 1*s.* per foot super for each side polished of slabs up to 2 inches thick.

Column Shafts, per foot run.

Diameter.	Dark Grey. Fine Sanded.		Dark Grey. Polished.		St. Acres and Kilkenny. Polished.		Victoria Red. Polished.		Pure Black. Polished.		Connemara Green. Polished	
	s.	*d.*	*s.*	*d.*	*s.*	*d.*	*s.*	*d.*	*s.*	*d.*	*s.*	*d.*
4 in. (& under)	3	9	5	0	5	6	5	9	6	6	9	6
4½ in. ,,	4	0	5	3	6	0	6	3	7	0	10	6
5 in. ,,	4	3	5	6	6	6	6	9	7	6	11	6
5½ in. ,,	4	6	6	0	7	0	7	3	8	3	12	9
6 in. ,,	4	9	6	6	7	6	7	9	9	0	14	0
6½ in. ,,	5	0	7	0	8	3	8	6	9	9	15	3
7 in. ,,	5	6	7	6	9	0	9	3	10	6	16	6
7½ in. ,,	6	0	8	3	9	9	10	0	11	3	17	9
8 in. ,,	6	6	9	0	10	6	11	0	12	0	19	0
8½ in. ,,	7	0	9	9	11	3	12	0	13	0	21	0
9 in. ,,	7	6	10	6	12	0	13	0	14	0	23	0
10 in. ,,	9	0	12	0	14	0	15	0	16	6	27	0
11 in. ,,	10	6	13	6	16	0	17	0	19	0	31	0
12 in. ,,	12	0	15	0	18	0	19	0	21	6	35	0
14 in. ,,	14	6	18	0	22	0	23	0	24	0	43	0

LIST OF GRANITES.

A FEW of the principal quarries in Great Britain may be given. Weight, from 162 lbs. to 182 lbs. per cubic foot:—

Cornwall.—Cheesewring, grey; De Lank, grey; Gunnislake, white and grey; Luxullian, grey; Penryn, grey; Penzance, greenish-grey; Trewthy, porphyritic.

Devonshire.—Freemator, grey; Haytor, grey; Pew Tor, reddish brown and grey; Trowlesworthy, red—the only red granite in the West of England.

Westmorland.—Shapfell, pink or reddish brown, with flesh-coloured crystals.

Aberdeen.—Birsmore, grey and pink; Bodham, grey; Correnie, salmon, grey, red; Clinterty, reddish-grey; Dancing Cairn, grey, sometimes red; Rubislaw, grey; Peterhead, red; Stirlinghill, red.

Argyleshire.—Ross of Mull, pink, red, grey.

Granite.

	Cornish.		Aberdeen.	
	s.	*d.*	*s.*	*d.*
In block, including waste, cartage, and profit within 4 miles of London depôt . . per foot cube	4	3	5	6
Ditto, including hoisting and scaffolding ,,	5	1	6	3
Ditto, ditto, and setting . . . ,,	5	9	7	0
Plain work to beds and joints . . per foot super	1	6	2	0
Ditto, face roughly axed . . . ,,	2	0	2	6
Ditto, ditto finely axed . . . ,,	2	6	3	0
Sunk work, rough . . . . ,,	2	3	2	9
Ditto, faced . . . . . ,,	3	6	4	6
Moulded work, ditto . . . . ,,	4	0	4	6
Ditto, ditto, circular . . . ,,	4	6	5	0

A new surface, called "finely emeried," has been recently introduced; the cost is the same as in polished work, as very little suffices to put the gloss on after being finely emeried.

Polished Granite Columns—Red, Blue, or Grey.

		s.	*d.*
3 in. diameter	per foot run	10	0
4 in. ditto	,,	12	0
5 in. ditto	,,	12	0
6 in. ditto	,,	12	0
7 in. ditto	,,	12	0
8 in. ditto	,,	14	0
9 in. ditto	,,	14	0
10 in. ditto	,,	15	0
11 in. ditto	,,	17	0
12 in. ditto	,,	20	0
14 in. ditto	,,	23	0
15 in. ditto	,,	26	0
	,,	28	0

The above prices are for columns of moderate length delivered in London. Fixing to be charged *extra*.

NOTE.—The use of polished granite dressings in modern buildings of a superior character is very noticeable. Such may be priced *approximately* at from 15*s.* per foot cube for a quite plain building, to 25*s.* per foot cube for better class structures, up to 40*s.* per foot cube where elaborate work or carving is introduced. During the last year or two a few very effective Norwegian granites have been introduced, *vide* Broad Street House, the Oxford Music Hall, Scott's Restaurant, Haymarket. The prices in these materials only run about 5 per cent. more than Aberdeen granites. Large quantities of these granites are always in stock in Aberdeen, so there is no risk of unnecessary delay.

TABLES OF DIAMETERS, CIRCUMFERENCES, AND AREAS OF CIRCLES.

Diameter.	Circumference.	Area.	Diameter.	Circumference.	Area.	Diameter.	Circumference.	Area.
$\frac{1}{8}$	·3927	·01227	$6\frac{3}{4}$	21·205	35·784	$13\frac{3}{8}$	42·018	140·500
$\frac{1}{4}$	·7854	·04909	$6\frac{7}{8}$	21·598	37·122	$13\frac{1}{2}$	42·411	143·139
$\frac{3}{8}$	1·1781	·1104	7	21·991	38·484	$13\frac{5}{8}$	42·804	145·802
$\frac{1}{2}$	1·5708	·1963	$7\frac{1}{8}$	22·383	39·871	$13\frac{3}{4}$	43·197	148·489
$\frac{5}{8}$	1·9635	·3068	$7\frac{1}{4}$	22·776	41·282	$13\frac{7}{8}$	43·589	151·201
$\frac{3}{4}$	2·3562	·4417	$7\frac{3}{8}$	23·169	42·718	14	43·982	153·938
$\frac{7}{8}$	2·7489	·6013	$7\frac{1}{2}$	23·562	44·178	$14\frac{1}{8}$	44·375	156·699
1	3·1416	·7854	$7\frac{5}{8}$	23·954	45·663	$14\frac{1}{4}$	44·767	159·485
$1\frac{1}{8}$	3·5343	·9940	$7\frac{3}{4}$	24·347	47·173	$14\frac{3}{8}$	45·160	162·295
$1\frac{1}{4}$	3·9270	1·2271	$7\frac{7}{8}$	24·740	48·707	$14\frac{1}{2}$	45·553	165·130
$1\frac{3}{8}$	4·3197	1·4848	8	25·132	50·265	$14\frac{5}{8}$	45·945	167·989
$1\frac{1}{2}$	4·7124	1·7671	$8\frac{1}{8}$	25·515	51·848	$14\frac{3}{4}$	46·338	170·873
$1\frac{5}{8}$	5·1051	2·0739	$8\frac{1}{4}$	25·918	53·456	$14\frac{7}{8}$	46·731	173·782
$1\frac{3}{4}$	5·4978	2·4052	$8\frac{3}{8}$	26·310	55·088	15	47·124	176·715
$1\frac{7}{8}$	5·8905	2·7611	$8\frac{1}{2}$	26·703	56·745	$15\frac{1}{8}$	47·516	179·672
2	6·2832	3·1416	$8\frac{5}{8}$	27·096	58·426	$15\frac{1}{4}$	47·909	182·654
$2\frac{1}{8}$	6·6759	3·5465	$8\frac{3}{4}$	27·489	60·132	$15\frac{3}{8}$	48·302	185·661
$2\frac{1}{4}$	7·0686	3·9760	$8\frac{7}{8}$	27·881	61·862	$15\frac{1}{2}$	48·694	188·692
$2\frac{3}{8}$	7·4613	4·4302	9	28·274	63·617	$15\frac{5}{8}$	49·087	191·748
$2\frac{1}{2}$	7·8540	4·9087	$9\frac{1}{8}$	28·667	65·396	$15\frac{3}{4}$	49·480	194·828
$2\frac{5}{8}$	8·2467	5·4119	$9\frac{1}{4}$	29·059	67·200	$15\frac{7}{8}$	49·872	197·933
$2\frac{3}{4}$	8·6394	5·9395	$9\frac{3}{8}$	29·452	69·029	16	50·265	201·062
$2\frac{7}{8}$	9·0321	6·4918	$9\frac{1}{2}$	29·845	70·882	$16\frac{1}{8}$	50·658	204·216
3	9·4248	7·0686	$9\frac{5}{8}$	30·237	72·759	$16\frac{1}{4}$	51·051	207·394
$3\frac{1}{8}$	9·8175	7·6699	$9\frac{3}{4}$	30·630	74·662	$16\frac{3}{8}$	51·443	210·597
$3\frac{1}{4}$	10·210	8·2957	$9\frac{7}{8}$	31·023	76·588	$16\frac{1}{2}$	51·836	213·825
$3\frac{3}{8}$	10·602	8·9462	10	31·416	78·540	$16\frac{5}{8}$	52·229	217·077
$3\frac{1}{2}$	10·995	9·6211	$10\frac{1}{8}$	31·808	80·515	$16\frac{3}{4}$	52·621	220·353
$3\frac{5}{8}$	11·388	10·320	$10\frac{1}{4}$	32·201	82·516	$16\frac{7}{8}$	53·014	223·654
$3\frac{3}{4}$	11·781	11·044	$10\frac{3}{8}$	32·594	84·540	17	53·407	226·980
$3\frac{7}{8}$	12·173	11·793	$10\frac{1}{2}$	32·986	86·590	$17\frac{1}{8}$	53·799	230·330
4	12·566	12·566	$10\frac{5}{8}$	33·379	88·664	$17\frac{1}{4}$	54·192	233·705
$4\frac{1}{8}$	12·959	13·364	$10\frac{3}{4}$	33·772	90·762	$17\frac{3}{8}$	54·585	237·104
$4\frac{1}{4}$	13·351	14·186	$10\frac{7}{8}$	34·164	92·885	$17\frac{1}{2}$	54·978	240·528
$4\frac{3}{8}$	13·744	15·033	11	34·557	95·033	$17\frac{5}{8}$	55·370	243·977
$4\frac{1}{2}$	14·137	15·904	$11\frac{1}{8}$	34·950	97·205	$17\frac{3}{4}$	55·763	247·450
$4\frac{5}{8}$	14·529	16·800	$11\frac{1}{4}$	35·343	99·402	$17\frac{7}{8}$	56·156	250·947
$4\frac{3}{4}$	14·922	17·720	$11\frac{3}{8}$	35·735	101·623	18	56·548	254·469
$4\frac{7}{8}$	15·315	18·665	$11\frac{1}{2}$	36·128	103·869	$18\frac{1}{8}$	56·941	258·016
5	15·708	19·635	$11\frac{5}{8}$	36·521	106·139	$18\frac{1}{4}$	57·334	261·587
$5\frac{1}{8}$	16·100	20·629	$11\frac{3}{4}$	36·913	108·434	$18\frac{3}{8}$	57·726	265·182
$5\frac{1}{4}$	16·493	21·647	$11\frac{7}{8}$	37·306	110·753	$18\frac{1}{2}$	58·119	268·803
$5\frac{3}{8}$	16·886	22·690	12	37·699	113·097	$18\frac{5}{8}$	58·512	272·447
$5\frac{1}{2}$	17·278	23·758	$12\frac{1}{8}$	38·091	115·466	$18\frac{3}{4}$	58·905	276·117
$5\frac{5}{8}$	17·671	24·850	$12\frac{1}{4}$	38·484	117·859	$18\frac{7}{8}$	59·297	279·811
$5\frac{3}{4}$	18·064	25·967	$12\frac{3}{8}$	38·877	120·276	19	59·690	283·529
$5\frac{7}{8}$	18·457	27·108	$12\frac{1}{2}$	39·270	122·718	$19\frac{1}{8}$	60·083	287·272
6	18·849	28·274	$12\frac{5}{8}$	39·662	125·184	$19\frac{1}{4}$	60·475	291·039
$6\frac{1}{8}$	19·242	29·464	$12\frac{3}{4}$	40·055	127·676	$19\frac{3}{8}$	60·868	294·831
$6\frac{1}{4}$	19·635	30·679	$12\frac{7}{8}$	40·448	130·192	$19\frac{1}{2}$	61·261	298·648
$6\frac{3}{8}$	20·027	31·919	13	40·840	132·732	$19\frac{5}{8}$	61·653	302·489
$6\frac{1}{2}$	20·420	33·183	$13\frac{1}{8}$	41·233	135·297	$19\frac{3}{4}$	62·046	306·355
$6\frac{5}{8}$	20·813	34·471	$13\frac{1}{4}$	41·626	137·886	$19\frac{7}{8}$	62·439	310·245

Diameter.	Circumference.	Area.	Diameter.	Circumference.	Area.	Diameter.	Circumference.	Area.
20	62·832	314·160	30½	95·818	730·618	45	141·372	1590·43
20⅛	63·224	318·099	30¾	96·604	742·644	45¼	142·157	1608·15
20¼	63·617	322·063	31	97·389	754·769	45½	142·942	1625·97
20⅜	64·010	326·051	31¼	98·175	766·992	45¾	143·728	1643·89
20½	64·402	330·064	31½	98·968	779·313	46	144·513	1661·90
20⅝	64·795	334·101	31¾	99·745	791·732	46¼	145·299	1680·01
20¾	65·188	338·163	32	100·531	804·249	46½	146·084	1698·23
20⅞	65·580	342·250	32¼	101·316	816·865	46¾	146·869	1716·54
21	65·973	346·361	32½	102·102	829·578	47	147·655	1734·94
21⅛	66·366	350·497	32¾	102·887	842·390	47¼	148·440	1753·45
21¼	66·759	354·657	33	103·672	855·30	47½	149·226	1772·05
21⅜	67·151	358·841	33¼	104·458	868·30	47¾	150·011	1790·76
21½	67·544	363·051	33½	105·243	881·41	48	150·796	1809·56
21⅝	67·937	367·284	33¾	106·029	894·61	48¼	151·582	1828·46
21¾	68·329	371·543	34	106·814	907·92	48½	152·367	1847·45
21⅞	68·722	375·826	34¼	107·599	921·32	48¾	153·153	1866·55
22	69·115	380·133	34½	108·385	934·82	49	153·938	1885·74
22⅛	69·507	384·465	34¾	109·170	948·81	49¼	154·723	1905·03
22¼	69·900	388·822	35	109·956	962·11	49½	155·509	1924·42
22⅜	70·293	393·203	35¼	110·741	975·90	49¾	156·294	1943·91
22½	70·686	397·608	35½	111·526	989·80	50	157·080	1963·50
22⅝	71·078	402·038	35¾	112·312	1003·78	50¼	157·865	1983·18
22¾	71·471	406·493	36	113·097	1017·87	50½	158·650	2002·96
22⅞	71·864	410·972	36¼	113·883	1032·06	50¾	159·436	2022·84
23	72·256	415·476	36½	114·668	1046·35	51	160·221	2042·82
23⅛	72·649	420·004	36¾	115·453	1060·73	51¼	161·007	2062·90
23¼	73·042	424·557	37	116·239	1075·21	51½	161·792	2083·07
23⅜	73·434	429·135	37¼	117·024	1089·79	51¾	162·577	2103·35
23½	73·827	433·731	37½	117·810	1104·46	52	163·363	2123·72
23⅝	74·220	438·363	37¾	118·595	1119·24	52¼	164·148	2144·19
23¾	74·613	443·014	38	119·380	1134·11	52½	164·934	2164·75
23⅞	75·005	447·699	38¼	120·166	1149·08	52¾	165·719	2185·42
24	75·398	452·390	38½	120·951	1164·15	53	166·504	2206·18
24¼	76·183	461·864	38¾	121·737	1179·32	53¼	167·290	2227·05
24½	76·969	471·436	39	122·522	1194·59	53½	168·075	2248·01
24¾	77·754	481·106	39¼	123·307	1209·95	53¾	168·861	2269·06
25	78·540	490·875	39½	124·093	1225·42	54	162·646	2290·22
25¼	79·325	500·741	39¾	124·878	1240·98	54¼	170·431	2311·48
25½	80·110	510·706	40	125·664	1256·64	54½	171·217	2332·83
25¾	80·896	520·769	40¼	126·449	1272·39	54¾	172·002	2354·28
26	81·681	530·930	40½	127·234	1288·25	55	172·788	2375·83
26¼	82·467	541·189	40¾	128·020	1304·20	55¼	173·573	2397·48
26½	83·252	551·547	41	128·805	1320·25	55½	174·358	2419·22
26¾	84·037	562·002	41¼	129·591	1336·40	55¾	175·144	2441·07
27	84·823	572·556	41½	130·376	1352·65	56	175·929	2463·01
27¼	85·608	583·208	41¾	131·161	1369·00	56¼	176·715	2485·05
27½	86·394	593·958	42	131·947	1385·44	56½	177·500	2507·19
27¾	87·179	604·807	42¼	132·732	1401·98	56¾	178·285	2529·42
28	87·964	615·753	42½	133·518	1418·62	57	179·071	2551·76
28¼	88·750	626·798	42¾	134·303	1435·36	57¼	179·856	2574·19
28½	89·535	637·941	43	135·088	1452·20	57½	180·642	2596·72
28¾	90·321	649·182	43¼	135·874	1469·13	57¾	181·427	2619·35
29	91·106	660·521	43½	136·659	1486·17	58	182·212	2642·08
29¼	91·891	671·958	43¾	137·445	1503·30	58¼	182·998	2664·91
29½	92·677	683·494	44	138·230	1520·53	58½	183·783	2687·83
29¾	93·462	695·128	44¼	139·015	1537·86	58¾	184·569	2710·85
30	94·248	706·860	44½	139·801	1555·28	59	185·354	2733·97
30¼	95·033	718·690	44¾	140·586	1572·81	59¼	186·139	2757·19

Diameter.	Circumference.	Area.	Diameter.	Circumference.	Area.	Diameter.	Circumference.	Area.
59½	186·925	2780·51	71¾	225·409	4043·28	84	263·894	5541·78
59¾	187·710	2802·92	72	226·195	4071·51	84¼	264·679	5574·80
60	188·496	2827·44	72¼	226·980	4099·83	84½	265·465	5607·95
60¼	189·281	2851·05	72½	227·766	4128·25	84¾	266·250	5641·16
60½	190·066	2874·76	72¾	228·551	4156·77	85	267·036	5674·51
60¾	190·852	2898·56	73	229·336	4185·39	85¼	267·821	5707·92
61	191·637	2922·47	73¼	230·122	4214·11	85½	268·606	5741·47
61¼	192·423	2946·47	73½	230·907	4242·92	85¾	269·392	5775·09
61½	193·208	2970·57	73¾	231·693	4271·83	86	270·177	5803·81
61¾	193·993	2994·77	74	232·478	4300·85	86¼	270·962	5842·60
62	194·779	3019·07	74¼	233·263	4329·95	86½	271·748	5876·55
62¼	195·564	3043·47	74½	234·049	4359·16	86¾	272·533	5910·52
62½	196·350	3067·96	74¾	234·834	4388·47	87	273·319	5944·69
62¾	197·135	2092·56	75	235·620	4417·87	87¼	274·104	5978·88
63	197·920	3117·25	75¼	236·405	4447·37	87½	274·890	6013·21
63¼	198·706	3142·04	75½	237·190	4476·97	87¾	275·675	6047·60
63½	199·491	3166·92	75¾	237·976	4506·67	88	276·460	6082·13
63¾	200·277	3191·91	76	238·761	4536·47	88¼	277·245	6116·72
64	201·062	3216·99	76¼	239·547	4566·36	88½	278·031	6151·44
64¼	201·847	3242·17	76½	240·332	4596·35	88¾	278·816	6186·20
64½	202·633	3267·46	76¾	241·117	4626·44	89	279·602	6221·15
64¾	203·418	3292·83	77	241·903	4656·63	89¼	280·387	6256·12
65	204·204	3318·31	77¼	242·688	4686·92	89½	281·173	6291·25
65¼	204·989	3343·88	77½	243·474	4717·30	89¾	281·958	6326·44
65½	205·774	3369·56	77¾	244·259	4747·79	90	282·744	6361·74
65¾	206·560	3395·33	78	245·044	4778·37	90¼	283·529	6399·12
66	207·345	3421·20	78¼	245·830	4809·05	90½	284·314	6432·62
66¼	208·131	3447·16	78½	246·615	4839·83	90¾	285·099	6468·16
66½	208·916	3473·23	78¾	247·401	4870·70	91	285·885	6503·89
66¾	209·701	3499·39	79	248·186	4901·68	91¼	286·670	6539·68
67	210·487	3525·66	79¼	248·971	4932·75	91½	287·456	6573·56
67¼	211·272	3552·01	79½	249·757	4963·92	91¾	288·242	6611·52
67½	212·058	3578·47	79¾	250·542	4995·19	92	289·027	6647·62
67¾	212·843	3605·03	80	251·328	5026·56	92¼	289·812	6683·80
68	213·628	3631·68	80¼	252·113	5058·00	92½	290·598	6720·07
68¼	214·414	3658·44	80½	252·898	5089·58	92¾	291·386	6756·40
68½	215·199	3685·29	80¾	253·683	5121·22	93	292·168	6792·92
68¾	215·985	3712·24	81	254·469	5153·00	93¼	292·953	6829·48
69	216·770	3739·28	81¼	255·254	5184·84	93½	293·739	6866·16
69¼	217·555	3766·43	81½	256·040	5216·82	93¾	294·524	6882·92
69½	218·341	3793·67	81¾	256·825	5248·84	94	295·310	6939·79
69¾	219·126	3821·02	82	257·611	5281·02	94¼	296·095	6976·72
70	219·912	3848·46	82¼	258·396	5313·28	94½	296·881	7013·81
70¼	220·697	3875·99	82½	259·182	5345·62	94¾	297·666	7050·92
70½	221·482	3903·63	82¾	259·967	5378·04	95	298·452	7088·23
70¾	222·268	3931·36	83	260·752	5410·62	95¼	299·237	7125·56
71	223·053	3959·20	83¼	261·537	5443·24	95½	300·022	7163·04
71¼	223·839	3987·13	83½	262·323	5476·00	95¾	300·807	7200·56
71½	224·624	4015·16	83¾	263·108	5508·84	96	301·593	7238·24

NOTE.—THE CIRCUMFERENCES OF LARGER CIRCLES (up to 200 ft.) than those above given may be found by taking one half of the diameter — finding the circumference of such half by the above table, and then multiplying by 2.

THE AREA OF CIRCLES OF LARGER DIAMETERS (up to 200 ft.) than those above given may be found by taking one half of the diameter of the proposed circle—finding the area of same by above table, and multiplying this area by 4. Circles being to each other as the squares of their diameters.

GLOSSARY OF TERMS.

Abacus.—The tablet or the upper member of the capital of a column; varying in the several orders and styles.

Abutment.—The solid part of a pier which receives the thrust or lateral pressure of the arch, and from which the arch immediately springs.

Alabaster.—A white translucent species of gypsum or sulphate of lime, composed of crystalline grains in a compact mass. It is capable of being worked to a high degree of finish, and taking a fine polish.

It is much used for interior decorations, monuments, &c.

Annular Vault.—A vault springing from two walls, each circular on plan.—*See* Plate XXVII.

Annulet.—A small fillet encircling a column, used either alone or in connection with other mouldings.

Arc.—In geometry, a portion of the circumference of a circle or other curve line.

Arcade.—A covered passage composed generally of a range of arches, supported either on columns or piers, and detached from or attached to the wall.

Arch.—A concave or hollow structure supported by its own curve.

A number of wedge-shaped stones disposed in the line of some curve, and supporting each other by their mutual pressure.

The arch itself is composed of voussoirs, or arch stones, the uppermost of which is called the key-stone.—*See* Plates IV. & V.

Architrave.—The lower of the three principal members of the entablature of an order, being the chief beam resting immediately on the columns.

A collection of mouldings round a door, window, or other aperture.—*See also* **Entablature.**

Archivolt.—The band of mouldings round the arch stones of an arch, which terminates horizontally upon the impost.

Arris.—The line or edge on which two surfaces forming an exterior angle meet each other, either plane or curved.

Ashlar.—A term for hewn or squared stone, as distinguished from unwrought material; it is generally used for facings, and set in horizontal courses, and bears various names according to the manner in which it is worked, such as Plain Ashlar, Tooled Ashlar, Rustic Ashlar, &c.—*See* Plate X.

Astragal.—A small moulding of a semicircular profile. The name is generally applied to the necking separating the capital from the column—*See also* **Moulding.**

Axis of a Cylinder.—A right line passing through the solid, from the centre of one of the circular ends to the centre of the other, and the line on which such a body may be conceived to revolve.

Axis of a Dome.—A right line perpendicular to the horizon, passing through the centre of its base.—*See* Plate XXXII.

Banker.—A block of stone forming a bench on which the stone is worked.

Base.—In geometry, the lower part of a figure or body.

The base of a solid is the surface on which it rests.

In masonry, the lower moulded part, between the shaft and the pedestal.

Batter.—A wall that inclines inward from a vertical or plumb line, so that the upper part of the surface falls within the base.

Bed.—The horizontal surface on which a stone lies. The beds of a stone are the surfaces where the stones meet ; the upper surface is called the top bed, and the under surface the bottom bed.—*See also* **Natural Bed.**

Billet Moulding.—A Norman moulding used in arches, strings, &c. ; it consists of small short lengths of beads or bars, cut in hollow mouldings, with spaces between equal to the length of the billet.—*See* Plate XLVII., Figs. 31 & 32. *See also* **Moulding.**

Blocking-course.—A course of stones placed on the top of a cornice, forming the summit of the wall.

Boasting.—Cutting the stone roughly to form of intended carving.

Bond.—The disposition or lapping of the stones so that vertical joints may not fall over one another, but fall directly over the middle of the stone below, in order to form an inseparable mass of building.

Bond-stone.—Stones whose longest horizontal direction is placed in the thickness of the work, for the purpose of binding the wall together.

Boning.—The art of testing a plane surface by the guidance of the eye and the aid of two straight-edges, by which it is seen whether the work is out of winding, or whether the surface be plane or twisted.—*See* Plate IX., Figs. 1 & 2.

Boss.—A sculptured or carved projection to conceal the intersection of the moulded ribs in a vault, or at the stop end of a string course or label.—*See* Plate XLI.

Breaking Joint.—The placing of a stone over the course below, in such a position that the joint above shall not fall vertically directly over the joint below it.

Buttress.—A pier of masonry projecting from a wall to support and strengthen it. Buttresses are employed in Gothic buildings to resist the thrust of the vaulting and roof, and also to stiffen walls and towers of great height.

Camber.—The slightly hollowed soffit given to a lintel or flat arch to correct the apparent sinking down in the centre.

Canopy.—An ornamental projection over windows, doors, niches, &c.

Cant.—An external splay angle cut off a square.

Cantilever.—A large projecting bracket to support cornices, balconies, eaves, &c.

Capital.—The head or uppermost member of a column, pier, or pilaster, in any part of a building, but generally applied to that of a column or pilaster of the several orders.—*See* CAPS, Plates XLVII. to LII.

Chamfer.—The arris of a solid cut to a bevelled plane.

Chevron.—A zigzag or V-shaped ornament used in mouldings, chiefly to arches in Norman work.—*See* Plate XLVII., Fig. 35.

Chiselled Work.—The surface of a stone formed by the chisel.

Chord.—In geometry, a straight line drawn from any point of an arc to any other point of that arc.

Circle.—A plane figure, of which its boundary is everywhere at an equal distance from a point within its surface, called its centre.

Its perimeter encloses the largest area of any figure.

Circular Work.—A term applied to any work with cylindric or spherical faces.

Circumference.—The curve line which bounds the area of a circle.

Circumscribe.—To draw a line round a figure so as to enclose it.

Closer.—The last stone fixed in a horizontal course which is usually of less dimensions than the others.

Coffer.—A sunk panel in vaults, domes, and arches. The name is also applied to any sunk panel in a ceiling or soffit.

Column.—A cylindrical or polygonal pier, which supports a superincumbent weight in a vertical direction; it is generally composed of a base, shaft, and capital.—*See also* **Pilaster.**

Concave.—A hollow line or surface, as the soffit of an arch, vault, or the inner surface of a sphere.

Concentric.—Having the same centre but different radii.

Conic Sections.—The figures formed by the intersections of a plane with a cone, which do not include the triangle or the circle. These three sections are the ellipse, parabola, and hyperbola.

Contour.—The outline of a figure or body; the line that bounds.

Convex.—A rising or swelling on the exterior surface into a round or spherical form, as the outside of a sphere, the extrados of an arch, &c.

Coping.—The highest and top covering course in a wall.

Corbel.—A small bracket projecting from the wall to support some superincumbent weight.

Cornice.—A horizontal projection, moulded, decorated, or otherwise, which crowns or terminates a wall, building, pedestal, or other piece of work.—*See* Plate IX., Fig. 4.

Course.—A row of stones of the same height generally placed on a level bed. The stones round the face and intrados of an arch, are also called a course of stones.

Coursing Joint.—The joint between two courses of stone.

Crown of an Arch.—The highest or central part of an arch or any arched surface.—*See* Plates IV. & V.

Cupola.—A concave ceiling or roof, hemispherical or nearly so. A small dome.

Curtail Step.—The first or bottom step of a stairs, generally of a curved form on plan, and a curved quoin end.

Curve Line.—A concave or convex line.

Cusp.—A triangular projection from an inner curve of a tracery arch or window. —*See* Plate XLVI., Fig. 10.

Cylinder.—A circular body of uniform diameter, whose ends or base form equal parallel circles, and whose curved surface is everywhere at an equal distance from its axis.

The cone, sphere, and cylinder have a relative value to each other, namely, that the cone is one-third the cylinder having the same base and height; and the inscribed sphere two-thirds of the cylinder, or the cone, sphere, and cylinder are to each other as the numbers 1, 2, 3.—*See* Plate IX., Fig. 3.

Cylindrical Work.—Any form of work which partakes of the shape of a cylinder.

Dentils.—The small square blocks or teeth cut in the bed mould of cornices, pediments, &c.—*See* Plate IX., Fig. 5.

Development.—The unrolling or laying out of a surface upon a plane, so that every point of the surface may coincide with the plane.

Diagonal.—A straight line drawn through a plane figure, joining two opposite angles.

Diameter.—A straight line passing through the centre of a curvilinear figure, and dividing the figure symmetrically into two equal parts, terminating in the circumference on each side, as that of a circle or ellipse.

Diminution of a Column.—The gradual contraction of the diameter of a column, so that the upper diameter is less than the lower.—*See* Plate XI., Figs. 7 & 8.

Dome.—The spherical or convex roof raised over a circular or polygonal building.

There is great variety in the forms of domes, both in plan and section. *See* Plate XXXII.—*See also* **Cupola.**

Draft.—A margin on the surface of a stone, dressed to the width of the chisel or bolster, for the purpose of directing its reduction to the required surface.

Dressed.—A term which expresses the preparation a stone has undergone, before fixing in its position in the building.

Edge.—The meeting in an external angle of two planes or surfaces of a solid.

Elevation.—A geometrical projection drawn on a plane perpendicular to the horizon.

Ellipse or Ellipsis.—One of the conic sections, produced by cutting a cone by a plane passing obliquely through the opposite sides. It may be divided into two equal and similar parts, by a diameter drawn in any direction.

Entablature.—The superstructure which lies horizontally upon architectural columns. It consists of three portions; the architrave, which rests immediately upon the columns, the frieze or central portion, and the cornice.

Entasis.—A refined and almost imperceptible swelling of the shaft of a column.—*See* Plate IX., Figs. 7 & 8.

Equiangular.—Having equal angles.

Equidistant.—At equal distances.

Equilateral.—Having equal sides.

Extrados.—The exterior or convex curve of an arch.—*See* Plate IV., Fig. 1.

Face-mould.—A pattern or templet defining the form to which a stone is to be worked. It is usually made of sheet zinc.

Fillet.—A small moulding of square section. Also the space between two flutings in a column or pilaster.

Finial.—The top or finishing terminal to a gable or pinnacle.

Flush.—The bedding of masonry blocks in mortar or cement, completely filling in all interstices in the beds and joints.

The term is also used to signify the breaking off or chipping any portion of a dressed stone.

Flute.—A perpendicular hollow or channel; used to decorate the shafts of columns or pilasters.

Flyers.—Steps in a flight of stairs, whose edges are parallel to each other.—*See* Plate XII.

Foci.—The two points in the major axis of an ellipse to which a string may be fixed so as to describe the curve.

Free-stone.—A stone which can be freely worked in any direction.

Gargoyle.—A projecting waterspout usually carved into a grotesque head.

Gauge.—The measure to which any dimension is confined.

Geometry.—The science which explains, and the art which shews, the construction of lines, angles, plane figures, and solids.

Grit-stone.—A coarse or fine-grained sandstone of various degrees of hardness. It is composed of small grains of sand united by a cementing material of an argillaceous, calcareous, or siliceous nature.

Groin.—The curved line formed by the intersection of two arches or vaults crossing each other at any angle.—*See* Plate XXVII.

Groined Vault.—" One formed by three or more curved surfaces, so that every two may form a groin, all the groins terminating at one extremity in a common point."—" Gwilt."—*See* Plate XXXIV. and following.

Ground Line.—The straight line upon which the vertical plane of projection is placed.

Grout.—A thin semi-liquid mortar composed of cement and sand or lime and sand, and run into the joints and beds of stonework, filling all interstices.

Gypsum.—" Crystals of native sulphate of lime. Being subjected to a moderate heat, to expel the water of crystallisation, it forms plaster of Paris, and, coming in contact with water, immediately assumes a solid form. Of the numerous species, alabaster is, perhaps, the most abundant."—" Gwilt."

Header.—Stones extending through the thickness of a wall, as bond-stones.

Heading.—The vertical side of a stone perpendicular to the face.

Heading Joint.—The thin stratum of mortar between the vertical surfaces of two adjacent stones.

Helix.—A spiral winding round the surface of a cylinder.— *See* Plate XIV.

Hemisphere.—One half of a globe or sphere, when divided through its centre by a plane.

Hypothenuse.—The longest side of a right-angled triangle. The side opposite to the right angle.

Impost.—The capital of a pier or pilaster from which an arch springs Its form varies in the different orders.

Inclination.—The angle contained between a line and a plane, or between two planes.

Intersection.—The point on which two lines meet and cut each other. The line in which two surfaces cut or meet each other.

Intrados.—The inner curve of an arch.—*See* Plate IV., Fig. 1.

Jambs.—The vertical sides of a window or door opening, which connect the two sides of a wall.

Joggle.—An indentation made in one stone, called the she joggle, to receive the projection on another termed the he joggle. *See* Plate VII.

Joint.—The surface of contact between two adjacent blocks of stone.

Jumper.—A long steel chisel used for drilling holes.—*See* Plate I., Fig. 18.

Key Course.—The horizontal range of stones in the summit of a vault, in which the course is placed.

Key Stone.—The highest central stone in the crown of an arch.—*See* Plate IV., Fig. 1. *See* **Arch.**

Label.—The drip or hood moulding over the apertures in Gothic windows and doors.

Lancet Arch.—Narrow window heads shaped like the point of a lancet, and characteristic of the Early English Gothic (13th century).

Landing.—The terminating floor of a flight of stairs, either above or below it ; or the level part of a staircase connecting one flight with another. *See* Plate XII., Fig. 2.

Level.—A line or surface horizontal or parallel to the horizon ; or a straight line perpendicular to a plumb line.

Line of Batter.—The line of section made by a plane and the surface of a battering wall, the plane being perpendicular both to the surface of the wall and to the horizon.

Lintel.—A stone which extends over the aperture of a door or window, and carries the superincumbent weight by means of its strength or resistance.

Marble.—" A term limited by mineralogists and geologists to the several varieties of carbonate of lime, having more or less of a granular and crystalline texture. It is susceptible of a very fine polish, and the varieties of it are extremely numerous."—" Gwilt."

Marble, Polishing of.—Marbles are of such a varied nature that one method of polishing cannot be adopted for all, although the following method will suffice for Statuary, Vein, Sicilian, St. Anne's, and most of the ordinary coloured marbles in general use.

The wrought surface is rubbed with fine sharp sand and water, until all the marks of the chisel or saw are removed, and an even face is produced; it is then "grounded," that is, rubbed with grit stones of varying degrees of fineness, commencing with the coarse or "first grit," next the "second grit," which is a little finer, and then finishing with "snake" or "Water of Ayr" stone. Particular care must be taken that in each process of "gritting" the marks or scratches of its predecessor are removed, so that when the surface is "snaked" no scratches whatever are visible, but left quite smooth, for upon the careful "gritting" depends the success of the ultimate polish.

The polishing is lastly effected by rubbing with a pad of felt sprinkled with putty powder (calcined tin) moistened with water, until the gloss or natural polish is obtained.

The polishing of marble adds greatly to its beauty, inasmuch as its delicate figuring, and gradations of rich colouring, are brought out and heightened by the process, which thus makes it so valuable as a decorative material.

Masonry.—The art of shaping, arranging, and uniting stones, in the construction of walls and other parts of buildings.

Metopes.—The square spaces between triglyphs in the frieze of the Doric order; sometimes applied to the sculptures fitted into these spaces.

Modillion.—A projecting enriched bracket in the soffit of the top bed of a cornice.

Monolith.—Consisting of one stone.

Mortise.—A sinking in a stone to receive a corresponding projection.

Mould.—A templet or pattern defining the form of the stone which is to be worked. It is usually made of sheet zinc.

Moulding.—The outline or contour given to an angle whether a projection or a cavity.

Mouldings may be generally resolved into three elementary forms—hollow, round, and square—and it is upon the choice, arrangement, and proportion of these forms that beauty or ugliness depends. Of the two main principles in connection with mouldings, namely, projection and recession, the former is generally adopted in Classical and Renaissance architecture, and the latter in Gothic. The most perfect profiles are such as are composed of few mouldings, varied and alternating both in form and size, fitly applied with regard to their uses, and so disposed that the straight and curved members succeed each other alternately. In every profile there should be a prominent member, to which all the others should be subservient, and appear to support and fortify, or to shelter it from injury by the weather.

The best known examples are as follows:—

Fillet, Listel or Square . 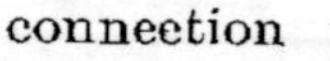

Astragal or Bead . . 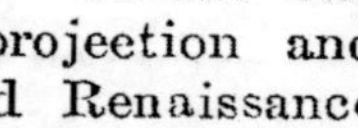

Ovolo or Quarter Round 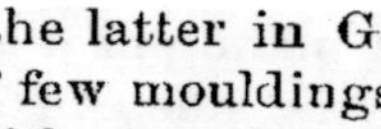

Torus or Tore . . 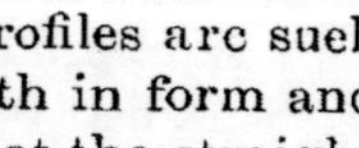

Ogee or Cyma Reversa . 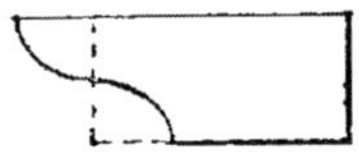

Cyma Recta or Cymatium 

Cavetto or Hollow . 

Scotia . . . 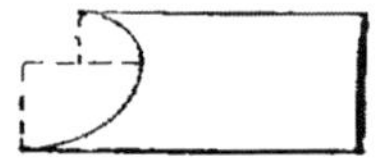

The above refer to mouldings of the Roman Orders.—*See also* Plates XLVII. to LII.

Mullion.—The upright post or bars of stone which subdivide a window into two or more lights. *See also* **Transom.**

Mural.—Belonging or attached to a wall.

Mutule.—A projecting ornament in a Doric cornice, somewhat resembling the end of a timber beam; it occupies the place of the modillion in the other orders.

Natural Bed of a Stone.—The direction in which the natural strata lie when in the quarry.

The line of the planes of cleavage.

Newel.—The vertical column or pillar about which, in a winding stair, the steps turn, and receive support from the bottom to the top.

The newel step in an open stair is the bottom one; it is generally curvilinear on plan.—*See* Plates XII. & XIV.

Niche.—A semicircular or hollow recess generally within the thickness of a wall, for a statue, vase, or other ornament.—*See* Plates XXV. & XXVI.

Normal.—A right line perpendicular to the tangent of a curve.

Ordinate.—"A line drawn from any part of the circumference of an ellipse or other conic section, perpendicular to, and across the axis to the other side." —"Gwilt."

Parabola.—One of the three conic sections.

An open curve of which both of its branches may be extended infinitely without ever meeting.

It is produced by cutting a cone by a plane parallel to one of its sides, and so named because its axis is parallel to the side of the cone.

Parallel.—Lines, surfaces, &c., that are in every part equidistant from each other, and extended in the same direction.

Pediment.—A triangular, or gabled termination to a building, sometimes also placed over doors, windows, porticoes, &c.

Perpendicular.—A line at right angles to a given line.

Pier, Pillar.—*See* **Column.**

Pilaster.—A square column usually attached to a wall from which it projects. In most cases it corresponds to the columns of its order, having a similar capital, shaft, and base.

Plane.—A perfectly flat or level surface, coinciding in every direction with a straight line.

Plinth.—The base of a wall, column, &c.

Profile.—The contour outline of mouldings taken at right angles to their length.

Projection.—The art of representing any object on a plane by means of straight lines, drawn from all visible parts of those objects to intersect the plane of projection.

Quadrant.—The fourth part of a circle ; an arc of ninety degrees.

Quoins.—The courses of stone to any external angle of a building.

Radiating Joints.—Those joints which tend to a centre.—*See* Plates IV. & V.

Radius.—A right line drawn from the centre to the circumference of a circle. The semidiameter of a circle or sphere.

Raking Mouldings.—Mouldings which run in an inclined position.—*See* Plate X., Figs. 11 & 12.

Rib.—A narrow arch-formed bar projecting beyond the surface of a vault, to mark its intersection and to add strength.—*See* Plate XXXVI., Fig. 10.

Rustic Quoins.—The coursed stones to the external angles of a building, projecting beyond the face of the wall.

Sandstone.—A stone composed of grains of sand, united with other mineral substances, cemented together by a material of an argillaceous, calcareous, or siliceous nature.

Scribe.—To scratch in on the stone, with a sharp pointed tool, the profile of a mould, templet, &c.

Section.—The figure formed by cutting a solid by a plane.

Segment of a Circle.—A portion of a circle contained by an arc and its chord.

Setting.—A term used to denote the fixing of dressed stones in their proper position in the walls of buildings.

Shaft.—The cylindrical part of a column between the base and the capital. *See* Plate XI., Figs. 7 & 8.

Soffit or Sofite.—The under surface of any part of a ceiling, architrave, arch, vault, stairs, &c.

Soffit Joints.—Those joints which appear on the under surface.

Span.—The distance or dimension across the opening of an arch, window, or aperture. *See* Plate IV., Fig. 1.

Spandrel.—A triangular-shaped piece. The irregular triangular space between the curve of an arch and the rectangle inclosing it ; or the space between the outer mouldings of two contiguous arches and a horizontal line above them.

Spiral.—The helix or screw.

A curve consisting of one or more revolutions round a fixed point and gradually receding from it.

Spire.—A steeple diminishing as it ascends, generally octagonal on plan.

Splay.—A slope making with the face of a wall an angle less than a right angle.

Stair.—One step of a series by means of which a person ascends or descends to a different landing.

A series of steps for passing from one part of a building to another. *See* Plates XII., XIII., XIV. & XV.

Staircase.—A flight of stairs with their supporting framework, casing, balusters, &c., which enable persons to ascend or descend from one floor to another. *See* Plate XII., Fig. 2.

Stilted Arch.—An arch in which the springing line or curve does not commence for some distance above the level of the impost.

Stone Cutting.—The art of hewing or dressing stones to their intended form.

Straight-Edge.—A rule whose edge coincides with a straight line.

Stretcher.—A stone laid with its longer face in the surface of the wall.

Tangent.—A straight line which touches a curve without cutting it.

Tangent Plane.—A plane which touches a curved surface without being able to cut it.

Templet.—A mould giving the contour to which stones are to be wrought.

Transom.—A horizontal bar across a window of two or more lights. *See also* **Mullion.**

Triangle.—A plane figure consisting of three sides.

Trihedral.—A solid angle consisting of three plane angles.

Trisection.—The division into three equal parts.

Tympanum.—The triangular face of a pediment included between the horizontal and raking mouldings.

Vault.—An arched roof or ceiling over an apartment, so constructed that the stones of which it is composed sustain and keep each other in their places. *See* Plates XXVII. to XXIX. & XXXIV. to XLI.

Vertical Plane.—A plane perpendicular to the horizon.

Volute.—A spiral scroll as in the Ionic capital.

Voussoir.—A wedge-shaped stone forming one of the blocks of an arch. *See* Plate IV., Fig. 1.

Weathering.—A sloping surface of stone employed to cover the set-off of a wall or buttress, and protect it from the effects of the weather.

Welch Groin.—A groin formed by the intersection of two cylindrieal vaults, one being of greater height than the other.

Winder.—One in a flight of steps which are curved on plan, having each tread broader at one end than the other. *See* Plates XIII. & XIV.

Wreathed Column.—Twisted in the form of a screw or spiral.

LIST OF WORKS

ON

ARCHITECTURE, BUILDING, DECORATIVE ARTS, CARPENTRY, TIMBER, SANITATION, ETC.

ACOUSTICS OF PUBLIC BUILDINGS: The Laws of Sound as applied to the Arrangement of Buildings. By Professor T. ROGER SMITH, F.R.I.B.A. New Edition revised. With numerous Illustrations. Crown 8vo, cloth ... ... **1s. 6d.**

ALPHABETS, ANCIENT AND MEDIÆVAL ORNAMENTAL. From the Eighth Century, with Numerals; including Gothic, Church-Text large and small, German, Italian, Arabesque, Initials for Illumination, Monograms, Crosses, etc., for the use of Architectural and Engineering Draughtsmen, Missal Painters, Masons, Decorative Painters, Lithographers, Engravers, Carvers, etc., etc. Collected and Engraved by F. DELAMOTTE, and printed in Colours. New and Cheaper Edition. Royal 8vo, oblong, ornamental boards ... **2s. 6d.**

ALPHABETS, PLAIN AND ORNAMENTAL, MODERN. Including German, Old English, Saxon, Italic, Perspective, Greek, Hebrew, Court Hand Engrossing, Tuscan, Riband, Gothic, Rustic, and Arabesque; with several Original Designs, and an Analysis of the Roman and Old English Alphabets, large and small, and Numerals, for the use of Draughtsmen, Surveyors, Masons, Decorative Painters, Lithographers, Engravers, Carvers, etc. Collected and Engraved by F. DELAMOTTE, and printed in Colours. New and Cheaper Edition Royal 8vo, oblong, ornamental boards ... ... **2s. 6d.**

"There is comprised in it every possible shape into which the letters of the alphabet and numerals can be formed, and the talent which has been expended in the conception of the various plain and ornamental letters is wonderful."—*Standard.*

ALPHABETS AND INITIALS, MEDIÆVAL. By F. G. DELAMOTTE. Containing 21 Plates and Illuminated Title, printed in Gold and Colours. With an Introduction by J. WILLIS BROOKS. Fifth Edition. Small 4to, ornamental boards ... ... *Net* **5s.**

ALPHABETS. See also ILLUMINATING.

ARCHES, PIERS, BUTTRESSES. By WILLIAM BLAND Crown 8vo, cloth **1s. 6d**

ARCHITECTURE—ORDERS. The Orders and their Æsthetic Principles. By W. H. LEEDS. Crown 8vo ... ... **1s. 6d.**

ARCHITECTURE—STYLES. The History and Description of the Styles of Architecture of Various Countries, from the Earliest to the Present Period. By T. TALBOT BURY, F.R.I.B.A., etc. Illustrated. Crown 8vo, cloth ... ... **2s.**

ORDERS AND STYLES OF ARCHITECTURE. In one Vol. ... **3s. 6d.**

ARCHITECTURE—DESIGN. The Principles of Design in Architecture, as deducible from Nature and exemplified in the Works of the Greek and Gothic Architects. By EDW. L. GARBETT, Architect. Crown 8vo, cloth ... ... **2s. 6d.**

"We know no work that we would sooner recommend to an attentive reader desirous to obtain clear views of the nature of architectural art. The book is a valuable one."—*Builder*.

*** *The three preceding Works in one handsome Vol., half-bound, entitled,* "MODERN ARCHITECTURE," *price* **6s.**

ARCHITECTURE OF MARCUS VITRUVIUS POLLIO. In Ten Books. Translated from the Latin by J. GWILT. With 23 Plates. Crown 8vo, cloth ... ... **5s.**

ARCHITECTURE—GRECIAN. An Inquiry into the Principles of Beauty in; with an Historical View of the Rise and Progress of the Art in Greece. By the EARL OF ABERDEEN. Crown 8vo, cloth **1s.**

*** *The two preceding Works in one handsome Volume, half-bound, entitled* "ANCIENT ARCHITECTURE," *price* **6s.**

ARCHITECTURE, MECHANICS OF. A Treatise on Applied Mechanics, especially Adapted to the Use of Architects. By E. W. TARN, M.A., Author of "The Science of Building," etc. Second Edition, Enlarged. Illustrated with 125 Diagrams. Crown 8vo, cloth **7s. 6d.**

"The book is a very useful and helpful manual of architectural mechanics."—*Builder*.

ARCHITECT'S GUIDE: Being a Text-Book of Useful Information for Architects, Engineers, Surveyors, Contractors, Clerks of Works, etc. By F. ROGERS. Crown 8vo, cloth ... ... **3s. 6d.**

ARCHITECTURAL MODELLING IN PAPER. The Art of. By T. A. RICHARDSON. Crown 8vo, cloth ... ... **1s. 6d.**

"A valuable aid to the practice of architectural modelling."—*Builders' Weekly Reporter*.

ARCHITECTURAL PERSPECTIVE. The whole Course and Operations of the Draughtsman in Drawing a Large House in Linear Perspective. Illustrated by 43 Folding Plates. By F. O. FERGUSON. Third Edition. 8vo, boards ... ... **3s. 6d.**

"It is the most intelligible of the treatises on this ill-treated subject that I have met with."—E. INGRESS BELL, ESQ., in the *R.I.B.A. Journal*.

ARCHITECTURAL PERSPECTIVE FOR BEGINNERS. For Students and Amateurs in Architecture, Painting, etc. By G. PYNE. Crown 8vo, cloth ... ... **2s.**

ARCHITECTURAL TERMS, DICTIONARY OF.— Building, Engineering, Mining, Metallurgy, Archæology, the Fine Arts, &c. By JOHN WEALE. Sixth Edition. Edited by ROBT. HUNT, F.R.S. Numerous Illustrations. Crown 8vo, cloth ... ... **5s.**

BRICKLAYING. General Principles of Practical Bricklaying; Arch Drawing, Cutting, Setting, and Pointing; Paving, Tiling, etc. By ADAM HAMMOND. With 68 Woodcuts. Crown 8vo, cloth **1s. 6d.**

BRICK-CUTTING AND SETTING. By ADAM HAMMOND. With 90 Engravings. Crown 8vo, cloth ... ... **1s. 6d.**

BRICKWORK. Embodying the General and Higher Principles of Bricklaying, Cutting and Setting; with the Application of Geometry to Roof Tiling, etc. By F. WALKER. Crown 8vo, cloth ... **1s. 6d.**

BRICKS AND TILES. Rudimentary Treatise on the Manufacture of. By E. DOBSON, Author of "Art of Building," etc. Twelfth Edition, fully revised, and several new Chapters added by ALFRED B. SEARLE, author of "Modern Brickmaking," Cantor Lecturer on Brickmaking, etc. 260 pages. Illustrated. Crown 8vo, cloth. **3s.** Extra cloth boards **3s. 6d.**

"The best handbook on the subject. We can recommend it as a good investment."—*Builder.*

BRICK AND TILE BOOK. Comprising Brick and Tile Making, by E. DOBSON, M.Inst.C.E.; Practical Bricklaying, by A. HAMMOND; Brick-Cutting and Setting, by A. HAMMOND. 550 pp., with 270 Illustrations, strongly half-bound ... ... **6s.**

BUILDERS' PRICES. See LOCKWOOD'S BUILDERS' PRICE BOOK, page 8.

BUILDING, SCIENCE OF. An Elementary Treatise on the Principles of Construction. By E. WYNDHAM TARN, M.A. Lond. Fourth Edition. Crown 8vo, cloth ... ... **3s. 6d.**

BUILDING, ART OF. General Principles of Construction, Character, Strength, and Use of Materials, Preparation of Specifications and Estimates, etc. By EDWARD DOBSON, M.Inst.C.E. Fifteenth Edition, revised by J. P. ALLEN, Lecturer on Building Construction at the Durham College of Science. Crown 8vo, cloth ... ... **2s.**

BUILDING. A Book on Civil and Ecclesiastical Building. By Sir EDMUND BECKETT, Bart., LL.D. Second Edition. Crown 8vo, cloth. **4s. 6d.**, cloth boards **5s. 6d.**

"A book which is always amusing and nearly always instructive."—*Times.*

BUILDING ESTATES. A Treatise on the Development, Sale, Purchase, and Management of Building Land. By F. MAITLAND. Fifth Edition. Crown 8vo, cloth ... ... **2s.**

"This book should undoubtedly be added to the library of every professional man dealing with building land."—*Land Agents' Record.*

BUILDING, COTTAGE. By C. BRUCE ALLEN. Twelfth Edition, with Chapter on Economic Cottages for Allotments by E. E. ALLEN, C.E. Crown 8vo, cloth ... ... **2s.**

BUILDING CONSTRUCTION (PRACTICAL). A Handbook for Students Preparing for Examinations, and a Book of Reference for Persons Engaged in Building. By JOHN PARNELL ALLEN, P.A.S.I., formerly Lecturer on Building Construction at the Armstrong College of Science, Newcastle-on-Tyne. Fifth Edition, Revised and Enlarged. 596 pp., with over 1,300 Illustrations. Medium 8vo, cloth. *Net* **7s. 6d.**

BRICKS AND THEIR COMPOSITION—BRICK BOND AND ITS APPLICATION—BRICK REVEALS AND ARCHES—DAMP AND ITS PREVENTION—BUILDING STONES—STONE DRESSINGS—WOOD FOR BUILDING PURPOSES—WOOD FLOORS—PARTITIONS—ROOFS—IRON AND STEEL—RIVETS AND RIVETING—IRON ROOFS—COVERINGS FOR ROOFS—FIREPROOF FLOORS—JOINTS AND MOULDINGS IN JOINERY—DOORS—WINDOWS—WOODEN STAIRS—SKYLIGHTS AND LANTERNS—PLASTERING AND PAINTING—CENTRING FOUNDATIONS, ETC.—STRESSES—CALCULATION OF STRAINS—SANITATION—FIREPLACES—WEIGHTS AND STRENGTHS—QUANTITIES AND PRICES, ETC., AND APPENDICES.

BUILDING INSPECTION, ELEMENTARY MANUAL OF; or, How to Become a Building Inspector. By WM. R. PURCHASE, Building Inspector to the Borough of Hove, Author of "Practical Masonry." 136 pp. With 9 Plates of Diagrams. Crown 8vo, cloth. *Net* **2s. 6d.**

DUTIES AND QUALIFICATIONS OF BUILDING INSPECTORS TO MUNICIPAL COUNCILS—MEMORANDUM OF THE LOCAL GOVERNMENT BOARD AS TO BYE-LAWS WITH RESPECT TO NEW STREETS, BUILDINGS, DRAINAGE, &C.—SETTING OUT A BUILDING—FOUNDATIONS IN "MADE-UP GROUND"—EXCAVATORS' MEMORANDA, FOUNDATIONS, &C.—BRICKS—STOCKS—PLACE—CHUFFS—BURRS—FOOTINGS OF A WALL—CHIMNEYS—FLUES—DAMP-PROOF COURSES—MORTAR—SETTING—BRICKWORK MEMORANDA—CEMENTS—RETAINING WALLS—STONE MASONRY—TERRA-COTTA—TIMBER—FLOORS — PILES — PILLARS — ROOF COVERINGS — PLASTERING — PLASTERERS' MEMORANDA — DRAINAGE—PLAN BOOK—APPENDIX CONTAINING USEFUL MEMORANDA FOR BUILDING INSPECTORS.

BUILDING—EVERY MAN HIS OWN BUILDER. A Book for Every Man who Owns a Piece of Land, giving Concise Directions How to Build a House from the Foundations to the Roof. Plastering, Floor Work, Plumbing, Draining, Wells and Well Sinking, &c. By G. GORDON SAMSON, Author of "How to Plan a House," and "Houses, Villas and Bungalows for Britishers and Americans abroad." Second Edition, Revised. 362 pages, with 292 Illustrations and Plans. Demy 8vo, cloth ... ... [*Just Published, Net* **5s.**

BUNGALOW RESIDENCES. A Handbook for all interested in building. By PERCIVAL T. HARRISON, A.M.I.C.E., M.R.S.I., Borough Engineer and Surveyor, Dorchester. 84 pages. Illustrated by 22 Plates and numerous Text Diagrams. Demy 8vo, cloth. *Net* **3s. 6d.**

BUNGALOWS. See also HOUSES, VILLAS, COTTAGES, AND BUNGALOWS. Page 7.

CABINET-MAKER'S GUIDE TO THE ENTIRE CONSTRUCTION OF CABINET WORK.—By RICHARD BITMEAD. Illustrated with Plans, Sections and Working Drawings. Crown 8vo, cloth ... ... **2s. 6d.**

CARPENTRY AND JOINERY. The Elementary Principles of Carpentry. Chiefly composed from the Standard Work of T. TREDGOLD. With Additions and a Treatise on Joinery by E. W. TARN, M.A. Eighth Edition. Crown 8vo, cloth ... ... **3s. 6d.**

ATLAS of 35 Plates to accompany and illustrate the foregoing book. With Descriptive Letterpress. 4to ... ... **6s.**

CIRCULAR WORK IN CARPENTRY AND JOINERY. A practical Treatise. By GEORGE COLLINS. Fifth Edition. Crown 8vo, cloth ... ... **2s. 6d.**

"Cheap in price, clear in definition, and practical in the examples selected."—*Builder.*

CLERK OF WORKS. A Handbook on the Supervision of Building Operations. By GEORGE METSON, Licentiate R.I.B.A., M.R.San.I., Member of the Concrete Institute; Lecturer on Building Construction (Higher Division) and Builders' Quantities (Ordinary and Honours Grade) at the Borough Polytechnic, 190 pages. Crown 8vo, cloth ... ... [*Just Published. Net* **2s. 6d.**

COLOURING, GRAMMAR OF. Applied to Decorative Painting and the Arts. By G. FIELD. New Edition, enlarged by E. A. DAVIDSON. With Coloured Plates. Crown 8vo, cloth ... ... **3s.**

COMPLETE MEASURER: Setting forth the Measurement of Boards, Glass, Timber, and Stone. By R. HORTON. Sixth Edition. Crown 8vo, cloth ... ... **4s.**

CONCRETE: ITS NATURE AND USES. A Book for Architects, Builders, Contractors, and Clerks of Works. By G. L. SUTCLIFFE, A.R.I.B.A. Second Edition, Revised and Enlarged. 396 pp., with Illustrations. Crown 8vo, cloth ... ... *Net* **9s.**

CONCRETE, REINFORCED. See page 11.

DECORATION (ELEMENTARY). As applied to Dwelling-Houses, etc. An Elementary Treatise. By J. W. FACEY. Cr. 8vo, cloth **2s.**

DECORATION (PRACTICAL). A Guide to the Art of Ornamental Painting, the arrangement of Colours in Apartments and the Principles of Decorative Design. By JAMES W. FACEY. Crown 8vo, cloth ... ... **2s. 6d.**

*** *The last two works in One handsome Vol., half-bound, entitled* "HOUSE DECORATION, ELEMENTARY AND PRACTICAL," *price* **5s.**

DECORATOR'S ASSISTANT. A Modern Guide for Decorative Artists and Amateurs, Painters, Writers, Gilders, etc. Containing upwards of 600 Receipts, Rules, and Instructions; with a variety of Information for General Work connected with every Class of Interior and Exterior Decorations, etc. Tenth Edition. Crown 8vo ... **1s.**

DRAWING. Practical Rules for the Builder and Young Student in Architecture. By G. PYNE. 4to, cloth ... ... **7s. 6d.**

DWELLING HOUSES. Their Erection. Illustrated by a Perspective View, Plans, Elevations, and Sections of a Pair of Villas, with the Specification, Quantities, and Estimates. By S. H. BROOKS. Crown 8vo, cloth ... ... **2s. 6d.**

EMBROIDERER'S BOOK OF DESIGN. Containing Initials, Emblems, Cyphers, Monograms, Ornamental Borders, Ecclesiastical Devices, Mediæval and Modern Alphabets, and National Emblems. Collected by F. DELAMOTTE and printed in Colours. Oblong royal 8vo, ornamental wrapper ... ... *Net* **2s.**

FARM BUILDINGS: Their Arrangement and Construction, with Plans and Estimates. By Professor J. SCOTT. Crown 8vo, cloth **2s.**

FIRE PROTECTION IN BUILDINGS. A Practical Treatise for Engineers, Architects, Surveyors and Property Owners. By HAROLD G. HOLT, A.R.I.B.A. 280 pages, with Diagrams and Illustrations. Demy 8vo, cloth ... ... [*Just Published.* *Net* **8s. 6d.**

FORESTRY, PRACTICAL: and its Bearing on the Improvement of Estates. By CHARLES E. CURTIS, F.S.I., Professor of Forestry, Field Engineering, and General Estate Management, at the College of Agriculture, Downton. Third Edition, Revised and Enlarged. Crown 8vo, cloth ... ... *Net* **3s. 6d.**

PREFATORY REMARKS—OBJECTS OF PLANTING—CHOICE OF A FORESTER—CHOICE OF SOIL AND SITE—LAYING OUT OF LAND FOR PLANTATIONS—PREPARATION OF THE GROUND FOR PLANTING—DRAINAGE—PLANTING—DISTANCES AND DISTRIBUTION OF TREES IN PLANTATIONS—TREES AND GROUND GAME—ATTENTION AFTER PLANTING—THINNING OF PLANTATIONS—PRUNING OF FOREST TREES—REALIZATION—METHODS OF SALE—MEASUREMENT OF TIMBER—MEASUREMENT AND VALUATION OF LARCH PLANTATION—FIRE LINES—COST OF PLANTING—AN ECONOMIC ESSAY ON THE PLANTING OF WASTE LANDS.

FORESTRY: COMPLETE YIELD TABLES FOR BRITISH WOODLANDS AND THE FINANCE OF BRITISH FORESTRY. By P. TRENTHAM MAW, P.A.S.I., Member of the Land Agents' Society, Author of "The Practice of Forestry," etc. 120 pp. Royal oblong 8vo, cloth ... ... *Net* **7s. 6d.**

FRETCUTTING, THE ART OF MODERN. By JOHN MAKINSON. 160 pages, with numerous Illustrations. Crown 8vo, cloth. *Net* **1s. 6d.**

GLASS STAINING, AND PAINTING ON GLASS. From the German of DR. GESSERT and EMANUEL OTTO FROMBERG. With an Appendix on the Art of Enamelling. Crown 8vo, cloth... **2s. 6d.**

GRAINING AND MARBLING. See VAN DER BURG'S "Imitation of Woods and Marbles," p. 10.

HANDRAILING. A Practical Treatise showing new and Simple Methods. By GEO. COLLINGS. Third Edition, including a Treatise on Stairbuilding. Crown 8vo, cloth ... ... **2s. 6d.**

HEALTH OFFICER'S POCKET-BOOK. A Guide to Sanitary Practice and Law. For Medical Officers of Health, Sanitary Inspectors, Members of Sanitary Authorities, etc. By EDWARD F. WILLOUGHBY, M.D. (Lond.), etc. Second Edition, Revised and Enlarged. Fcap. 8vo, leather ... ... *Net* **10s. 6d.**

HEATING BY HOT WATER. See STEAM AND HOT WATER HEATING AND VENTILATION.

HINTS TO YOUNG ARCHITECTS. By GEORGE WIGHTWICK, Architect, Author of "The Palace of Architecture," etc. Sixth Edition, revised and enlarged by G. HUSKISSON GUILLAUME, Architect. Crown 8vo, cloth ... ... **3s. 6d.**

HOUSE-OWNER'S ESTIMATOR; or, What will it Cost to Build, Alter, or Repair? A Price Book for Unprofessional People as well as the Architectural Surveyor and Builder. By J. D. SIMON. Edited by F. T. W. MILLER, A.R.I.B.A. Sixth Edition. Crown 8vo, cloth ... ... *Net* **3s. 6d.**

HOUSE PAINTING, GRAINING, MARBLING, AND SIGN WRITING. With a Course of Elementary Drawing and a Collection of Useful Receipts. By E. A. DAVIDSON. Tenth Edition. Coloured Plates. Crown 8vo, cloth ... ... **5s.**

*** *The above, in cloth boards, strongly bound,* **6s.**

HOUSE PLANNING—HOW TO PLAN A HOUSE. A Book for all about to Build. By G. GORDON SAMSON. Second Edition, Revised. 150 pages. With Plans and numerous Folding Plates. Demy 8vo, cloth ... ... [*Just Published. Net* **2s.**

GENERAL REMARKS ON THE PLANNING AND ARRANGEMENT OF HOUSES—PLANS IN DETAIL—HOUSES WITH FOUR RECEPTION ROOMS—HOUSES WITH THREE RECEPTION ROOMS—DETACHED VILLAS—SEMI-DETACHED VILLAS—TERRACE HOUSES—COTTAGE DWELLINGS FOR THE WORKING CLASSES—STABLES—HINTS ON LAYING OUT GARDENS—HINTS ON PLAN DRAWING.

HOUSE PROPERTY. A Popular and Practical Handbook to the Purchase, Tenancy, and Compulsory Sale of Houses and Land, including Dilapidations and Fixtures, with Examples of all kinds of Valuations, Information on Building and on the right use of Decorative Art. By E. L. TARBUCK, Architect and Surveyor. Seventh Edition. 12mo, cloth ... ... **5s.**

"The advice is thoroughly practical."—*Law Journal.*

"For all who have dealings with house property this is an indispensable guide."—*Decoration.*

"Carefully brought up to date, and much improved by the addition of a division on fine art. A well-written and thoughtful work."—*Land Agents' Record.*

HOUSES, VILLAS, COTTAGES, AND BUNGALOWS. For Britishers and Americans Abroad. A book showing how they should be built, and what they ought to cost. By G. GORDON SAMSON, Author of "How to Plan a House," etc. 147 pages, with 39 Full-page and many other Illustrations, including Plans and External Views of 18 different Houses, Bungalows, and Villas. Demy 8vo, cloth. *Net* **3s. 6d**

ILLUMINATING AND MISSAL PAINTING ON PAPER AND VELLUM. A Practical Treatise on Manuscript Work, Testimonials, and Herald Painting. With Chapters on Lettering and Writing and on Mediæval Burnished Gold. With 2 Coloured Plates. By PHILIP WHITHARD, First Class Diploma for Illuminating and Herald Painting, Printing Trades Exhibition, 1906. New and Cheaper Edition. 156 pages. Crown 8vo, cloth ... ... *Net* **1s. 6d.**

ILLUMINATION, ART OF. A Primer for the Use of Beginners; with a Rudimentary Treatise on the Art, Practical Directions for its Exercise, and Examples taken from Illuminated MSS., printed in Gold and Colours. By F. DELAMOTTE. New and Cheaper Edition. Small 4to, ornamental boards ... ... **6s.**

JOINTS MADE AND USED BY BUILDERS. By W. J. CHRISTY. With 160 Woodcuts. Crown 8vo, cloth ... ... **3s.**

LAW FOR ARCHITECTS, BUILDERS, &c. See EVERY MAN'S OWN LAWYER. A Handybook of the Principles of Law and Equity. By a Barrister. Fiftieth (1913) Edition, Revised and Enlarged. Including Abstracts of the Legislation of 1912 of especial interest to Architects and Builders, such as The Insurance Act, relating to sickness, invalidity, and unemployment, which is one of great interest and importance, and many other recent Acts. Large Crown 8vo, cloth, 850 pp. [*Published Annually. Net* **6s. 8d.**

LETTER PAINTING MADE EASY. By J. G. BADENOCH. With 12 full-page Engravings of Examples. Crown 8vo, cloth 1s. 6d.

"Any intelligent lad who fails to turn out decent work after studying this system has mistaken his vocation."—*English Mechanic.*

LIGHT: An Introduction to the Science of Optics. Designed for the Use of Students of Architecture, Engineering, and other Applied Sciences. By E. W. TARN, M.A. Crown 8vo, cloth ... 1s. 6d.

LIGHTNING CONDUCTORS, MODERN. An Illustrated Supplement to the Report of the Lightning Research Committee of 1905, also the Phœnix Fire Office 1910 Rules, with Notes as to the Methods of Protection, and Specifications. By KILLINGWORTH HEDGES, M.Inst.C.E., M.I.E.E., Honorary Secretary to the Lightning Research Committee. Second Edition, with additions. Medium 8vo, cloth ... *Net* 6s. 6d.

"The work now appears with some additions that noticeably enhance its value."—*Scotsman.*

"The new edition embodies the rules for lightning rods which have been issued by the Phœnix Fire Office, together with additional sections dealing with the effect of lightning on mankind, upward discharges of lightning, lightning on the high Alps, and an historical summary of the subject-matter from the year 1717. There are several new illustrations, including a remarkable picture of the interior of Barham Church, which was struck with lightning on February 8, 1906."—*Ironmonger.*

"Some 77 illustrations are included, many of which are of a particularly interesting nature, especially those showing the effect of lightning strokes on protected and unprotected buildings."—*Hardware Trade Journal.*

"The information given in the volume is most valuable."—*Electrical Engineer.*

LIMES, CEMENTS, MORTARS, CONCRETES, MASTICS, PLASTERING, etc. By G. R. BURNELL, C.E. Fifteenth Edition. Crown 8vo, cloth ... ... 1s. 6d.

LOCKWOOD'S BUILDER'S PRICE BOOK. A Comprehensive Handbook of the Latest Prices and Data for Builders, Architects, Engineers, and Contractors. Re-constructed, re-written, and Greatly Enlarged. By FRANCIS T. W. MILLER. 800 pages. Crown 8vo, cloth ... ... [*Published Annually.* 4s.

LATEST PRICES OF EVERY KIND OF MATERIAL AND LATEST RATES OF LABOUR IN TRADES CONNECTED WITH BUILDING—TABLES FOR VALUATION OF LEASES, ESTATES, ETC.—WAGES TABLES—LEGAL NOTES AND MEMORANDA—THE FORM OF BUILDING CONTRACT ISSUED BY THE R.I.B.A.—FULL SECTION ON ELECTRIC LIGHTING, BY A. P. HASLAM, M.I.E.E.—SUPPLEMENT CONTAINING THE LONDON BUILDING ACTS, 1894 TO 1908, WITH CAREFUL ANNOTATIONS ON ACTS NOW IN FORCE—NOTES OF IMPORTANT DECISIONS IN THE SUPERIOR COURTS, BY A. J. DAVID, K.C., B.A., LL.M., OF THE INNER TEMPLE, BARRISTER-AT-LAW—BY-LAWS AND OTHER REGULATIONS NOW IN FORCE—AN INDEX TO THE ACTS AND REGULATIONS.

"An excellent book of reference."—*Architect.*

"Comprehensive, reliable, well arranged, legible and well bound."—*British Architect.*

MASONRY. A Practical Guide to the Art of Stone Cutting. Comprising the Construction, Setting-Out, and Working of Stairs, Circular Work, Arches, Niches, Domes, Pendentives, Vaults, Tracery Windows, &c.; to which are added Supplements relating to Masonry Estimating and Quantity Surveying, and to Building Stones and Marbles, and a glossary of terms. For the Use of Students, Masons and Craftsmen. By W. R. PURCHASE, Building Inspector to the Borough of Hove. Fifth Edition, Enlarged. Royal 8vo, 226 pp., with 52 Plates, comprising over 400 Diagrams, cloth ... ... *Net* 7s. 6d.

"The book is a practical treatise. Most of the examples given are from actual work carried out. It should be found of general utility to architectural students and others, as well as to those to whom it is specially addressed."—*Journal of the Royal Institute of British Architects.*

MASONRY AND STONECUTTING. The Principles of Masonic Projection, and their Application to Construction. By E. DOBSON, M.R.I.B.A. Crown 8vo, cloth ... ... 2s. 6d.

MARBLE AND MARBLE WORKING. A Handbook for Architects, Sculptors, Marble Quarry Owners and Workers, and all engaged in the Building and Decorative Industries. Containing numerous Illustrations and 13 Coloured Plates. By W. G. RENWICK, Author of "The Marble Industry," "The Working of Marble for Decorative Purposes," &c. 240 pp. Medium 8vo, cloth ... **15s.**

THE CHEMISTRY OF MARBLE—ITS GEOLOGICAL FORMATION—A SHORT CLASSIFICATION OF MARBLES—ANTIQUITY OF THE MARBLE INDUSTRY—ANCIENT QUARRIES AND METHODS OF WORKING—MODERN QUARRIES AND QUARRYING METHODS—MACHINERY USED IN QUARRYING—EUROPEAN AND AMERICAN SYSTEMS COMPARED—MARBLE AS BUILDING MATERIAL—USES OF MARBLE OTHER THAN FOR BUILDING PURPOSES—SOURCES OF PRODUCTION: ITALIAN, FRENCH, BELGIAN AND GREEK MARBLES, &C.; MARBLES OF THE UNITED KINGDOM AND BRITISH COLONIES—CONTINENTAL MARBLE WORKING—MARBLE WORKING MACHINERY—MARBLE WORKING IN THE UNITED STATES—AMERICAN MACHINERY DESCRIBED AND COMPARED—MARBLE WORKING: A BRITISH INDUSTRY—MARBLE SUBSTITUTES AND IMITATIONS—PRACTICAL POINTS FOR THE CONSIDERATION OF ARCHITECTS—HINTS ON THE SELECTION OF MARBLE—LIST OF MARBLES IN ORDINARY USE, WITH DESCRIPTIVE NOTES AND INSTANCES OF THEIR APPLICATION.

MARBLE DECORATION. And the Terminology of British and Foreign Marbles. A Handbook for Students. By GEORGE H. BLAGROVE, Author of "Shoring and its Application," etc. With 28 Illustrations. Crown 8vo, cloth ... ... **3s. 6d.**

MEASURED DRAWINGS. Issued by the School of Architecture of the University of Liverpool, under the direction of Professor C. H. REILLY. Containing measured drawings (including detailed drawings and contours of mouldings) of notable buildings in Great Britain and Ireland, and on the Continent. With full-page plates and descriptive letterpress.

Either loose in a cloth Portfolio or bound in cloth.

Per volume, *net* **21s**

Vol. I. contains a complete External Survey of the following buildings with detail drawings to a large scale:—THE TOWN HALL, LIVERPOOL, 7 PLATES.—THE PALACE OF THE PETIT TRIANON, VERSAILLES, 5 PLATES.—THE PALACE OF THE GRAND TRIANON, VERSAILLES, 4 PLATES.—THE CUSTOM HOUSE, DUBLIN, 4 PLATES.—THE ORANGERY, KENSINGTON PALACE, 3 PLATES.—THE SENATE HOUSE, CAMBRIDGE, 3 PLATES.—THE HOUSE OF PROVIDENCE, DINGLE LANE, LIVERPOOL, 1 PLATE.—LODGE TO THE HOUSE OF PROVIDENCE, 1 PLATE.—MAIN DOORWAY UNDER COLONNADE, ST. GEORGE'S HALL, LIVERPOOL, 1 PLATE.—JACOBEAN OAK CHIMNEY PIECE, HALL-'I-TH'-WOOD MUSEUM, BOLTON, 1 PLATE.

Vol. II. contains a complete External Survey of the following buildings with detail drawings to a large scale: THE BANK OF ENGLAND, CASTLE STREET, LIVERPOOL, 3 PLATES.—BRONZE INTERNAL DOORS, ST. GEORGE'S HALL, LIVERPOOL, 1 PLATE.—ST. PAUL'S CHURCH, LIVERPOOL, 5 PLATES.—THE QUEEN ANNE BLOCK, GREENWICH PALACE, 8 PLATES.—MORDEN COLLEGE, BLACKHEATH, 7 PLATES.—THE UNIVERSITY LIBRARY, CAMBRIDGE, 3 PLATES.—THE SCREEN IN THE CHAPEL, LINCOLN COLLEGE, OXFORD, 2 PLATES.—THE PALACE OF THE PETIT TRIANON, VERSAILLES, COURTYARD DETAILS, 1 PLATE.—PALAZZO BEVILACQUA, VERONA, 1 PLATE.—PORTA NUOVA, VERONA, 3 PLATES.—SPEKE HALL, LANCASHIRE, 6 PLATES.—PORTA PALIO, VERONA, 5 PLATES.

MEASURING AND VALUING ARTIFICERS' WORK. A Students' Guide containing Directions for taking Dimensions, Abstracting the same, and bringing the Quantities into Bill, with Tables of Constants for Valuation of Labour, and for the Calculation of Areas and Solidities. Originally edited by E. DOBSON, Architect. With Additions by E. W. TARN, M.A. Seventh Edition, Revised. Crown 8vo, cloth. **7s. 6d.**

PACKING-CASE TABLES. Showing the number of Superficial Feet in Boxes or Packing-Cases, from 6 ins. square and upwards. By W. RICHARDSON, Timber Broker. Fourth Edition. Oblong 4to, cloth. **3s. 6d.**

PAINTING. THE IMITATION OF WOODS AND MARBLES. As Taught and Practised by A. R. VAN DER BURG and P. VAN DER BURG, Directors of the Rotterdam Painting Institution. Royal folio, cloth, 18½ by 12½ in. Illustrated with 24 full-size Coloured Plates; also 12 plain Plates, comprising 154 Figures. Fifth Edition. *Net* £1 5s.

LIST OF PLATES.—1. Various Tools Required for Wood Painting.—2, 3. Walnut: Preliminary Stages of Graining and Finished Specimen.—4. Tools Used for Marble Painting and Method of Manipulation.—5, 6. St. Remi Marble: Earlier Operations and Finished Specimen.—7. Methods of Sketching Different Grains, Knots, etc.—8, 9. Ash: Preliminary Stages and Finished Specimen.—10. Methods of Sketching Marble Grains.—11, 12. Breche Marbles: Preliminary Stages of Working and Finished Specimen.—13. Maple: Method of Producing the Different Grains.—14, 15. Bird's-eye Maple: Preliminary Stages and Finished Specimen.—16. Methods of Sketching the Different Species of White Marble.—17, 18. White Marble: Preliminary Stages of Process and Finished Specimen.—19. Mahogany: Specimens of Various Grains and Methods of Manipulation.—20, 21. Mahogany: Earlier Stages and Finished Specimen.—22, 23, 24. Sienna Marble: Varieties of Grain, Preliminary Stages and Finished Specimen.—25, 26, 27. Juniper Wood: Methods of Producing Grain, etc.; Preliminary Stages and Finished Specimen.—28, 29, 30. Vert de Mer Marble, etc., etc.

PAINTING POPULARLY EXPLAINED. By THOMAS JOHN GULLICK, Painter, and JOHN TIMBS, F.S.A. Including Fresco, Oil, Mosaic, Water-Colour, Water-Glass, Tempera, Encaustic, Miniature, Painting on Ivory, Vellum, Pottery, Enamel, Glass, etc. Sixth Edition. Crown 8vo, cloth ... ... 5s.

PLANNING OF HOUSES. See HOUSE PLANNING.

PLASTERING. A Practical Compendium of Plain and Ornamental Plaster Work. By W. KEMP. Crown 8vo, cloth ... 2s.

PLUMBING, STEAM AND HOT WATER HEATING. A Modern Work for the Plumber, the Heating Engineer, the Architect, and the Builder. By J. J. LAWLER. With 284 Illustrations. 4to, cloth ... ... *Net* 21s.

PLUMBING: A Text-Book to the Practice of the Art or Craft of the Plumber. With Chapters upon House Drainage and Ventilation. By WM. PATON BUCHAN. Ninth Edition, with 512 Illustrations. Crown 8vo, cloth ... ... 3s. 6d.

PORTLAND CEMENT FOR USERS. By the late HENRY FAIJA, M.Inst.C.E. Fifth Edition. Revised and Enlarged by D. B. BUTLER, A.M.Inst.C.E. Crown 8vo, cloth ... ... 3s.

PORTLAND CEMENT, THE MODERN MANUFACTURE OF. A Handbook for Manufacturers, Users, and all interested in Portland Cement. By PERCY C. H. WEST, Fellow of the Chemical Society and of the Society of Chemical Industry. Vol. I., "Machinery and Kilns." 280 pp., with 159 Illustrations and numerous Tables. Royal 8vo, cloth ... ... *Net* 12s. 6d.

PUBLIC WORKS CALCULATOR. Containing Tables showing at sight the Cubic Contents of Square or Round Stone, &c. Also Tables of Superficial Measure and Weight of Mild Steel Bars and Angles. Compiled specially for Indian and Colonial requirements by a Public Works Officer. Second Edition, Enlarged. 7 ins. × 3 ins., cloth ... ... [*Just Published. Net* 2s. 6d.

QUANTITIES AND MEASUREMENTS. In Bricklayers', Masons', Plasterers', Plumbers', Painters', Paperhangers', Gilders', Smiths', Carpenters' and Joiners' Work. By A. C. BEATON, Surveyor. Crown 8vo, cloth ... ... 1s. 6d.

RATING AND ASSESSMENT, THE LAW AND PRACTICE OF. A Handbook for Overseers, Members of Assessment Committees, Surveyors, and others interested in Rating and Valuation. By CLARENCE A. WEBB, P.A.S.I., Valuer and Rating Surveyor. Author of "The Valuation of Real Property," etc. 250 pages. Demy 8vo, cloth. *Net* 7s. 6d.

REINFORCED CONCRETE. A Handbook for Architects, Engineers and Contractors. By F. D. WARREN, Massachusetts Institute of Technology, with Illustrations, 271 pages. Crown 8vo, cloth. *Net* 10s. 6d.

EXTRACT FROM PREFACE.

The book is divided into four parts. Part I. gives a general but concise *résumé* of the subject from a practical standpoint, bringing out some of the difficulties met with in practice and suggesting remedies. Under Part II. is compiled a series of tests justifying the use of various constants and co-efficients in preparing the tables under Part III. Part III. contains a series of Tables from which it is hoped the designer may obtain all necessary information to meet the more common cases in practice. Part IV. treats of the design of trussed roofs from a practical standpoint.

REINFORCED CONCRETE DESIGN. A Graphical Handbook by JOHN HAWKESWORTH, C.E., consisting of a series of Plates showing graphically, by means of plotted curves, the required design for Slabs, Beams and Columns, under various conditions of external loading, together with practical examples explaining the method of using each Plate. 64 Pages. 15 full-page Plates. 4to, cloth ... ... *Net* 12s.

REINFORCED CONCRETE DESIGN SIMPLIFIED. Diagrams, Tables, and other data for designing and checking accurately and speedily. By JOHN C. GAMMON, B.Sc. Eng. (London), Assoc. City Guilds Institute, Member of the Concrete Institute, Assistant Engineer, Public Works Department, India. With an Introduction by H. KEMPTON DYSON, Secretary of the Concrete Institute, Lecturer on Reinforced Concrete, London County Council School of Building, Consulting Engineer and Architect. Second Edition, Revised. Demy 4to, cloth, with Thumb Index ... ... *Net* 10s. 6d.

ROOF CARPENTRY. Practical Lessons in the Framing of Wood Roofs. For the use of Working Carpenters. By GEO. COLLINGS. Crown 8vo, cloth ... ... 2s.

SANITARY WORK IN SMALL TOWNS AND VILLAGES. By CHARLES SLAGG, A.M.Inst.C.E. Third Edition, Enlarged. Crown 8vo, cloth ... ... 3s.

SANITATION, WATER SUPPLY AND SEWAGE DISPOSAL OF COUNTRY HOUSES. By WM. PAUL GERHARD, C.E. 350 pages with 113 Illustrations. Crown 8vo, cloth. *Net* 8s. 6d.

SAW MILLS. Their Arrangement and Management, and the Economical Conversion of Timber. By M. POWIS BALE, M.Inst.C.E. Third Edition, Revised. Crown 8vo, cloth ... ... 10s. 6d.

SEWAGE, PURIFICATION OF: being a Brief Account of the Scientific Principles of Sewage Purification, and their Practical Application. By SIDNEY BARWISE, M.D. (Lond.), B.Sc., M.R.C.S., D.P.H. (Camb.), Fellow of the Sanitary Institute, Medical Officer of Health to the Derbyshire County Council. Second Edition, Revised and Enlarged, with an Appendix on the Analysis of Sewage and Sewage Effluents. With numerous Illustrations and Diagrams. Demy 8vo, cloth .. .. *Net* 10s. 6d.

SEWAGE, PURIFICATION OF—*continued.*

SUMMARY OF CONTENTS:—SEWAGE: ITS NATURE AND COMPOSITION—THE CHEMISTRY OF SEWAGE—VARIETIES OF SEWAGE AND THE CHANGES IT UNDERGOES—RIVER POLLUTION AND ITS EFFECTS—THE LAND TREATMENT OF SEWAGE—PRECIPITATION, PRECIPITANTS, AND TANKS—THE LIQUEFACTION OF SEWAGE—PRINCIPLES INVOLVED IN THE OXIDATION OF SEWAGE—ARTIFICIAL PROCESSES OF PURIFICATION—AUTOMATIC DISTRIBUTORS AND SPECIAL FILTERS—PARTICULARS OF SEWERAGE AND SEWAGE DISPOSAL SCHEMES REQUIRED BY LOCAL GOVERNMENT BOARD—USEFUL DATA—*Appendix:* THE APPARATUS REQUIRED FOR SEWAGE ANALYSIS—STANDARD SOLUTIONS USED IN THE METHOD OF SEWAGE ANALYSIS.—*Tables:* ESTIMATION OF AMMONIA—NITROGEN AS NITRATES—INCUBATOR TEST, OXYGEN ABSORBED—TO CONVERT GRAINS PER GALLON TO PARTS PER 100,000.

SEWERAGE OF SEA COAST TOWNS. By HENRY C. ADAMS, A.M.Inst.C.E., M.I.Mech.E., A.M.I.E.E., M.R.San.Inst., etc. 132 pages, with Illustrations. Demy 8vo, cloth ... ... *Net* **5s.**

SEWERAGE SYSTEMS. Their Design and Construction. A Practical Treatise upon the principles of the Design, Construction, and Maintenance of Town Sewerage Systems, with examples of existing works. By HUGH S. WATSON, A.M.Inst.C.E., with Legal Notes on the Principal Acts of Parliament and the legal procedure relating to the Provision of Works of Sewerage by ELIDGE B. HERBERT, Barrister-at-Law. Illustrated by 150 Diagrams and Working Drawings. Royal 8vo, 330 pages, cloth ... ... *Net* **10s. 6d.**

SEWAGE. See also SANITATION, WATER SUPPLY AND SEWAGE DISPOSAL OF COUNTRY HOUSES.

SHORING, and its Application. By G. H. BLAGROVE. Crown 8vo, cloth... ... ... **1s. 6d.**

A SHORT SPECIFICATION. Of Materials, Labour, and Goods, for Works connected with Building. By JAMES CUBITT, Architect. 114 pages. Oblong demy 4to. New and Cheaper Edition. *Net* **2s.**

SPECIFICATIONS IN DETAIL. By FRANK W. MACEY, Architect, Author of "Conditions of Contract." Second Edition, Revised and Enlarged, containing 644 pp., and 2,000 illustrations. Royal 8vo, cloth ... ... *Net* **21s.**

GENERAL NOTES—SPECIFICATION OF WORKS AND LIST OF GENERAL CONDITIONS—PRELIMINARY ITEMS (INCLUDING SHORING AND HOUSE BREAKER)—DRAINAGE (INCLUDING RAIN-WATER WELL AND REPORTS)—EXCAVATOR (INCLUDING CONCRETE FLOORS, ROOFS, STAIRS AND WALLS)—PAVIOR—BRICKLAYER (INCLUDING FLINTWORK, RIVER AND OTHER WALLING, SPRING-WATER WELLS, STORAGE TANKS, FOUNTAINS, FILTERS, TERRA COTTA AND FAIENCE)—MASON—CARPENTER, JOINER AND IRONMONGER (INCLUDING FENCING AND PILING)—SMITH AND FOUNDER (INCLUDING HEATING, FIRE HYDRANTS, STABLE AND COW-HOUSE FITTINGS)—SLATER (INCLUDING SLATE MASON)—TILER—STONE TILER—SHINGLER—THATCHER—PLUMBER (INCLUDING HOT-WATER WORK)—ZINCWORKER—COPPERSMITH—PLASTERER—GASFITTER—BELLHANGER—GLAZIER—PAINTER—PAPERHANGER—GENERAL REPAIRS AND ALTERATIONS—VENTILATION—ROAD-MAKING—ELECTRIC LIGHT—INDEX.

SPECIFICATIONS FOR PRACTICAL ARCHITECTURE. A Guide to the Architect, Engineer, Surveyor, and Builder. Upon the Basis of the Work by A. BARTHOLOMEW, Revised by F. ROGERS. 8vo, cloth ... ... **15s.**

STEAM AND HOT WATER HEATING AND VENTILATION. A Modern Work on Steam and Hot Water Heating and Ventilation, with Descriptions and Data of all Materials and Appliances used in the Construction of such Apparatus, Rules, Tables, &c. By A. G. KING. 400 pp., over 300 Illustrations. Demy 8vo, cloth. *Net* **12s. 6d.**

SUPERFICIAL MEASUREMENT. Tables calculated from 1 to 200 inches in length, by 1 to 108 inches in breadth. A Guide for the use of Architects, Surveyors, Engineers, Timber Merchants, Builders, etc. By J. HAWKINGS. Fifth Edition. Crown 8vo, cloth ... **3s. 6d.**

TECHNICAL GUIDE, MEASURER, AND ESTIMATOR. For Builders and Surveyors. Containing Technical Directions for Measuring Work in all the Building Trades, Complete Specifications for Houses, Roads, and Drains, and an Easy Method of Estimating the parts of a Building collectively. By A. C. BEATON. Tenth Edition. Waistcoat-pocket size ... ... **1s. 6d.**

TIMBER IMPORTER'S, TIMBER MERCHANT'S, AND BUILDER'S STANDARD GUIDE. By R. E. GRANDY. Crown 8vo, cloth ... ... **2s.**

TIMBER MERCHANT'S and BUILDER'S COMPANION. Containing New and Copious Tables of the Reduced Weight and Measurement of Deals and Battens, of all sizes, and other Useful Tables for the use of Timber Merchants and Builders. By WILLIAM DOWSING. Fifth Edition. Revised and Corrected. Crown 8vo, cloth ... **3s.**

TIMBER MERCHANT. Being a Practical Guide for the Use of Building Contractors, Surveyors, Builders, etc., comprising useful Tables for all purposes connected with the Timber Trade, Marks of Wood, Essay on the Strength of Timber, Remarks on the Growth of Timber, etc. By W. RICHARDSON. Second Edition. Fcap. 8vo, cloth **3s. 6d.**

VALUATION OF REAL PROPERTY: A Guide to the Principles of Valuation of Land and Buildings, etc., for various Purposes, including the taxation of Land Values. With numerous examples. By CLARENCE A. WEBB, Valuer and Rating Surveyor, Professional Associate of the Surveyors' Institution; Author of "The Law and Practice of Rating and Assessment" and "Rates and Taxes." 3rd Edition. Revised and Enlarged by ARTHUR HUNNINGS, F.S.I. 340 pp. Demy 8vo, cloth [*Just Published. Net* **7s. 6d.**

GENERAL PRINCIPLES OF VALUATION—VALUATION OF LAND AND BUILDINGS SEPARATELY—VALUATION FOR MORTGAGE—TIMBER MEASURING AND VALUING—ARBITRATION—COMPENSATION FOR COMPULSORY PURCHASE—VALUATION FOR RATING—VALUATION FOR TAXATION—LAND TAX—INHABITED HOUSE DUTY—INCOME TAX—LAND VALUES TAXATION—DUTIES ON LIQUOR LICENCES—ENFRANCHISEMENT OF COPYHOLDS—COMPENSATION UNDER LICENSING ACT, 1904—VALUATION FOR FIRE INSURANCE CLAIMS—CONSTRUCTION OF VALUATION TABLES—THE PRINCIPAL VALUATION TABLES; PART I. OF THE FINANCE (1909-10) ACT, 1910.

"We know of no other volume of such handy size which covers so wide a scope, and we can confidently recommend it to those who desire to obtain a knowledge of the methods of valuing real property for various purposes without a detailed study of complicated legal questions."—*Westminster Gazette.*

VENTILATION. A Text-Book to the Practice of the Art of Ventilating Buildings. By W. P. BUCHAN. With 170 Illustrations. Crown 8vo, cloth ... ... **3s. 6d.**

VENTILATION. See also STEAM AND HOT WATER HEATING AND VENTILATION.

WATER AND ITS PURIFICATION. A Handbook for the Use of Local Authorities, Sanitary Officers, and others interested in Water Supply. By S. RIDEAL, D.Sc.Lond., F.I.C. Second Edition, Revised, with Additions, including numerous Illustrations and Tables. Large Crown 8vo, cloth... ... ... *Net* **9s.**

WATER SUPPLY OF CITIES AND TOWNS. By WILLIAM HUMBER, A.M.Inst.C.E. and M.Inst.M.E., Author of "Cast and Wrought Iron Bridge Construction," etc., etc. Illustrated with 50 Double Plates, 1 Single Plate, Coloured Frontispiece, and upwards of 250 Woodcuts, and containing 400 pp. of Text. Imperial 4to, elegantly and substantially half-bound in morocco ... ... *Net* £6 6s.

I. HISTORICAL SKETCH OF SOME OF THE MEANS THAT HAVE BEEN ADOPTED FOR THE SUPPLY OF WATER TO CITIES AND TOWNS.—II. WATER AND THE FOREIGN MATTER USUALLY ASSOCIATED WITH IT.—III. RAINFALL AND EVAPORATION.—IV. SPRINGS AND THE WATER-BEARING FORMATIONS OF VARIOUS DISTRICTS.—V. MEASUREMENT AND ESTIMATION OF THE FLOW OF WATER.—VI. ON THE SELECTION OF THE SOURCE OF SUPPLY.—VII. WELLS.—VIII. RESERVOIRS.—IX. THE PURIFICATION OF WATER.—X. PUMPS.—XI. PUMPING MACHINERY.—XII. CONDUITS.—XIII. DISTRIBUTION OF WATER.—XIV. METERS, SERVICE PIPES, AND HOUSE FITTINGS.—XV. THE LAW AND ECONOMY OF WATER WORKS.—XVI. CONSTANT AND INTERMITTENT SUPPLY.—XVII. DESCRIPTION OF PLATES—APPENDICES, GIVING TABLES OF RATES OF SUPPLY, VELOCITIES, ETC., ETC., TOGETHER WITH SPECIFICATIONS OF SEVERAL WORKS ILLUSTRATED, AMONG WHICH WILL BE FOUND: ABERDEEN, BIDEFORD, CANTERBURY, DUNDEE, HALIFAX, LAMBETH, ROTHERHAM, AND OTHERS.

WATER SUPPLY OF TOWNS AND THE CONSTRUCTION OF WATER-WORKS. A Practical Treatise for the Use of Engineers and Students of Engineering. By W. K. BURTON, A.M.Inst. C.E., Consulting Engineer to the Tokyo Waterworks. Third Edition, Revised. Edited by ALLAN GREENWELL, F.G.S., A.M.Inst.C.E. With numerous Plates and Illustrations. Super-royal 8vo, buckram £1 5s.

I. INTRODUCTORY.—II. DIFFERENT QUALITIES OF WATER.—III. QUANTITY OF WATER TO BE PROVIDED.—IV. ON ASCERTAINING WHETHER A PROPOSED SOURCE OF SUPPLY IS SUFFICIENT.—V. ON ESTIMATING THE STORAGE CAPACITY REQUIRED TO BE PROVIDED.—VI. CLASSIFICATION OF WATERWORKS.—VII. IMPOUNDING RESERVOIRS.—VIII. EARTHWORK DAMS.—IX. MASONRY DAMS.—X. THE PURIFICATION OF WATER.—XI. SETTLING RESERVOIRS.—XII. SAND FILTRATION.—XIII. PURIFICATION OF WATER BY ACTION OF IRON, SOFTENING OF WATER BY ACTION OF LIME, NATURAL FILTRATION.—XIV. SERVICE OR CLEAN WATER RESERVOIRS—WATER TOWERS—STAND PIPES.—XV. THE CONNECTION OF SETTLING RESERVOIRS, FILTER BEDS AND SERVICE RESERVOIRS—XVI. PUMPING MACHINERY.—XVII. FLOW OF WATER IN CONDUITS—PIPES AND OPEN CHANNELS.—XVIII. DISTRIBUTING SYSTEMS.—XIX. SPECIAL PROVISIONS FOR THE EXTINCTION OF FIRES.—XX. PIPES FOR WATERWORKS.—XXI. PREVENTION OF WASTE OF WATER.—XXII. VARIOUS APPLIANCES USED IN CONNECTION WITH WATERWORKS.

APPENDIX I. BY PROF. JOHN MILNE, F.R.S.—CONSIDERATIONS CONCERNING THE PROBABLE EFFECTS OF EARTHQUAKES ON WATERWORKS AND THE SPECIAL PRECAUTIONS TO BE TAKEN IN EARTHQUAKE COUNTRIES.

APPENDIX II. BY JOHN DE RIJKE, C.E. ON SAND DUNES AND DUNE SANDS AS A SOURCE OF WATER SUPPLY.

WATER SUPPLY, RURAL. A Practical Handbook on the Supply of Water and Construction of Water-works for small Country Districts. By ALLAN GREENWELL, A.M.I.C.E., and W. T. CURRY, A.M.I.C.E. Revised Edition. Crown 8vo, cloth... ... ... 5s.

WATER SUPPLY. See also SANITATION, WATER SUPPLY AND SEWAGE DISPOSAL OF COUNTRY HOUSES.

WATER ENGINEERING. A Practical Treatise on the Measurement, Storage, Conveyance, and Utilisation of Water for the Supply of Towns. By C. SLAGG, A.M.Inst.C.E. ... ... 7s. 6d.

WOOD-CARVING FOR AMATEURS. With Hints on Design. By A LADY. With 10 Plates. New and Cheaper Edition. Crown 8vo, in emblematic wrapper... ... ... 2s.

WOODWORKING MACHINERY. Its Rise, Progress, and Construction. With Hints on the Management of Saw Mills and the Economical Conversion of Timber. Illustrated with Examples of Recent Designs by leading English, French, and American Engineers. By M. POWIS BALE, M.Inst.C.E., M.I.Mech.E. Second Edition, Revised, with large Additions, large crown 8vo, 440 pp., cloth ... ... 9s.

PUBLICATIONS OF THE ENGINEERING STANDARDS COMMITTEE.

The Reports are Foolscap Folio, Sewed, except where otherwise stated.

Reports already published :—

1. BRITISH STANDARD SECTIONS (9 lists). (*Included in No.* 6).—ANGLES, EQUAL AND UNEQUAL—BULB ANGLES, TEES AND PLATES—Z AND T BARS—CHANNELS—BEAMS ... ... **1s.** *Net.*
2. TRAMWAY RAILS AND FISH-PLATES ... ... **21s.** *Net.*
3. REPORT ON THE INFLUENCE OF GAUGE LENGTH. By Professor W. C. UNWIN, F.R.S. ... ... **5s.** *Net.*
4. PROPERTIES OF STANDARD BEAMS. (*Included in No.* 6.) *Demy 8vo, sewed* ... ... **1s.** *Net.*
5. STANDARD LOCOMOTIVES FOR INDIAN RAILWAYS. *Superseded.*
6. PROPERTIES OF BRITISH STANDARD SECTIONS. Diagrams and Definitions, Tables, and Formulæ. *Demy 8vo, cloth* **2s. 6d.** *Net.*
7. TABLES OF BRITISH STANDARD COPPER CONDUCTORS ... ... **5s.** *Net.*
8. TUBULAR TRAMWAY POLES ... ... **5s.** *Net.*
9. BULL-HEADED RAILWAY RAILS ... ... **21s.** *Net.*
10. TABLES OF PIPE FLANGES ... ... **2s. 6d.** *Net.*
11. FLAT-BOTTOMED RAILWAY RAILS ... ... **21s.** *Net.*
12. SPECIFICATION FOR PORTLAND CEMENT ... **5s.** *Net.*
13. STRUCTURAL STEEL FOR SHIPBUILDING ... **5s.** *Net.*
14. STRUCTURAL STEEL FOR MARINE BOILERS ... **5s.** *Net.*
15. STRUCTURAL STEEL FOR BRIDGES AND GENERAL BUILDING CONSTRUCTION ... ... **5s.** *Net.*
16. SPECIFICATIONS AND TABLES FOR TELEGRAPH MATERIALS ... ... **21s.** *Net.*
17. INTERIM REPORT ON ELECTRICAL MACHINERY *Superseded.*
19. REPORT ON TEMPERATURE EXPERIMENTS ON FIELD COILS OF ELECTRICAL MACHINES ... **10s. 6d.** *Net.*
20. BRITISH STANDARD SCREW THREADS ... **2s. 6d.** *Net.*
21. BRITISH STANDARD PIPE THREADS ... **2s. 6d.** *Net.*
22. REPORT ON EFFECT OF TEMPERATURE ON INSULATING MATERIALS ... ... **5s.** *Net*
23. STANDARDS FOR TROLLEY GROOVE AND WIRE **1s.** *Net.*
24. MATERIAL USED IN THE CONSTRUCTION OF RAILWAY ROLLING STOCK ... ... **21s.** *Net.*
25. ERRORS IN WORKMANSHIP. Based on Measurements carried out for the Committee by the National Physical Laboratory **10s. 6d.** *Net.*
26. SECOND REPORT ON STANDARD LOCOMOTIVES FOR INDIAN RAILWAYS ... ... *Superseded.*
27. STANDARD SYSTEMS OF LIMIT GAUGES FOR RUNNING FITS ... ... **5s.** *Net.*
28. NUTS, BOLT-HEADS, AND SPANNERS ... **2s. 6d.** *Net.*
29. INGOT STEEL FORGINGS FOR MARINE PURPOSES. **5s.** *Net.*
30. INGOT STEEL CASTINGS FOR MARINE PURPOSES. **5s.** *Net.*
31. STEEL CONDUITS FOR ELECTRICAL WIRING ... **5s.** *Net.*
32. STEEL BARS (for use in Automatic Machines) ... ... **2s. 6d.** *Net.*
33. CARBON FILAMENT GLOW LAMPS ... ... **5s.** *Net.*

P.T.O.

PUBLICATIONS OF THE ENGINEERING STANDARDS COMMITTEE—*(contd.)*

35. COPPER ALLOY BARS (for use in Automatic Machines) **2s. 6d.** *Net.*
36. STANDARDS FOR ELECTRICAL MACHINERY. **2s. 6d.** *Net.*
37. CONSUMERS' ELECTRIC SUPPLY METERS (Motor Type for Continuous and Single-Phase Circuits) ... ... **5s.** *Net.*
38. LIMIT GAUGES FOR SCREW THREADS ... ... **5s.** *Net.*
39. COMBINED REPORTS ON SCREW THREADS (containing Reports Nos. 20, 28, 38) ... ... **7s. 6d.** *Net.*
40. CAST IRON SPIGOT AND SOCKET LOW PRESSURE HEATING PIPES ... ... **2s. 6d.** *Net.*
41. CAST IRON SPIGOT AND SOCKET FLUE OR SMOKE PIPES ... ... **2s. 6d.** *Net.*
42. RECIPROCATING STEAM ENGINES FOR ELECTRICAL PURPOSES ... ... **5s.** *Net.*
43. CHARCOAL IRON LAPWELDED BOILER TUBES **2s. 6d.** *Net.*
44. CAST-IRON PIPES FOR HYDRAULIC POWER ... **5s.** *Net.*
45. STANDARD DIMENSIONS FOR THE THREADS OF SPARKING PLUGS (FOR INTERNAL COMBUSTION ENGINES) **2s. 6d.** *Net.*
46. KEYS AND KEYWAYS ... ... **2s. 6d.** *Net.*
47. STEEL FISHPLATES FOR BULL-HEAD AND FLAT-BOTTOM RAILWAY RAILS ... ... **10s. 6d.** *Net.*
48. WROUGHT IRON OF SMITHING QUALITY FOR SHIPBUILDING (Grade D) ... ... **2s. 6d.** *Net.*
49. AMMETERS AND VOLTMETERS ... ... **5s.** *Net.*
50. THIRD REPORT ON STANDARD LOCOMOTIVES FOR INDIAN RAILWAYS. Incorporating Reports Nos. 5 and 26. **21s.** *Net.*
51. WROUGHT IRON FOR USE IN RAILWAY ROLLING STOCK. "Best Yorkshire" and Grades A., B. and C. ... ... **10s. 6d.** *Net.*
52. BAYONET SOCKET LAMP-HOLDERS AND CAPS ... **5s.** *Net.*
53. COLD DRAWN WELDLESS STEEL TUBES FOR LOCOMOTIVE BOILERS ... ... **2s. 6d.** *Net.*
54. THREADS, NUTS AND BOLT HEADS FOR USE IN AUTOMOBILE CONSTRUCTION ... ... **2s. 6d.** *Net.*
55. HARD-DRAWN COPPER AND BRONZE WIRE **10s. 6d.** *Net.*
56. DEFINITIONS OF YIELD POINT AND ELASTIC LIMIT. *Gratis.*
57. HEADS FOR SMALL SCREWS ... ... **2s. 6d.** *Net.*
58. CAST IRON SPIGOT AND SOCKET SOIL PIPES ... **5s.** *Net.*
59. SPIGOT AND SOCKET WASTE AND VENTILATING PIPES FOR OTHER THAN SOIL PURPOSES ... ... **5s.** *Net.*
60. REPORT OF EXPERIMENTS ON TUNGSTEN FILAMENT GLOW LAMPS (in two parts) ... ... **21s. 0d.** *Net.*
61. COPPER TUBES AND THEIR SCREW THREADS ... **2s. 6d.** *Net.*
62. SCREWING FOR MARINE BOILER STAYS ... ... *Gratis.*
63. SIZES OF BROKEN STONE AND CHIPPINGS **3s. 0d.** *Net.*
64. STEEL FISHBOLTS AND NUTS FOR RAILWAY RAILS. **5s. 0d.** *Net.*

London: Crosby Lockwood & Son,

7, STATIONERS' HALL COURT, LUDGATE HILL, E.C.

and 5, Broadway, Westminster, S.W.